COMPUTER PROGRAMMING IN BASIC

Peter Bishop

Second Edition

Thomas Nelson and Sons Ltd
Nelson House   Mayfield Road
Walton-on-Thames   Surrey
KT12 5PL   UK

51 York Place
Edinburgh
EH1 3JD   UK

Thomas Nelson (Hong Kong) Ltd
Toppan Building 10/F
22A Westlands Road
Quarry Bay   Hong Kong

Distributed in Australia by

Thomas Nelson Australia
480 La Trobe Street
Melbourne   Victoria 3000
and in Sydney, Brisbane, Adelaide and Perth

© Peter Bishop 1978, 1983

First published by Thomas Nelson and Sons Ltd 1978

Reprinted six times

Second edition 1983

Reprinted 1983, 1985, 1986, 1987

ISBN 0-17-438358-4

NCN 20-KCS-3439-05

Designed by the New Book Factory, London
Phototypesetting by Parkway Group, London and Abingdon
Printed in Hong Kong

Preface

In the six years since the first edition of *Computer Programming in BASIC* was written, much has happened in computing and computer education. On the hardware side, microcomputers have become the norm, and their numbers and capabilities are increasing daily. 'Micro-mainframes' and local area networks, linking microcomputers and other items of equipment in the same building, are just around the corner. On the software side, BASIC has become Basic, the principles of programming have become more widely understood, and the requirements of a well written program have become more exacting. In education, the potential of the computer as a teaching aid, in almost every subject from Art to Zoology is being realised. 'Computer literacy' is coming to be recognised as an essential educational requirement for all pupils. The teaching of programming is only one of many computer-related activities within a school. Furthermore, the age at which pupils are introduced to some form of computing is decreasing; currently it is well into the primary school range.

All these factors pose considerable problems in writing the second edition of a book which has been, and continues to be, extremely successful, although it is patently out of date in certain respects. They have required that a finely balanced compromise be struck between retaining existing ideas and introducing new material. An essential requirement has been to preserve those qualities of the book which made it a success in the first place. In the process of satisfying these requirements, the entire text of the book has had to be redrafted. However, most of the 'old favourite' material remains, albeit in a different form.

The overall objectives of the book remain virtually unchanged from the first edition: This book is an introduction to Basic language computer programming, intended mainly for pupils doing an O-level or CSE course in Computer Studies. It caters for pupils of a wide range of interests and abilities, and its use can be varied accordingly. It is also ideal for the hobbyist who wants a more methodical approach to acquiring the skills of programming than given in most introductory texts.

Three skills are taught:
- Understanding a task and working out a way of carrying it out on a computer.
- Expressing the method of carrying out the task as a flow diagram comprising logically connected steps, or as an algorithm written in clear, concise English.
- Translating these steps into a Basic language computer program.

The emphasis remains on a methodical approach to writing programs. Flow diagrams are retained in a slightly more marginal role, their main function being to illustrate the logical structure of a program. (However it is essential to note that examination boards remain strongly committed to flow diagrams.)

As before, the language is introduced in gradual stages. Each section introduces a new feature, or a new technique using existing features. In each section there is a worked example, with a description of the method, a flow diagram, the program and, in most cases, a sample run of the program. Then follows an exercise giving pupils practice in the technique introduced in the section, and sometimes extending the technique by the introduction of a few associated ideas.

Although no previous knowledge of programming is assumed, the sections and questions in exercises are carefully graded to take account of various ages, ability levels and amounts of previous experience on the part of the pupils. More able pupils, or ones with previous programming experience, can pass fairly quickly through earlier sections, and concentrate on more advanced topics. Sections and questions in exercises of above average difficulty are marked □.

The examples and exercises cover a very wide range of computing tasks. The emphasis is, as far as possible, on actual computer applications. The mathematical content of the tasks is kept to a minimum. Any formulae required are supplied with the specification of the task. At the end of each chapter is an exercise of a more general nature, linking topics introduced in the chapter, and revising previous work. At the end of the book is a general revision exercise, consisting entirely of questions from past examination papers. There is also a series of suggestions for more substantial programming tasks, which may form the basis of the projects required by most examination boards, or provide the inevitable computer enthusiasts with some substantial programming tasks of a useful nature to work on.

In response to comments on the first edition, the average rate of introduction of new material has been slightly speeded up. This enables three new chapters, on subprograms, graphics and file handling, to be incorporated without increasing the length of the text too much. In addition, there are new sections covering the general topics of checking and documenting programs, and of program structure. These new topics are treated fairly lightly, as the temptation of introducing too much material into an already crowded syllabus must be avoided at all costs.

One of the biggest problems confronting a text of this nature is the fact that every type of computer supporting Basic language uses a slightly different version. Differences are particularly marked in the new and exciting programming areas, such as graphics, file handling, voice recognition, sound generation, speech synthesis etc. The only possible approach, in dealing with this situation, is to introduce a machine-independent subset of Basic for the elementary programming operations, and select the version used by a popular microcomputer where standardisation is impossible. For this purpose, Research Machines Extended Basic Version 5 has been chosen. If the underlying concepts of programming are properly mastered, switching from one version of Basic to another should not pose too great a problem.

Example programs have been run on a Research Machines 380Z computer. Magnetic disks containing these examples are available for this computer, and for the Commodore Pet, Apple and BBC microcomputers.

My thanks go to Mr Jeffrey Lake, whose material on climatic classification has been included in the text, and to Miss Carole Duell who typed the entire text.

Peter Bishop
21st December 1981

Acknowledgements

Thanks are due to the following examination boards for their kind permission to reproduce questions from past examination papers:

The Associated Examining Board
Associated Lancashire Schools Examining Board
East Anglian Examinations Board
East Midland Regional Examinations Board
Joint Matriculation Board
London Regional Examination Board

North West Regional Examinations Board
Oxford Delegacy of Local Examinations
South East Regional Examinations Board
South Western Examinations Board
Southern Regional Examinations Board
The West Midlands Examination Board
Southern Universities Joint Board
University of Cambridge Local Examinations Syndicate
University of London University Entrance and School
   Examinations Council
Welsh Joint Education Committee
Yorkshire Regional Examinations Board

Contents

Introduction

This book will teach you how to program a computer, using Basic language. It will also teach you how to prepare a task to be programmed, how to check a program, and how to write a description of the workings of a program. You will also learn about some of the many ways in which a computer can be used.

This chapter introduces the subject of programming in stages, by very briefly investigating the questions 'What is a computer?', 'What can and can't a computer do?' and 'What is a program?' A few general features of Basic language are also discussed.

1A What is a computer?

Before starting to learn about programming a computer, it is important to find out (or be reminded of) a few essential facts about computers.

Briefly stated:

> A computer is an automatic, electronic data processing machine.

There are quite a number of technical words in this description! Each of them deserves a word or two of explanation.

Automatic means that a computer can carry out a sequence of operations on its own. In this respect, a computer is rather like an automatic washing machine or automatic pilot. Furthermore, this is where programming comes in. In order to function automatically, a computer needs a set of instructions, which are stored in its memory, and direct its step-by-step operation. A program is a set of instructions to a computer.

Electronic means that a computer is made from solid-state electronic components, commonly known as **chips**. Pocket calculators, hi-fi sets and television sets are other examples of electronic devices. An important fact about electronic devices is that they need no moving parts for their operation. This is why computers work so quickly and use very little electricity.

Data is another word for information. It is used to describe information in a form which can be processed by a computer. Computers can only accept information in certain forms, generally as characters (letters, numbers or punctuation marks), which may be in some code. Sounds and pictures cannot be processed by computers directly; they must first be expressed as a suitable type of data, in some code.

Processing describes the types of work done by a computer. Processing includes storing, locating, selecting and sorting data, doing calculations and making simple decisions. Notice that computers can do much more than just calculate, and that the data stored by a computer does not have to be numbers.

Machine is a reminder that a computer is a device which does something. In this respect a computer is like a car, sewing machine or electric toothbrush. Like all machines, computers require maintenance and can break down. However, computers are different from most other machines in one important way. Whereas most machines can only perform one task, or a small range of tasks, computers are **general-purpose** machines. They can perform a very wide variety of tasks. The particular task carried out by a computer at any one time depends on how it has been programmed.

To summarise, the previous few paragraphs have presented a very brief answer to the question 'What is a computer?'. It is possible to answer this question in much more detail, but the description presented here is adequate for this course. One final point is, however, worth mentioning. In addition to performing a wide variety of tasks, computers come in a wide variety of sizes. Large computers are called **mainframe** computers, smaller ones are called **minicomputers**, and the smallest (and newest) computers are called **microcomputers**. Most of the computers used in schools are microcomputers.

1B   What can a computer do?

Having briefly discussed the nature of a computer, it is important to be clear about what a computer can and cannot do. This section investigates the things which a computer can do; the next section looks at things which a computer cannot do.

Most of the things which a computer can do are summarised by the words **input**, **processing**, and **output**. The idea of processing has already been discussed; input and output are introduced below.

Input is the act of supplying data to a computer from its environment. It is a computer's way of receiving information from the outside world. Data can be input to a computer in a number of ways. For a microcomputer, the usual input method is via its keyboard. Other input methods include punched cards, paper tape and bar codes (found on many items purchased in shops).

Output is the act of supplying data from a computer to its environment. This can be achieved in several ways. Microcomputers generally output data via their display screens; printers, graph plotters, voice synthesisers and microfilm are some of the other common methods of output. In addition to the input, processing and output of data, most computers can also **store** and **retrieve** data, and **communicate** with other computers or suitable devices.

Data is generally stored on magnetic disks or tapes. Most microcomputers use ordinary cassette tapes or small disks called **floppy disks**. Larger computers use disks and tapes with capacities of thousands of millions of characters. Data can be stored or retrieved in large

quantities, very quickly. These stores of data are sometimes called **data banks**.

Data **communication** is one of the newest and fastest growing areas of computing. Data can be sent at high speeds from one computer to another, or from a computer to a device such as a **terminal**, which consists of a keyboard and a display screen or printer. Data communication can be within the same building or across a continent. Telephone lines, radio and satellite links and fibre optics cables are all used for data communication.

To summarise this section, a computer can input, process, store, retrieve and output data, and communicate data with other computers or suitable devices. Figure 1B1 illustrates the parts of a typical microcomputer which carry out these operations.

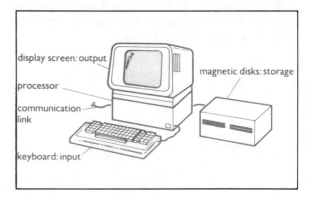

Figure 1B1   The parts of a computer

1C   What can't a computer do?

Most of the misunderstandings which a great many people have about computers are due to a lack of knowledge about the limitations of computers. Having been introduced, in the previous section, to some of the things which computers can do, it is important to balance the picture by outlining some of the things they cannot do.

Because everything which a computer does is in response to instructions in a program, a computer cannot respond to unforeseen circumstances or take initiatives. For example, if a computer does not have a standby power supply such as batteries, a power failure will cause it to shut down, in most cases losing the information it was processing at the time.

Although a computer can take simple decisions, based on questions which have 'yes' or 'no' answers, or combinations of such questions, a computer cannot think for itself. For example, if a computer is processing data consisting of people's names, it will not generally know if a name is spelled wrongly. Similarly, a computer cannot make moral judgements. A computer has no way of deciding whether war is a bad thing, or whether the means justifies the end.

Finally, computers cannot understand natural languages like English. Computers are quite capable of storing text in natural languages, and processing it in certain ways such as locating a particular word or counting the frequencies of letters. However, computers cannot respond to requests in a natural language. All the programming languages, such as Basic, used to instruct computers, are simpler than natural languages, even though they might contain complicated mathematical formulae.

These, then, are some of the most important limitations of computers. Not only are they limitations today, but they will continue to be beyond the scope of computers in the future, unless a completely new basis for the design of computers is discovered.

1D   Programs

Programs have been mentioned several times in the previous sections. In this section the idea of a program is examined a little more closely.

A program is a set of instructions to a computer. Each instruction controls one step of the task carried out by the computer. Before a computer can carry out a task, the program for the task is loaded into the computer. The computer then automatically works through the instructions of the program, one at a time.

Corresponding to each type of operation that a computer can carry out, there is a type of program instruction. Thus there are instructions for the input, output, storage and retrieval of data, and for the various types of processing – particularly performing calculations and making simple decisions.

A program sets up a computer to do a specific task. The person writing the program must understand the task, both as a whole, and in a fair amount of detail. In theory, the person must be able to carry out the task by hand, although it might take a very long time.

Most programs are designed to be run not once, but a number of times. It is therefore essential that a program is correct in every way, and is properly designed for repeated running. Like a computer, a program must be robust, able to withstand accidental or deliberate misuse.

1E   Basic language

Basic (short for Beginner's All-purpose Symbolic Instruction Code) language originated in the USA. It was developed by Thomas Kurtz and John Kemeny at Dartmouth College, as a simple language for teaching programming to students, particularly those without a scientific background. The first Basic program was run in May 1964.

Basic soon proved to be ideal for its purpose. Its use has spread to schools and universities throughout the world. It is also an established language for scientific and commercial programming. It is particularly suitable for the programming of microcomputers, a fact which has enhanced its popularity in recent years. Today Basic is the third most popular programming language in the world (after Cobol and Fortran).

The one problem with Basic language is that a large number of versions of it have been written. Each type of computer has its own version, slightly different from the rest. However, the versions are similar enough for a common version to be introduced here which will work on a wide range of computers, and certainly on the popular models used in schools. In the few areas where a common language is not possible, the version used is Research Machines Extended Basic Version 5.

1F   Programs in Basic

As mentioned previously, a program is a set of instructions to a computer. An instruction in a Basic program is called a **statement**. Each statement is generally written as a separate line, starting with a **line number**. For example:

```
100   REM EXAMPLE PROGRAM 1F
105   REM
110   REM A BASIC PROGRAM CONSISTS
115   REM OF A NUMBER OF STATEMENTS
120   REM
125   REM EACH STATEMENT IS WRITTEN
130   REM ON A SEPARATE LINE, STARTING
135   REM WITH A LINE NUMBER
140   REM
145   REM THE WORD "REM" IN THESE
150   REM STATEMENTS IS SHORT FOR
155   REMARK
160   END
```

This program consists entirely of **remarks**, starting with the word **REM**. Remarks are used to identify a program and explain steps in it. They are not acted on by the computer in any way. The word **END** marks the end of the program.

Notice how the line number increases in steps of 5. Steps of 5 or 10 are usual, so that additional lines can easily be inserted later.

1G   End-of-chapter summary

This chapter has introduced you to (or reminded you of) a number of important points about computers and programs. If any of the points are not clear, it is worth thinking about them again before proceeding further. To assist with this, the main points made in the chapter are summarised below.

- A computer is an automatic, electronic, data processing machine.
- Solid-state electronic components are known as chips.
- Data is information in a form which can be stored on and processed by a computer.
- Processing includes storing, locating, selecting and sorting data, doing calculations and making simple decisions.
- Large computers are called mainframe computers, smaller computers are called minicomputers and the smallest computers are called microcomputers.
- Input is the act of supplying data to a computer from its environment.
- Output is the act of supplying data from a computer to its environment.
- Many computers can store and retrieve data in large quantities, using magnetic disks and tapes.
- Data communication is one of the newest and fastest growing areas of computing.
- Computers cannot take initiatives, respond to unforeseen circumstances, make moral judgements or understand natural languages like English.
- A program is a set of instructions to a computer.
- A computer automatically works through the steps of a program one at a time.
- A program sets up a computer to do a specific task.
- Basic is a programming language designed especially for beginners.
- A Basic program consists of a number of statements.
- Each statement of a Basic program is written on a separate line, starting with a line number.

- Programs must be robust, able to withstand repeated running, often under difficult conditions.

Exercise 1G

1   Write down the meanings of the following words or phrases: computer, chip, data, processing, mainframe, input, output, data bank, terminal, program, statement.
2   What is wrong with this portion of a Basic program?

```
100  REM  THERE IS
105  REM  SOMETHING WRONG
100  REM  WITH ONE OF
115  REM  ONE OF THESE LINES
```

3   Do you think that a computer can be programmed to:
   a) Translate sentences from one language to another?
   b) Accept voice input and print a copy of the words spoken?
   c) Predict next week's weather?
   d) Assist in the design of another computer?
   e) Decide whether some people should have more than one vote?
   f) Determine the effects of world air pollution?
4   Basic, Fortran and Cobol are three programming languages mentioned in the text. Find out the names and uses of some other programming languages.
5   In addition to computers, there are a number of other devices which can be programmed. Examples are traffic lights and automatic washing machines. Extend this list.

2
The first steps

The previous chapter explained very briefly what a computer is, and introduced some preliminary ideas about programs and Basic language. This chapter starts to put these ideas into practice. It introduces the first steps of programming in Basic.

Two operations are introduced, which occur in almost every program. They are **input** and **output**, the meanings of which are explained in the previous chapter. In addition, a technique for preparing a task for programming is introduced. This technique is drawing a **flow diagram**, also known as a **flowchart**. It is not absolutely essential that you learn how to draw flow diagrams, though many examinations in Computer Studies require some knowledge of them. Flow diagrams are, however, very useful in explaining the logic of a program. They are used throughout this book.

2A Input and output

As mentioned in the previous chapter, input is the act of supplying data to a computer from its environment. Output is the opposite process, that of supplying data from a computer to its environment. On most computers used in schools, input is from the keyboard, and output is to the display screen or printer. The Basic instructions for input and output of this type are introduced here.

Each item of data used by a program is known as a **variable**. Variables are given **names**, which consist of a capital letter, sometimes followed by a dollar sign ($). Some versions of Basic permit more than one letter for a variable name; this practice is not followed here.

The operations of input and output are now introduced by means of an example.

Example 2A

Input a person's name and telephone number.
Display or print this information.

Method
The two steps of this task are:
    Input the information
    Display or print it.

Variables
Two variables are required, the person's name and the telephone number. The variable names chosen are:

N$ name
T   telephone number.

Notice that the variable for the person's name has a $ sign. This is because the name consists of letters. Variables of this type are called **literal** variables. Literal variable names in Basic end with a $ sign.

The variable for the telephone number does not end with a $ sign. This is because the variable is a number. Variables of this type are called **numeric** variables.

Flow diagram
A flow diagram is drawn, containing one box for each step of the task. The shape of each box indicates the type of step it represents. See figure 2A1.

Program

```
100  REM EXAMPLE PROGRAM 2A
105  REM INPUT AND OUTPUT NAME
```

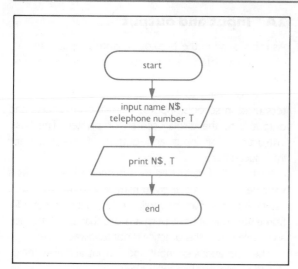

Figure 2A1   Flow diagram for example program 2A

```
110  REM AND TELEPHONE NUMBER
115  INPUT N$, T
120  PRINT N$, T
125  END
```

Points to notice

- Only capital letters are used.
- Each statement begins with a **line number**. These start at a convenient number and increase in steps of 5. Any step size can be used, but 5 and 10 are the most common. The steps are so that other lines can be filled in later if necessary.
- The line number is followed by an **instruction word**. This program introduces four instruction words:

REM   for **remark**. A remark is for the conveni-
          ence of someone reading a program. It is
          not acted on by the computer in any way.

INPUT   is the instruction word for input. It is
          followed by a list of the variables whose
          values are to be input. Variable names are
          separated by commas.

PRINT   is the instruction word for output.
          Whether the output appears on the
          screen or is printed (or both) depends on
          the way the computer is set up. The
          instruction word **PRINT** is used in either
          case. The word **PRINT** is followed by the
          names of the variables whose values are
          to be output, separated by commas.

END   marks the end of the program.

- The variable names used in the **INPUT** and **PRINT** statements are the same, as the same data is input and output.

Sample run

A sample run of the program is shown below. Input from the keyboard is underlined.

```
?  STEVEN MARKHAM, 4772

   STEVEN MARKHAM     4772
```

Notice that there is a comma between the two data items typed.

Exercise 2A

1   Write down the meanings of the following words or phrases: variable, literal variable, numeric variable.

2   a) How are literal and numeric variable names represented in Basic?
    b) For each of the following variable names, say whether it is numeric, literal or incorrect:

    K   N$. $A.   J.   AB.   5.   ?$

Copy the flow diagrams and programs for questions 3 and 4, filling in the missing parts.

3   Input the names of three football teams, and the number of points they have in the Football League. Print this information.

Variables

N$	first team name	A	first team's points
P$	second team name	B	second team's points
R$	third team name	C	third team's points

Flow diagram
See figure 2A2.

Program

```
100  REM EXERCISE 2A QUESTION 3
105  REM INPUT AND PRINT TEAM
110  REM NAMES AND POINTS
115  INPUT N$, A, P$, __, __, C
120  PRINT N$, A
125  PRINT __, __
130  _____
135  END
```

Notice that if you run this program, each **PRINT** statement will start a new line of output.

4   Input the name of a book, its author, year of publication and price. Print this information.

Variables

N$	name of book	A$	author
D	year of publication	P	price

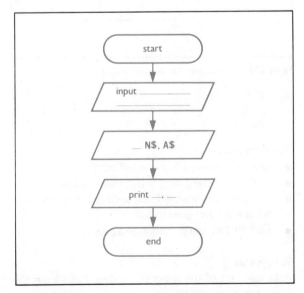

Figure 2A2 Flow diagram for exercise 2A, question 3

Flow diagram
See figure 2A3.

Figure 2A3 Flow diagram for exercise 2A, question 4

Program

```
100  REM EXERCISE 2A QUESTION 4
105  REM INPUT AND PRINT BOOK TITLE,
110  REM AUTHOR, YEAR OF PUBLICATION
115  REM AND PRICE
120  INPUT __, __, __, __
125  _____ N$, A$
130  PRINT __, __
135  END
```

Note that if you run the program, a £ sign should not be typed with the price.

Draw flow diagrams and write programs for the tasks in questions 5 and 6.

5 Input the names and prices of four cars. Print this information.
6 a) Input, as separate variables, the words **OUTNUMBERED**, **OUR**, **THE**, **ARMY**, **POWERFUL**, **DEFEATED**, **ENEMY**. Output several sentences, using some of all of the words in different arrangements. Use a new **PRINT** statement for each sentence.
   b) Repeat part (a) using different input words.

Rewrite the program for the task in question 7, correcting all the mistakes. Remember that a computer will not run a program if there are any mistakes in it.

7 Input the names and populations (in millions of people) of three countries. Output this information.

Variables
A$, B$, C$ name of countries
P, Q, R   their populations

Program

```
100  REM EXERCISE 2A QUESTION 7
105  INPUT AND OUTPUT NAMES AND
110  POPULATIONS OF THREE COUNTRIES
115  INPUT A, P, B, Q, C, R
120  PRINT A$, P
125  PRINT B$, Q
130  PRINT C$ AND R
135  THE END
```

2B Prompts

The previous section introduced the Basic instruction words for input and output, and showed how they can be used in simple programs. When you ran programs from section 2A, you will have noticed that an **INPUT** statement produces a question mark on the screen, and the computer waits for you to type something. But how do you know what to type? What kind of information is the computer expecting? This is where a **prompt** comes in.

A prompt is a word or two of explanation, displayed on the screen before an input is requested. The prompt tells the person using the computer what kind of input the computer is expecting. Prompts are one aspect of a very important quality of programs, namely that they are as easy as possible to use. Programs with this quality are said to be **user-friendly**.

A prompt is created by a **PRINT** statement containing the words of the prompt in inverted commas, immediately before the **INPUT** statement to which the prompt refers. Some versions of Basic allow the prompt to be placed in the **INPUT** statement, but this practice is not followed here.

Example 2B

Input a person's name and address (three lines plus postcode) and print this information as an address label. Provide suitable prompts.

Method
The steps of this task are as follows:
Display name prompt and input name.
Display address prompt and input three lines of address.
Display postcode prompt and input postcode.
Output name, address (3 lines) and postcode.

Variables
N$	name
A$, B$, C$	three lines of address
P$	postcode

Flow diagrams
See figure 2B1. Notice that a prompt and the corresponding input are generally placed in the same box.

```
155  PRINT  A$
160  PRINT  B$
165  PRINT  C$
170  PRINT  P$
175  END
```

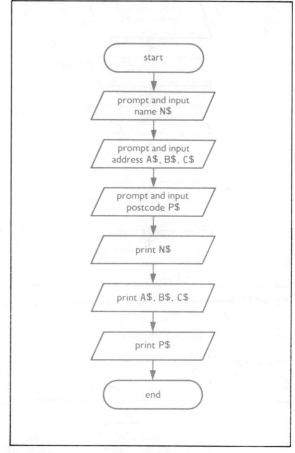

Figure 2B1   Flow diagram for example program 2B

Program

```
100  REM  EXAMPLE PROGRAM 2B
105  REM  INPUT AND PRINT NAME,
110  REM  ADDRESS AND POSTCODE
115  PRINT "NAME"
120  INPUT N$
125  PRINT "ADDRESS (3 LINES)"
130  INPUT A$, B$, C$
135  PRINT "POSTCODE"
140  INPUT P$
145  PRINT
150  PRINT N$
```

Points to notice
- Line 145 causes a blank line of output.
- The text of the prompts is in inverted commas.
- The prompts are brief, but sufficient to tell the user what input is required next.
- Each **PRINT** starts output on a new line.

Sample run
A sample run of the program follows. Input from the keyboard is underlined.

```
NAME
?  GREGORY ANDREWS

ADDRESS (THREE LINES)
?  17 THE VALE
?  ACTON
?  LONDON

POSTCODE
?  W10 5JR

   GREGORY ANDREWS
   17 THE VALE
   ACTON
   LONDON
   W10 5JR
```

Exercise 2B

1 Write down the meanings of the terms prompt and user-friendly.
2 Briefly explain why prompts in a program are important.

Copy and complete the flow diagram and program for the task described in question 3.

3 Input and print a person's name and date of birth, using suitable prompts. Print the information. The date must be in the form 01/04/81 (representing 1st April 1981).

Variables
N\$ name   **D\$** date of birth

Flow diagram
See figure 2B2.

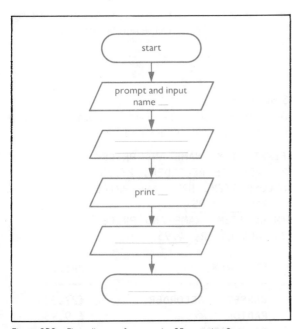

Figure 2B2 Flow diagram for exercise 2B, question 3

Program

```
100  REM EXERCISE 2B QUESTION 3
105  REM INPUT AND PRINT NAME
110  REM AND DATE OF BIRTH
115  PRINT "NAME"
120  INPUT _____
125  PRINT _____
130  PRINT "LIKE THIS : 01/04/81"
135  PRINT "FOR 1ST APRIL 1981"
140  _____
145  PRINT
150  PRINT _____
155  _____
160  ____
```

Notice that the prompt for the date of birth occupies three lines.

Draw flow diagrams and write programs for the tasks in questions 4 and 5.

4 Input the name and wavelength of a radio station and display the information on the screen.
5 The amount of money a person has in the bank is called the balance of that person's account. Each account also has an account number. Input a person's name, bank account number and balance, and print the information.
6 Choose a program from section 2A, and rewrite it, including suitable prompts.

2C Headings and units

The previous section concentrated on the input of information. It showed you how to display suitable prompts to help the person using a program to type the correct input information. This section concentrates on the output of information. It introduces some ways of improving the appearance of output by printing or displaying headings, and including units where appropriate.

Like prompts, headings and units are placed between inverted commas in **PRINT** statements. Units may occur in the same **PRINT** statements as variable names. Care must be taken with the punctuation of such statements, as they can become quite complicated.

Example 2C

Input the names and prices of three items for sale at a shop. Print this information under suitable headings, including units where appropriate.

Method
The steps of this task are as follows:
    Prompt and input first item name and price.
    Prompt and input second item name and price.

Prompt and input third item name and price.
Display headings.
Display first item name and price.
Display second item name and price.
Display third item name and price.

Note that several steps of this task are repeated. In a later chapter of this book you will learn how to instruct a computer to carry out steps of a task repeatedly, using only a few program instructions.

Variables
I\$, J\$, K\$ names of the three items
P, Q, R their prices

Flow diagram
See figure 2C1.

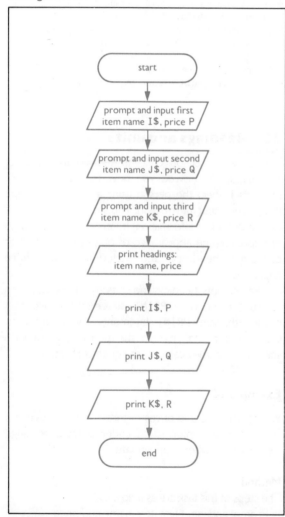

Figure 2C1 Flow diagram for example program 2C

Program

```
100  REM EXAMPLE PROGRAM 2C
105  REM INPUT AND DISPLAY NAMES
110  REM AND PRICES OF THREE ITEMS
115  PRINT "FIRST ITEM, NAME AND PRICE"
120  INPUT I$, P
125  PRINT "SECOND ITEM, NAME AND PRICE"
130  INPUT J$, Q
135  PRINT "THIRD ITEM, NAME AND PRICE"
140  INPUT K$, R
145  PRINT
150  PRINT "ITEM NAME", "PRICE"
155  PRINT "---------", "-----"
160  PRINT
165  PRINT I$, "£";P
170  PRINT J$, "£";Q
175  PRINT K$, "£";R
180  END
```

Points to notice
- The headings are printed in line 150 and underlined in line 155.
- The commas in the **PRINT** statements in line 150 and 155, and lines 165 to 175 cause the output to appear in two columns.
- The semicolons in lines 165 to 175 cause the £ sign to be placed close to the number behind it.

Sample run
A sample run of the program is shown below. Input from the keyboard is underlined.

```
FIRST ITEM, NAME AND PRICE
? CASSETTE RECORDER, 27.50
SECOND ITEM, NAME AND PRICE
? RADIO, 9.95
THIRD ITEM, NAME AND PRICE
? CALCULATOR, 4.95


ITEM NAME              PRICE
---------              -----

CASSETTE RECORDER      £27.50
RADIO                  £ 9.95
CALCULATOR             £ 4.95
```

Exercise 2C

I How is close spacing of output achieved in a **PRINT** statement?

Copy and complete the flow diagram and program for the task in question 2.

2 Input the departure times, flight numbers and destinations of three aircraft. Display this information under suitable headings, with destinations preceded and followed by ★'s.

Variables

T, U, V	departure times
F$, G$, H$	flight numbers (note that they are literal variables)
C$, D$, E$	destinations

Flow diagram
See figure 2C2.

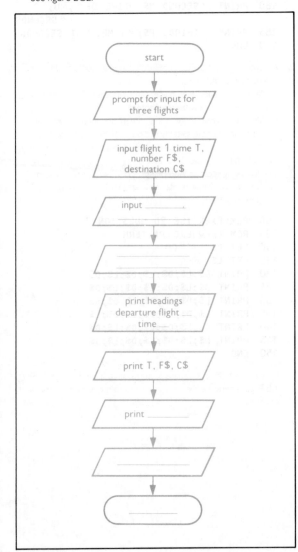

Figure 2C2 Flow diagram for exercise 2C, question 2

Program

```
100  REM EXERCISE 2C QUESTION 3
105  REM INPUT AND OUTPUT FLIGHT
110  REM NUMBERS AND DEPARTURE TIMES
115  PRINT "FOR THE FLIGHTS, INPUT"
120  PRINT "DEPARTURE TIME, FLIGHT NUMBER"
125  PRINT "AND DESTINATION"
130  INPUT T, F$, C$
135  INPUT __, __, __
140  _____
145  PRINT
150  PRINT "DEPARTURE", "FLIGHT", ____
155  PRINT "TIME", _____
160  _____
165  PRINT T, F$, "*";C$;"*"
170  PRINT __, __, __;__;__
175  _____
180  __
```

Notice that there is only one (three-line) prompt for the input, and that the headings for the output occupy two lines.

Draw a flow diagram and write a program for the task described in question 3.

3 Input the titles and performers of the current top three hit singles, and output this information, making the output as attractive as possible.

4 Choose a program from section 2B, and modify it to include headings and units in the output.

5 The program below is written to input a person's name, date of birth and National Insurance number, and output this information with suitable headings. Copy the program, correcting all the errors.

```
100  REM EXERCISE 2C QUESTION 5
105  REM INPUT NAME, DATE OF BIRTH
110  REM AND N.I. NUMBER, AND
110  REM OUTPUT THIS INFORMATION
120  PRINT "NAME"
125  INPUT N$
130  PRINT "DATE OF BIRTH"
135  PRINT D$
140  PRINT "NATIONAL INSURANCE NUMBER
145  INPUT I$
150  PRINT "NAME", N
155  PRINT "DATE OF BIRTH, D$"
160  PRINT "NATIONAL INSURANCE NUMBER" I$
165  END.
```

Note that each 'heading' occurs next to the corresponding output. (This is not a program error.)

6 A number of interesting shapes can be displayed on the screen simply by using consecutive **PRINT** statements, particularly if your computer has a set of graphics characters. An example is shown below.

```
100  REM EXERCISE 2C QUESTION 6
105  REM DISPLAY LARGE SHAPE
110  PRINT "    *    "
115  PRINT "   A   "
```

```
120  PRINT  "    AAA    "
125  PRINT  "   AAAAA   "
130  PRINT  "    AAA    "
135  PRINT  "   AAAAA   "
140  PRINT  "  AAAAAAA  "
145  PRINT  "   AAAAA   "
150  PRINT  "  AAAAAAA  "
155  PRINT  " AAAAAAAAA "
160  PRINT  "     I     "
165  PRINT  "     I     "
170  PRINT  "     I     "
175  END
```

Use this method to produce interesting screen displays of your own. Suggested displays are large characters, cartoon figures, maps, plans and diagrams. A simple outline of the UK is a particularly challenging possibility. (See chapter 11 for further examples and suggestions.)

2D End-of-chapter summary

This chapter has introduced ways of programming input and output operations. A number of ideas associated with input and output have been discussed. The main points of the chapter are as follows:

- The Basic instruction for input contains the word **INPUT**, followed by a list of variables whose values are to be typed at the keyboard. Variables are separated by commas.

- The Basic instruction for output contains the word **PRINT**, followed by a list of variables whose values are to be displayed or printed, or text to be output, enclosed in inverted commas. Commas between output items cause the output to be arranged in columns. Semicolons cause close spacing of output.

- It is good programming practice to include prompts before **INPUT** statements, explaining to the user what input is required.

- Output should be arranged in columns, with headings and units, where appropriate.

- The presentation of input and output is an important aspect of the user-friendliness of programs.

Exercise 2D

This exercise covers various topics introduced in this chapter.

1 The program below is designed to input the names and times of the first three athletes in a race, and display the information, suitably laid out. Rewrite the program, correcting all the errors.

```
100  REM EXERCISE 2D QUESTION 1
105  REM NAMES AND TIMES OF
110  REM FIRST THREE ATHLETES
```

```
115  REM IN A RACE
120  PRINT  "NAME OF RACE?
125  PRINT R$
130  PRINT  "NAME AND TIME OF
                         FIRST ATHLETE"
135  INPUT N$;T; "SECONDS"
140  PRINT  "NAME AND TIME OF
                         SECOND ATHLETE"
145  INPUT N$, U
150  PRINT  "NAME AND TIME OF
                         THIRD ATHLETE",
155  PRINT P$, V$
160  PRINT
165  PRINT RESULTS OF R$
170  PRINT
170  PRINT  "FIRST:";N$,  "TIME:";T;
                             "SECONDS"
180  PRINT  "SECOND M$, TIME OF", U,
                             "SECONDS
185  PRINT  "THIRD, P$; "TIME:"  T SECONDS
190  END.
```

2 An entry in a school Accident Book generally contains the following information:

Date, time of accident, place, name of person involved, injuries sustained, names of witnesses, notes.

Write a program to input this information, providing suitable prompts, and print it, suitably laid out. This program can later form part of a larger program which stores this information on a magnetic tape or disk.

3 The following short section of a program demonstrates a simple method of printing or displaying a pattern. It produces a chequered pattern.

```
100  REM EXERCISE 2D QUESTION 3
105  REM CHEQUERED PATTERN
110  LET D$ = "OO"
115  LET L$ = "  "
120  PRINT D$;L$;D$;L$;D$;L$;D$
125  PRINT D$;L$;D$;L$;D$;L$;D$
130  PRINT L$;D$;L$;D$;L$;D$;L$
135  PRINT L$;D$;L$;D$;L$;D$;L$
140  PRINT D$;L$;D$;L$;D$;L$;D$
145  PRINT D$;L$;D$;L$;D$;L$;D$
150  END
```

Use this technique to create patterns of your own design. (The **LET** statement used in lines 110 and 115 is described in the next chapter.)

3
Calculations

As mentioned in chapter 1, one of the most important aspects of information processing is doing calculations. This chapter introduces calculations in Basic language. You will see that they are carried out in a way which is very similar to ordinary mathematics. The programs introduced in this chapter make use of the operation of input and output introduced in the previous chapter.

This chapter does not require any special knowledge of mathematics. All the formulae required by the programs are supplied in the text.

3A The LET statement

The Basic instruction for a calculation contains the word **LET**. Some examples are:

120 LET A = 3

The variable **A** takes on the value **3**.

135 LET B = C

The variable **B** takes on the value of the variable **C**.

150 LET X = P+Q

The variable **X** takes on the sum of the values of variables **P** and **Q**.

The **LET** statement may also be used with literal variables. For example:

110 LET I$ = J$

The literal variable **I$** takes on the value of the literal variable **J$**.

120 LET K$ = "GIGO"

The variable **K$** takes on the value **GIGO**.

Some general points about **LET** statements are worth mentioning at this stage:

- A **LET** statement contains the word **LET**, followed by a variable, an equals sign, and a number, another variable or an expression.
- The value of the number, variable or expression on the right of the equals sign is **assigned** to the variable on the left of the equals sign. For this reason, a **LET** statement is also known as an **assignment** statement.
- A **LET** statement cannot assign a literal value to a numeric variable, or vice versa. Thus the following statement is wrong:

125 LET A = X$

- In many versions of Basic, the word **LET** can be omitted from assignment statements. For example:

185 J = K+1

In this book, the word **LET** is always included.

Example 3A

Input the length and breadth of a rectangle. Calculate and output its area. Use metres and square metres as units.

Method

The steps of the task are as follows:

Prompt and input length of rectangle.
Prompt and input breadth of rectangle.
Calculate area, using the formula
area = length × breadth.
Output area, with units.

Note that a brief written description of the steps of a task in clear, concise English, as shown above, is called an **algorithm**. An algorithm is often used in place of a flow diagram to express the logic of a program.

Variables

L   length (metres)
B   breadth (metres)
A   area (square metres)

Formula

$A = L \times B$

Flow diagram

See figure 3A1. Notice the shape of the box for the calculation.

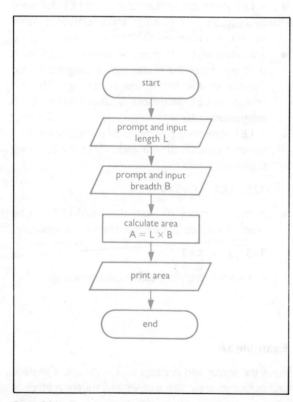

Figure 3A1   Flow diagram for example program 3A

Program

```
100   REM EXAMPLE PROGRAM 3A
105   REM CALCULATE AREA OF RECTANGLE
110   PRINT  " LENGTH (METRES) "
115   INPUT L
120   PRINT  " BREADTH (METRES) "
125   INPUT B
130   LET A = L*B
135   PRINT  " AREA: " ;A; " SQUARE METRES "
140   END
```

Points to notice

- The symbol for multiplication is *. The Basic symbols for the four arithmetic operations are:

	Arithmetic	Basic
add	+	+
subtract	−	−
multiply	×	*
divide	÷	/

- The order of working is
  multiplication and division first,
  addition and subtraction afterwards.
- Semicolons are used for closely spaced output in line 135.

Sample run

A sample run of the program is shown below. Input from the keyboard is underlined.

```
LENGTH (METRES)
?  16.8
BREADTH (METRES)
?  7
AREA: 117.6 SQUARE METRES
```

Exercise 3A

1   Briefly explain the meanings of the words assignment and algorithm.
2   Write **LET** statements for the following expressions:

Examples:

$E = 3A - 2$ becomes
LET E = 3*A − 2

$X = \dfrac{YZ}{4}$ becomes
LET X = Y*Z/4

a) $C = 5B$
b) $K = 10 - 3L$
c) $M = \dfrac{P \times Q}{R}$
d) $H = 0.37 \times J$

e) $S = 10 - \dfrac{T}{5}$

f) $G = ABC$

g) $X = 3Y + 2Z$

h) $W = \dfrac{0.4}{X} - \dfrac{0.7}{Y}$

i) $J = 3 + 5H - 2K$

j) $C = 1.712D - 1.119E$

3 If $A = 20$, $B = 5$, $C = 7$ and $D = 1.5$, write down the value of E after each of the following **LET** statements.

Examples: **LET E = A + 2*B**

$\qquad\qquad E = 20 + 2 \times 5$ (multiplication

$\qquad\qquad E = 20 + 10$ done before

$\qquad\qquad E = 30$ addition)

$\qquad$ **LET E = C/D**

$\qquad\qquad E = 7 \div 1.5$

$\qquad\qquad E = 4.667$ (to 3 decimal places)

a) **LET E = A − C**

b) **LET E = A/B**

c) **LET E = B*D − C**

d) **LET E = C/B + D**

e) **LET E = B*C − D*A**

4 A **LET** statement can be used to change the value of a variable. For example, if $A = 10$, the statement

LET A = A + 1

assigns the value 11 to A. The old value of A is used to work out the expression on the right of the equals sign. The result then becomes the new value of A.

    If X has the value 6, work out the new value of X after each of the following **LET** statements. (The old value of X is 6 in all cases.)

a) **LET X = X + 1**

b) **LET X = 8 − X**

c) **LET X = X*X**

d) **LET X = 12/X + X/12**

e) **LET X = 10 − 2*X**

Copy and complete the flow diagrams and programs for the tasks in questions 5 and 6.

5 Input three numbers and calculate and print their average.

Method

    Prompt and input the numbers.

    Add up the total.

    Divide the total by 3 to get the average.

    Output the average.

Variables

A, B, C numbers   **T** total   **M** average

Formulae

$T = A + B + C$

$M = T \div 3$

Flow diagram

See figure 3A2.

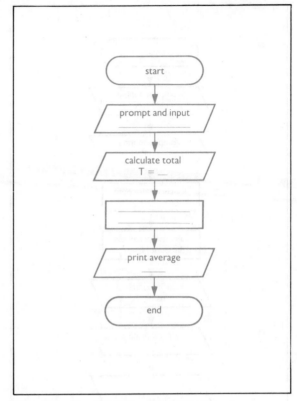

Figure 3A2 Flow diagram for exercise 3A, question 5

Program

```
100  REM EXERCISE 3A QUESTION 5
105  REM INPUT THREE NUMBERS, CALCULATE
110  REM AND OUTPUT AVERAGE
115  PRINT "TYPE THREE NUMBERS"
120  INPUT __, __, __
125  LET T = _____
130  _____
135  PRINT "AVERAGE";____
140  END
```

6 Input the name of an article and its price. Calculate the discount on this price at 15%, and the price less discount. Output the name, price, discount and price less discount.

Variables

A\$	name of article	**P**	price (£)
D	discount (£)	**N**	price less discount (£)

Formulae

$D = 0.15 \times P$ (15% as a decimal fraction is 0.15).

$N = P - D$

Flow diagram

See figure 3A3.

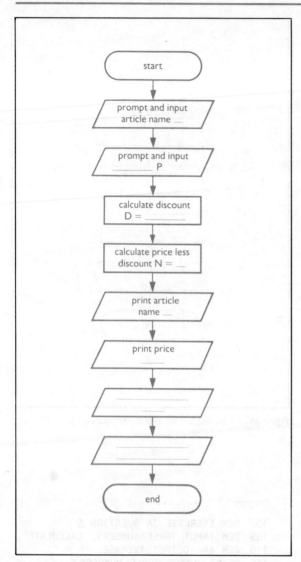

Figure 3A3   Flow diagram for exercise 3A, question 6

Program

```
100  REM EXERCISE 3A QUESTION 6
105  REM CALCULATE DISCOUNT AND PRICE
110  REM LESS DISCOUNT ON ARTICLE
115  PRINT "ARTICLE NAME"
120  INPUT _____
125  PRINT _____
130  INPUT P
135  LET D = _____
140  LET N = _____
145  PRINT "ARTICLE NAME";_____
150  PRINT "PRICE £";_____
155  PRINT _____
160  PRINT _____
165  END
```

Draw flow diagrams and write programs for the tasks in questions 7 to 11. Provide a prompt for each input, and headings and units for each output.

7   Cement is sold at £3.72 per bag. Input an order number and quantity ordered. Calculate the cost, and print the order number, quantity and cost.

Variables
R   order number   **N**   quantity ordered
C   cost (£)

Formula
C = 3.72 × N

8   Input a length in inches and convert it to millimetres. Output the number of millimetres (1 inch = 25.4 millimetres).

9   The profit of a company is taxed at 40%. Input the name of a company and its profit. Calculate the tax and the amount left (the profit after tax). Output all the information.

Variables
C$ name of company   **P**   profit (£)
T   tax (£)   **N**   profit after tax (£)

Formulae
T = 0.40 × P
N = P − T

10   A lorry carries 1132 kg of sand. Input the name of a month and the number of loads the lorry has carried that month. Calculate the number of kilograms the lorry has carried. Output the month, the number of loads and the number of kilograms.

Variables
M$ month   **L**   number of loads
K   kilograms

Formula
K = 1132 × L

11   A salesman is paid 20% commission on his sales. Input the invoice numbers and amounts for three sales. Add up the amounts and calculate the commission. Print a table of the invoice numbers and amounts. Also print the total amount and commission.

Variables
I, J, K   invoice numbers
A, B, C   amounts
T   total
D   commission

Formulae
T = A + B + C
D = 0.20 × T

3B   Arithmetic in Basic

The previous section introduced simple calculations in Basic. This section discusses the topic in more detail, showing how more complicated calculations can be carried out.

A detailed list of the arithmetic operations in Basic language is as follows:

	Arithmetic	Basic
add	+	+
subtract	−	−
multiply	×	*
divide	÷	/
or fraction, e.g.	$\frac{1}{4}$	1/4
brackets	( )	( )

brackets within brackets are permitted

powers and roots, e.g.	x^2	X↑2
	$\sqrt{x} = x^{1/2}$	X↑(1/2)

These operations are carried out in the following order:

1 Powers or roots
2 Multiplication or division
3 Addition or subtraction
4 Any calculations in brackets done first of all, in the above order inside the brackets.

It is preferable to write powers as repeated multiplications if possible, as this way is quicker for the computer to work out. For example:

A↑2 is better written as A*A
Y↑3 is better written as Y*Y*Y

Example 3B

Use Pythagoras' Theorem to calculate the length of the hypotenuse of a right-angled triangle, given the length of the other two sides.

Method
The steps of the task are:
  Prompt and input the lengths of the two sides.
  Calculate the length of the hypotenuse.
  Output the length of the hypotenuse.

Variables
H   length of the hypotenuse
F, G   lengths of the other two sides

Formula
$$H = \sqrt{F^2 + G^2}$$

Flow diagram
See figure 3B1.

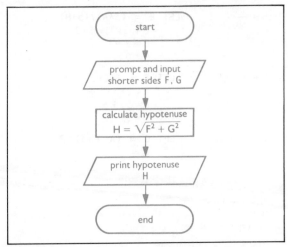

Figure 3B1   Flow diagram for example program 3B

Program

```
100  REM EXAMPLE PROGRAM 3B
105  REM USE OF PYTHAGORAS THEOREM
110  PRINT "TYPE LENGTH OF SHORTER"
115  PRINT "SIDES OF A RIGHT ANGLED"
120  PRINT "TRIANGLE"
125  INPUT F, G
130  LET H = (F*F + G*G)↑(1/2)
135  PRINT "HYPOTENUSE:"; H
140  END
```

Points to notice
● The method of squaring a number by multiplying it by itself is used in line 130.

Sample run

```
TYPE LENGTH OF SHORTER
SIDES OF A RIGHT ANGLED
TRIANGLE
?  7, 24
   HYPOTENUSE : 25
```

Exercise 3B

1 Write the formulae below as **LET** statements. Calculate the left-hand variable if A = 1, B = 3, C = 5, X = 10 and Y = 4.

Examples
Note carefully the order of calculations.

D = 5 + 2B   LET D = 5 + 2*B
                     D = 5 + 2×3
                     D = 5 + 6
                     D + 11

$E = \dfrac{3A}{5B}$

```
LET E = (3*A)/(5*B)
```
$E = (3 \times 1) \div (5 \times 3)$
$E = 3 \div 15$
$E = 0.2$

$F + 2C^2 + 5$

```
LET F = 2*C*C + 5
```
$F = 2 \times 5 \times 5 + 5$
$F = 50 + 5$
$F = 55$

$G = (A + 3)^2$

```
LET G = (A + 3)↑2
```
$G = (1 + 3)^2$
$G = 4^2$
$G = 16$

a) $D = B + 3C$
b) $W = 5(X + Y)$
c) $U = Y^2 - 2X$
d) $V = \dfrac{4}{3} \times 3.14159 \times B^3$
e) $C = \dfrac{A}{X} + \dfrac{B}{Y}$
f) $D = \dfrac{A+B}{2C}$
g) $E = \dfrac{A}{2C}$
h) $J = \dfrac{12}{A+2}$
i) $Z = 3X + 4Y$
j) $K = (AC)^B$

Copy and complete the flow diagram and program for question 2.

2 A chemical is supplied in 25 kg and 50 kg bags. Input the number of bags of each type in an order, together with the order number. Calculate the weight of the order. Output all the information, suitably labelled.

Variables

N   order number
X   number of 25 kg bags
Y   number of 50 kg bags
T   total weight (kg)

Formula

$T = 25X + 50Y$

Flow diagram

See figure 3B2.

Program

```
100  REM EXERCISE 3B QUESTION 2
105  REM CALCULATE TOTAL WEIGHT OF
110  REM SACKS OF CHEMICALS
115  PRINT "ORDER NUMBER"
120  INPUT _____
125  PRINT "NUMBER OF 25 KG SACKS"
130  INPUT _____
135  _____
140  _____
145  LET _____
150  PRINT "ORDER NUMBER: ";_____
```

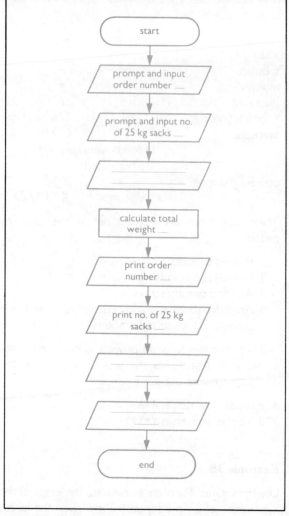

Figure 3B2   Flow diagram for exercise 3B, question 2

```
155  PRINT "25 KG SACKS: ";_____
160  PRINT _____
165  PRINT _____; "KG"
170  END
```

Draw flow diagrams and write programs for questions 3 to 6.

3 The average number of hours that people spent watching television per week was 18.9 in February 1972 and 19.7 in February 1975. Input these figures, or more up to date ones, and calculate the percentage increase.

Variables

A   earlier number of hours per week
B   later number of hours per week
P   percentage increase

Formula

$P = \dfrac{(B-A) \times 100}{A}$

4 At a warehouse, the following data is input each week for each item stored.

	Variable
item number	N
item name	A$
number in stock the previous week	P
number added during the week	L
number removed during the week	R

Use this data to calculate the number currently in stock.

Formula
$C = P + L - R$
C current number in stock.

5 A number of programs can be written concerning area, perimeter or volume. Below are some useful formulae:

Rectangle	area: $A = L \times B$
	perimeter: $P = 2 \times L + 2 \times B$
	L: length B: breadth
Triangle	area: $A = B \times H \div 2$
	B: base H: height
Circle	area: $A = 3.142 \times R \times R$
	circumference: $C = 2 \times 3.142 \times R$
	R: radius
Cylinder	volume: $V = 3.142 \times R \times R \times H$
	R: radius H: height
Cone	volume: $V \times 3.142 \div 3 \times R \times R \times H$
	R: radius H: height
Sphere	volume: $V = 4 \div 3 \times 3.142 \times R \times R \times R$
	surface area: $A = 4 \times 3.142 \times R \times R$
	R: radius

☐ **6** Calculate the volume of earth that must be removed to dig the entrance to the railway tunnel shown in figure 3B3. Work out the formulae yourself. No extra lengths need to be calculated.

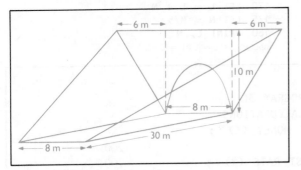

Figure 3B3 Entrance to railway tunnel

3C Checking programs: dry runs

By now you will probably have realised that a program will not run on a computer and produce correct results unless it is correct in every respect. For this reason it is essential to check a program very carefully before attempting to run it.

There are a number of techniques for checking programs. This section introduces one of the commonest, called **dry running**. A dry run is carried out by working through a program statement by statement, doing each operation by hand as it would be done by the computer. A dry run is sometimes a very slow process, but it is often the only way of locating an error in a program, or of ensuring that the program is correct.

Example 3C

Interest is paid on a sum of money if it is saved in a bank or building society for a period of time. The formula for calculating the interest is:

$$I = \frac{PRT}{100}$$

P sum of money ($£$)	**R** interest rate (%)
T time saved (years)	**I** interest ($£$)

Input a sum of money, interest rate and time, calculate the interest and output all the information with suitable headings and units.

A flow diagram is drawn and a program written for this task. The program is then dry run.

Flow diagram
See figure 3C1.

Program

```
100  REM EXAMPLE PROGRAM 3C
105  REM INTEREST CALCULATION
110  PRINT "SUM OF MONEY (£)";
115  INPUT P
120  PRINT "INTEREST RATE (%)";
125  INPUT R
130  PRINT "TIME (YEARS)";
135  INPUT T
140  LET I = P*R*T/100
145  PRINT "SUM OF MONEY :£"; P
150  PRINT "INTEREST RATE :"; R; "%"
155  PRINT "TIME :"; T; "YEARS "
160  PRINT "INTEREST :£"; I
165  END
```

Points to notice
● The semicolons at the ends of lines 110, 120 and 130 cause the input to be on the same line as the prompt in each case.

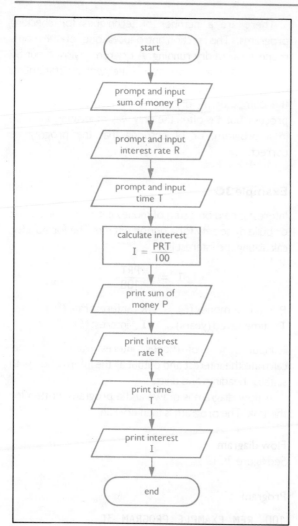

Figure 3C1 Flow diagram for example program 3C

Dry run

The program is dry run by drawing columns next to a copy of the program, one column for each variable. Next to each program line, the current values of the variables are written. Simple values are chosen, to make calculations easy to carry out by hand. See figure 3C2.

Points to notice

- The number output in each of lines 145 to 160 is underlined.
- A table of this nature is sometimes called a **trace table**.

Exercise 3C

1 What is a dry run and why are dry runs important?

Dry run the portions of programs in questions 2 to 4, using the input values given.

```
2  150  INPUT A, B, C
   155  LET D = B - A
   160  LET E = B*C + A
   165  PRINT D, E
```
Input values: A = 7, B = 9, C = 5

```
3  125  INPUT X, Y
   130  LET Z = 25 - X
   135  LET U = X + 2*Y - 5
   140  PRINT U, Z
```
Input values: X = 13, Y = 9

```
4  160  LET K = 5
   165  INPUT L, M
   170  LET L = L + M
   175  LET N = M/5
   180  PRINT L, N
```
Input values: L = 4, M = 15

	P	R	T	I
100 REM EXAMPLE PROGRAM 3C				
105 REM INTEREST CALCULATIONS				
110 PRINT "SUM OF MONEY (£)";				
115 INPUT P	200			
120 PRINT "INTEREST RATE (%)";	200			
125 INPUT R	200	15		
130 PRINT "TIME (YEARS)";	200	15		
135 INPUT T	200	15	2	
140 LET I = P*R*T/100	200	15	2	60
145 PRINT "SUM OF MONEY :£"; P	200	15	2	60
150 PRINT "INTEREST RATE :"; R; "%"	200	15	2	60
155 PRINT "TIME :"; T; "YEARS "	200	15	2	60
160 PRINT "INTEREST :£"; I	200	15	2	60
165 END	200	15	2	60

Figure 3C2 Dry run of example program 3C

5 a) The portion of a program shown below contains two errors. Dry run the program, using inputs A = 10, B = 4, to identify the errors.

```
125  INPUT A, B
130  LET C = 3*(A - B)
135  LET D = E - A
140  LET E = A/(4 - B)
145  PRINT C, D, E
```

b) One of the errors will only occur under certain conditions. State which error it is, and under what conditions it will occur.

6 Dry run programs that you have written for previous exercises.

3D End-of-chapter summary

This chapter has shown how calculations are performed in Basic, and introduced the **LET** statement. A method of checking programs, called dry running, has also been discussed. The main points made during the chapter are as follows:

- An algorithm is a written description of the steps of a task in clear, concise English.
- A **LET** statement assigns a value to a variable. This variable is on the left of an equals sign, which is followed by a constant (a number or string of characters in quotes), another variable or an expression.
- A **LET** statement can be used with literal or numeric variables, but not with a mixture of the two.
- The order in which operations are carried out in Basic is the same as that in arithmetic.
- Squares and cubes of numbers are best written as repeated multiplication.

Exercise 3D

This exercise covers various topics introduced in this chapter.

1 Write the following expressions as **LET** statements. Work out the value of each left-hand variable if D = 2, E = 3, F = 0, G = −2.

a) P = 20 + 3E
b) R = 2E ÷ (D + 1)
c) S = E + G
d) T = DE + EF
e) U = 4(D² − G)

Copy and complete the flow diagram and program for the task in question 2.

2 Input a temperature in degrees Centigrade and convert it to degrees Fahrenheit.

Variables
C degrees Centigrade   F degrees Fahrenheit

Formula

$$F = 32 + \frac{C \times 9}{5}$$

Flow diagram
See figure 3D1.

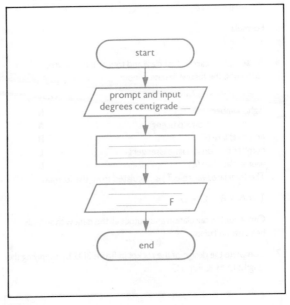

Figure 3D1 Flow diagram for exercise 3D, question 2

Program

```
100  REM EXERCISE 3D QUESTION 2
105  REM CONVERSION FROM CENTIGRADE
110  REM TO FAHRENHEIT
115  PRINT "DEGREES CENTIGRADE";
120  INPUT _____
125  LET _____
130  PRINT _____; F
135  END
```

Dry run the portions of programs in questions 3 and 4, using the input values given.

3
```
135  INPUT A, B, C, D
140  LET T = A + B + C + D
145  LET M = T/4
150  PRINT T, M
```
Input values: A = 3, B = 5, C = 7, D = 1

4
```
120  INPUT P, Q, R
125  LET A = P*Q
130  LET B = 3*P - 2*R
135  LET C = P + Q - R
```
Input values: P = 7, Q = 9, R = 5

Draw flow diagrams and write programs for the tasks in questions 5 to 7. Dry run the programs, using suitable test data.

5 Input the distance from your home to school, and the number of times you make this journey in a year (there are about 190 school

days in a year). Calculate the total distance you travel to and from school in a year. Print, with suitable headings and units, the distance to school, the number of journeys and the total distance travelled.

Variables

D distance to school   **J** number of journeys
T total distance

Formula

T = D × J

6 An aeroplane carries first class and tourist class passengers. For each flight, the following data is input:

	Variable
flight number	N
number of first class passengers	A
first class fare (£)	B
number of tourist class passengers	C
tourist class fare (£)	D

The total fare (variable **T**) is calculated from the formula

T = A × B + C × D

Carry out this calculation and output all the data with suitable headings and units.

7 Complete the design of the rocket in figure 3D2 by supplying the lengths D, H, K, F and G.

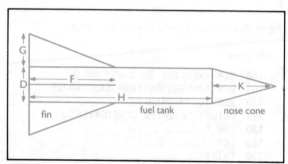

Figure 3D2 A rocket

Input these lengths and calculate:

Overall length: L = H + K

Fuel tank capacity: $C = \dfrac{3.142 \times D^2 \times H}{4}$

Fuel tank surface area: S = 3.142 × D × H

Nose cone volume: $V = \dfrac{3.142 \times D^2 \times K}{12}$

Nose cone surface area: $R = \dfrac{3.142 \times D}{2} \times \sqrt{\dfrac{D^2}{4} + K^2}$

Output all the information with suitable headings and units.

8 Rewrite the program for this task, correcting all the errors.
   Input a person's name and his or her weekly wage. Calculate the year's wage by multiplying the weekly wage by 52. Print the name and both wages.

```
100  REM EXERCISE 3D QUESTION 8
105  REM ANNUAL WAGE CALCULATION
110  PRINT  "NAME;"
115  INPUT  N
120  PRINT  "WEEKLY WAGE ;
125  INPUT  W
130  LET Y = 52W
135  PRINT  "NAME"  N
140  PRINT  "WEEKLY WAGE" , W
150  PRINT  "ANNUAL WAGE"; A
150  END.
```

4

Branches

One of the capabilities of a computer mentioned in chapter 1 is the ability to make simple decisions. This chapter introduces the way decision making is put into effect using Basic language. In Basic, a computer may be instructed to **branch** to one part of a program or another, depending on one or more **conditions**. This is known as **conditional branching**. **Unconditional branching** is also possible, where control is always transferred to another part of the program. The Basic statements for conditional and unconditional branching are introduced in this chapter. A number of uses for these statements are discussed.

4A IF...THEN and GO TO statements

The Basic statement for conditional branching contains the phrase **IF...THEN**. Figure 4A1 shows a portion of a flow diagram and the corresponding program segment for a conditional branch.

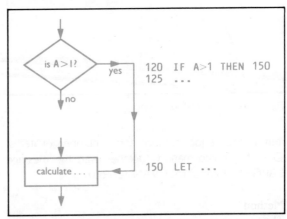

Figure 4A1 A conditional branch

In figure 4A1, if the condition is **true**, i.e. if A is greater than 1, then control passes to statement 150. If the condition is **false**, i.e. A is not greater than 1, then control passes to statement 125, the one following the **IF** statement.

In general, an **IF...THEN** statement has a condition after the word **IF** and a statement number after the word **THEN**. If the condition is true, then control passes to the statement indicated after the word **THEN**. If the condition is false, control passes to the statement after the **IF...THEN** statement.

An **IF...THEN** statement corresponds to a **decision box** in a flow diagram. In the flow diagram, the condition is generally expressed as a question, with different arrows for the answers **YES** and **NO**.

The Basic statement for unconditional branching contains the phrase **GO TO**, followed by a statement number. An example of a **GO TO** statement is shown in figure 4A2.

In figure 4A2, control passes from statement 150 to statement 170.

There is no flow diagram box corresponding to a **GO TO** statement. It is shown by the layout of the arrows.

Example 4A

A furniture removal firm has two sizes of vans: small vans for up to 30 items and large vans for more than 30

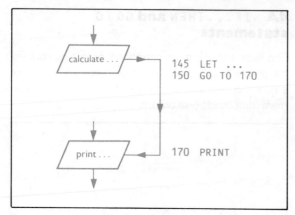

```
145  LET ...
150  GO TO 170

170  PRINT
```

calculate ...

print ...

Figure 4A2   An unconditional branch

items. Input a job number and a number of items. Output this information, together with the message LARGE VAN or SMALL VAN as required.

Method
The most convenient condition is:
   Is the number of items more than 30?
   in which case a large van is required.
Accordingly, the steps of the program are as follows:
   Prompt and input a job number and number of items.
   If the number of items is greater than 30
      then print the information with the message LARGE VAN
      else print the information with the message SMALL VAN

Variables
J   job number   I   number of items

Flow diagram
See figure 4A3.

Program
```
100  REM EXAMPLE PROGRAM 4A
105  REM SMALL OR LARGE VAN?
110  PRINT "JOB NUMBER";
115  INPUT J
120  PRINT "NUMBER OF ITEMS";
125  INPUT I
130  IF I > 30 THEN 145
135  PRINT "JOB :"; J;  "ITEMS :"; I;
                        "SMALL VAN"
140  GO TO 150
```

```
145  PRINT "JOB :"; J;  "ITEMS :"; I;
                        "LARGE VAN"
150  END
```

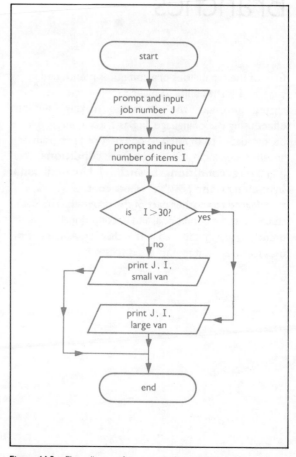

Figure 4A3   Flow diagram for example program 4A

Points to notice
● Notice how the program statements correspond to the layout of the boxes in the flow diagram.
● The **GO TO** statement in line 140 prevents line 145 being executed when it is not wanted.

Sample run
```
JOB NUMBER ? 4691
NUMBER OF ITEMS ? 37
JOB: 4691  ITEMS 37  LARGE VAN
```

Relations used in IF ... THEN statements
A condition always contains a comparison between two quantities. The following relations may be used to express the comparison.

Symbol	Meaning
>	greater than
<	less than
>=	greater than or equal to
<=	less than or equal to
=	equal to
<>	not equal to

An **IF...THEN** statement may also be used with literal variables. In this case, the relations refer to alphabetical ordering of letters as follows:

Symbol	Meaning
>	later in alphabetical order
<	earlier in alphabetical order
>=	later than or equal to
<=	earlier than or equal to
=	equal to
<>	not equal to

Exercise 4A

1 Write down the meanings of the phrases conditional branch and unconditional branch.
2 In each of the following cases, state whether or not control will pass to statement 150.

Example
```
IF  A  >  2*B  THEN  150        A = 11   B = 5
```

Comparison
11 > 2 × 5
11 > 10   true   Control *will* pass to statement 150

a) `IF  3*X  <  17  THEN  150`
   where X = 6
b) `IF  10  -  Y  <>  X  +  5  THEN  150`
   where Y = 4 and X = 0
c) `IF  X*X  >  100  THEN  150`
   where X = 9.9
d) `IF  3*(A  +  B)/5  =  21  THEN  150`
   where A = 29 and B = 6
e) `IF  A  +  B  >  0  THEN  150`
   where A = 6 and B = 9
f) `IF  A$  <  "M"  THEN  150`
   where A$ = "J"
g) `IF  A$  <>  B$  THEN  150`
   where A$ = "NO" and B$ = "YES"
h) `IF  P$  >=  "DAAAA"  THEN  150`
   where P$ = "DAAAB"

In questions 3 to 7 write program segments corresponding to the flow diagrams.

Example

Flow diagram
Figure 4A4.

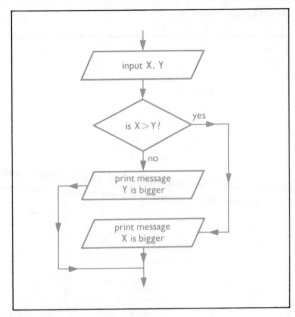

Figure 4A4 Exercise 4A, example

Program
```
130  INPUT  X,  Y
135  IF  X  >  Y  THEN  150
140  PRINT  "Y  IS  BIGGER"
145  GO  TO  155
150  PRINT  "X  IS  BIGGER"
155  REM  CONTINUE
```

3 Figure 4A5.

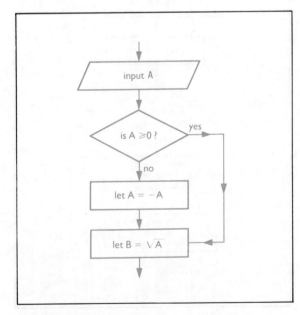

Figure 4A5 Exercise 4A, question 3

4 Figure 4A6.

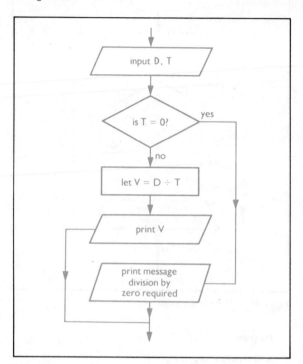

Figure 4A6 Exercise 4A, question 4

6 Figure 4A8.

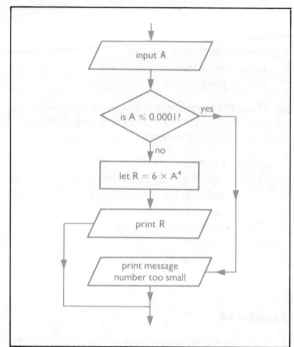

Figure 4A8 Exercise 4A, question 6

5 Figure 4A7.

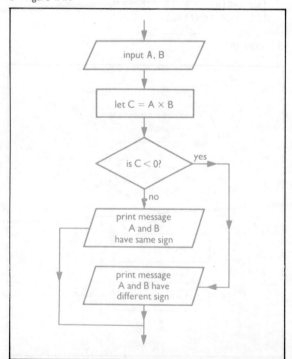

Figure 4A7 Exercise 4A, question 5

7 Figure 4A9.

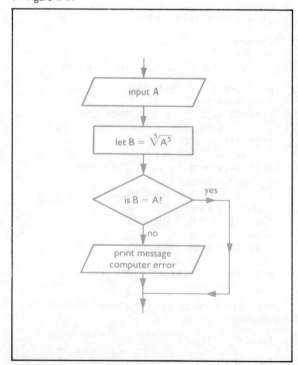

Figure 4A9 Exercise 4A, question 7

Draw flow diagrams and write programs for the tasks in questions 8 and 9.

8   The heating system at a factory is switched on if the average temperature at three points is less than 13°C. Input the temperatures at the three points, calculate their average and print the average with the message HEATING ON or HEATING OFF as required.

9   A triangle is right-angled if the relation $a^2 = b^2 + c^2$ holds for it, where a is the length of the longest side, and b and c are the lengths of the other sides. Input the three lengths, and print them with the words RIGHT-ANGLED or NOT RIGHT-ANGLED as required.

4B   More about conditions

In a great many cases, a condition is used in a program where the alternatives are to carry out some action, or to do nothing. Careful choice of the relation to be used in the **IF...THEN** statement can often simplify the structure of the program under these circumstances. What is generally required is a condition which is true when a portion of the program is to be skipped, in other words a condition for taking no action. In many cases, the condition stated in the program specification must be 'turned around' to achieve this effect.

The example program and exercise in this section demonstrate ways of simplifying the structure of a program by an appropriate choice of condition.

Example 4B

A salesman is entitled to a bonus of £20 if his commission for a week's sales is more than £100. Input a salesman's name and commission, and add the bonus if necessary. Output the salesman's name and commission.

Method

The condition for paying the bonus is:
    Is the commission more than £100?
Therefore the condition for taking no action is:
    Is the commission less than or equal to £100?

Notice that the reverse of 'more than' is 'less than or equal to'. This 'turned around' condition is the one used in the program.

The steps of the program are as follows:
    Input the name of the salesman and his commission.
    If the commission is less than or equal to £100
        then do nothing
        else add £20 to the commission.
    Output the salesman's name and the commission payable.

Variables
N\$ salesman's name   **C**   commission (£)

Flow diagram
See figure 4B1.

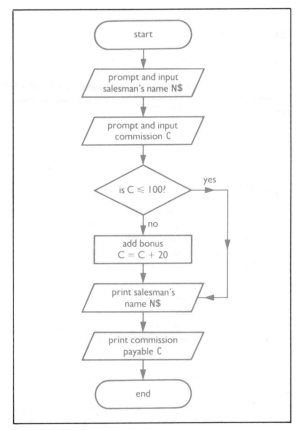

Figure 4B1   Flow diagram for example program 4B

Program

```
100   REM  EXAMPLE PROGRAM 4B
105   REM  SALES COMMISSION BONUS
110   PRINT  " SALESMAN " ;
115   INPUT  N$
120   PRINT  " WEEKS COMMISSION " ;
125   INPUT  C
130   IF C <= 100 THEN 140
135   LET C = C + 20
140   PRINT  " COMMISSION PAYABLE £ " ; C
150   END
```

Points to notice
●   The condition in line 130 is the one for avoiding line 135.
●   The value of variable C is changed in line 135.

Sample run

```
SALESMAN ? A. J. IRONSIDE
WEEKS COMMISSION ? 147.50
SALESMAN: A. J. IRONSIDE
COMMISSION PAYABLE: £167.50
```

Exercise 4B

1 Briefly explain why conditions are sometimes 'turned around' so that they are true when no action is to be taken.
2 The opposite of 'greater than' ($>$) is 'less than or equal to' ($<=$). Write down the opposite of each of the following relations, using Basic symbols.
  a) $<$
  b) $=$
  c) $>=$
  d) $<>$

Draw flow diagrams and write programs for questions 3 and 4.

3 A shop gives a 10% discount on sales totalling more than £50. Input the prices of five items sold and calculate their total. If the total is more than £50, calculate the discount, and the total less discount. Output the total, and the discount and total less discount if necessary.

Variables
P, Q, R, S, W	prices of items (£)
T	total (£)
D	discount (£)
N	total less discount (£)

Formulae
$D = 0.10 \times T$
$N = T - D$

4 At a bank, a charge of 12p per transaction is made on amounts where the average balance is less than £100. Input an account number, average balance and number of transactions. If necessary, calculate the charge (charge = number of transactions $\times$ 0.12). Print all the information, and the charge where there is one.

4C Checking programs: test data

In section 3C, the importance of correctness of programs was discussed, and a technique for checking programs called dry running was introduced. This section introduces another technique for checking programs, namely the use of **test data**.

Test data is input data which is chosen, not to produce useful results, but to ensure that a program is working correctly, or assist in locating a program error. In most cases, several sets of test data are used, for the following purposes:
- Simple data, so that results can easily be checked by hand.

- Sets of data to test each logical path in the program.
- Data which is deliberately 'awkward' and tries to make the program fail.

For a complicated program, the amount of test data required in the second category can be large.

Example 4C

A hired car is charged at 17p a mile for the first 100 miles and 8p a mile for the rest, plus a fixed charge of £6.50. Input a distance travelled, and calculate the total charge.

Devise suitable test data for the program.

Variables
M	mileage	T total charge (£)

Formulae
If the mileage is less than 100, the formula is:

$$T = 0.17 \times M + 6.50$$

Otherwise, the first 100 miles cost 100×0.17 and the rest ($M - 100$) costs $0.08 \times (M - 100)$, so the formula is:

$$T = 0.17 \times 100 + 0.08 \times (M - 100) + 6.50.$$

The steps of the program are:
  Input the miles travelled
  If the mileage is greater than 100
    then use the second formula above to calculate the charge,
    else use the first formula.
Output the mileage and the charge.

Flow diagram
See figure 4C1.

Program
```
100  REM EXAMPLE PROGRAM 4C
105  REM HIRED CAR CALCULATIONS
110  PRINT "MILES TRAVELLED";
115  INPUT M
120  IF M > 100 THEN 135
125  LET T = .17*M + 6.50
130  GO TO 140
135  LET T = .17*100
               + .08*(M - 100) + 6.50
140  PRINT "MILES TRAVELLED :"; M
145  PRINT "CHARGE: £"; T
150  END
```

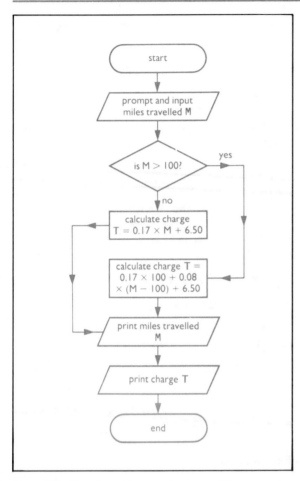

Figure 4C1   Flow diagram for example program 4C

Points to notice

● Both branches of the program lead to the same **PRINT** statements, in lines 140 and 145.

Test data

'Simple' data includes the values 0 miles and 10 miles, where results can be checked by hand.

Data to test each logical branch of the program includes values below and above 100, say 80 miles and 120 miles.

'Awkward' data includes values very close to 100, such as 99.5, 100 and 100.5. The charges must be nearly the same in all these cases. Negative numbers and very large numbers can also be tried.

Sample runs

Sample runs of the program are shown following, using the values of the test data mentioned above.

Run I
MILES TRAVELLED ? 0
MILES TRAVELLED : 0
CHARGE : £6.50

Run 2
MILES TRAVELLED ? 10
MILES TRAVELLED : 10
CHARGE : £8.20

Run 3
MILES TRAVELLED ? 80
MILES TRAVELLED : 80
CHARGE : £20.10

Run 4
MILES TRAVELLED ? 120
MILES TRAVELLED : 120
CHARGE : £25.10

Run 5
MILES TRAVELLED ? 99.5
MILES TRAVELLED : 99.5
CHARGE : £23.42

Run 6
MILES TRAVELLED ? 100.5
MILES TRAVELLED : 100.5
CHARGE : £23.54

Exercise 4C

1 Explain in your own words what test data is and why it is important.
2 What advantage does the use of test data have over dry running as a method of checking programs?
3 A plumber charges £4.75 per hour for his working time, plus a materials charge, with a minimum of £25.00 for each job. Input a job number, materials charge and number of hours worked, and calculate the total charge, making it £25.00 where necessary.

Variables
J   job number   H   hours
M   materials charge (£)   C   charge (£)

Formula
$C = H \times 4.75 + M$

The program written for this task, shown below, contains a logical error. Devise a suitable set of test data and either dry run the program or run it on your computer, using the test data, in order to locate and correct the error.

Program

```
100  REM EXERCISE 4C QUESTION 3
105  REM PLUMBERS CHARGES
110  PRINT "JOB NUMBER";
```

```
115  INPUT J
120  PRINT "HOURS WORKED";
125  INPUT H
130  PRINT "MATERIALS CHARGE";
135  INPUT M
140  LET C = H*4.75 + M
145  IF C < 25.00 THEN 155
150  LET C = 25.00
155  PRINT "CHARGE: £"; C
160  END
```

Draw flow diagrams and write programs for questions 4 and 5. Devise suitable sets of test data for the programs.

4 Workers are paid at ordinary rate for the first 40 hours worked per week, and at overtime rate for the rest. Input a worker's name, works number, ordinary rate and overtime rate and hours worked. Calculate the worker's wage, and output all the information.

Variables

N$	name	M	works number
R	ordinary rate (£ per hour)	V	overtime rate (£ per hour)
H	hours worked	W	wage (£)

Formulae

For no overtime:
$W = R \times H$

With overtime:
$W = 40 \times R + V \times (H - 40)$

5 Write a program to find the roots x_1 and x_2 of a quadratic equation $ax^2 + bx + c = 0$ by the formulae:

$$x_1 = \frac{-b + \sqrt{b^2 - 4ac}}{2a}$$

$$x_2 = \frac{-b - \sqrt{b^2 - 4ac}}{2a}$$

Input values of a, b and c, and test if $b^2 - 4ac$ is negative. If so, there are no roots.

4D Combinations of conditions

It frequently happens that decisions must be made in programs on the basis of a combination of conditions. This section introduces the facilities provided by Basic language for combining conditions, and demonstrates how they are used.

Conditions in an **IF...THEN** statement may be combined by the words **AND** and **OR**, or negated by the word **NOT**. All these words have their usual English meanings, but it is useful to include a table of the workings of **AND** and **OR**, so that there is no uncertainty.

A	B	A OR B	A AND B
false	false	false	false
false	true	true	false
true	false	true	false
true	true	true	true

The table is interpreted as follows: **A** and **B** are individual conditions, which may be true or false. Each line of the table shows how individual values of the conditions affect combinations of them. For example, the third line means that if **A** is true and **B** is false, then **A OR B** is true, but **A AND B** is false.

For example, the combination of conditions required to test whether a number is in the range 1 to 10 (inclusive) is:

```
IF X >= 1 AND X <= 10 THEN ...
```

Trying a few values of **X**:

If $X = 0$, the first condition is false and the second condition is true. Therefore the combination is false.

If $X = 12$, the first condition is true and the second condition is false. Therefore the combination is false.

If $X = 6$, both conditions are true, and therefore the combination is true.

Example 4D

An examination consists of two papers. A candidate fails if his or her percentage for either paper is less than 30%. Input a candidate number, name and the two percentages. Output the information, with the words PASS or FAIL as appropriate.

Method

If the two percentages are variables P and Q, the combined condition for a candidate failing is:

Is P less than 30?
OR Is Q less than 30?

The steps of the program are as follows:
Input a candidate number, name and two percentages.
Print this information.
If the first percentage is less than 30 **OR** the second percentage is less than 30
then print FAIL
else print PASS.

Variables

N   candidate number   N$ name

P, Q   percentages

Flow diagram

See figure 4D1.

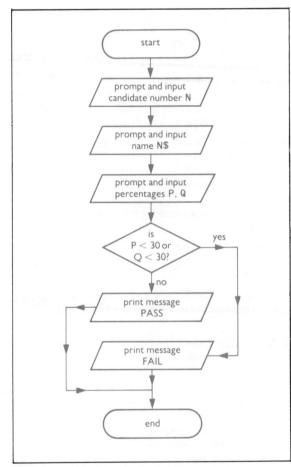

Figure 4D1   Flow diagram for example program 4D

Program

```
100  REM EXAMPLE PROGRAM 4D
105  REM EXAMINATION RESULTS
110  PRINT "CANDIDATE NUMBER";
115  INPUT N
120  PRINT "NAME";
125  INPUT N$
130  PRINT "PERCENTAGES";
135  INPUT P, Q
140  PRINT
145  PRINT "CANDIDATE NUMBER :"; N
150  PRINT "NAME :"; N$
155  PRINT "PERCENTAGES :"; P; "%";
                       Q ; "%"
160  PRINT "RESULT :";
165  IF P < 30 OR Q < 30 THEN 180
170  PRINT "PASS"
175  GO TO 185
180  PRINT "FAIL"
185  END
```

Points to notice

● The combined condition translates directly to an `IF...THEN` statement.

Sample run

```
CANDIDATE NUMBER ? 3169
NAME ? A. J. K. JOSEPHSON
PERCENTAGES ? 57, 29

CANDIDATE NUMBER : 3169
NAME : A. J. K. JOSEPHSON
PERCENTAGES : 57% 29%
RESULT : FAIL
```

Exercise 4D

1 If $A = 10$ and $B = 6$, state whether each of the following combinations of conditions is true or false.
a) `A < 20 AND B > 1`
b) `A = 5 OR B = 6`
c) `A <> 10 AND B < 8`
d) `A <= 10 OR B >= 6`
e) `A*B < 100 AND A*B > 60`
f) `A < B OR B < A`

Copy and complete the flow diagram and program for question 2.

2 Examination percentages are graded as follows: Over 80%: grade A, 55% to 80%: grade B, 30% to 54%: grade C, less than 30%: fail. Input a candidate's name and percentage, and output the corresponding grade.

Method

This program requires several separate conditions, rather than a single combined condition. The conditions are related as follows:
    If percentage greater than 80 then grade A,
    Else if percentage greater than or equal to 55 then grade B,
    Else if percentage greater than or equal to 30 then grade C,
    Else fail.

Variables

N$ name   P   percentage

Flow diagram

See figure 4D2.

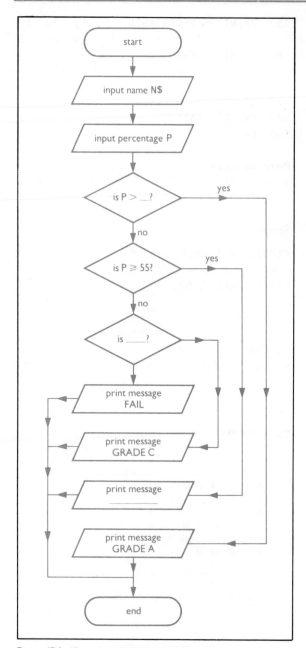

Figure 4D2 Flow diagram for exercise 4D, question 2

Program

```
100  REM EXERCISE 4D QUESTION 2
105  REM EXAMINATION GRADES
110  PRINT " NAME " ;
115  INPUT N$
120  PRINT " PERCENTAGE " ;
125  INPUT P
130  IF P _____ THEN 175
135  IF P _____ THEN _____
140  IF _____
```

```
145  PRINT " FAIL "
150  GO TO 180
155  PRINT " GRADE C "
160  GO TO _____
165  PRINT _____
170  _____
175  PRINT " GRADE A "
180  END
```

Draw flow diagrams and write programs for questions 3 to 5.

3 At a steel mill, three tests are carried out on each batch before it is despatched. The results of the three tests are numbers in the range 0 to 10. The batch is passed if the result for test A is less than 0.3, the result for test B is greater than 7 and the result for test C is 5 or more. Input an identification number for the batch and the results of the three tests. Output the message ACCEPT or REJECT according to the results of the tests.

4 The percentage impurities of a chemical is calculated from the formula:

$$\text{percentage impurities} = \frac{\text{mass of impurities}}{\text{mass of sample}} \times 100$$

The chemical is graded according to the percentage impurities as follows:

less than 1%   : grade 1
1% to 5%   : grade 2
more than 5% : grade 3

Input a batch number, mass of impurities and mass of sample. Calculate the percentage impurities, and display this figure together with the grade.

5 **Climatic Classification**
To determine the type of climate at a place, the following information is required:

altitude
temperatures:
    annual average
    hottest monthly temperature
    coldest monthly temperature
    annual temperature range
rainfall:
    total annual rainfall
    whether there is a summer or a winter maximum
    rainfall of driest summer month

Use the flow diagram (figure 4D3) to write a program to input this data and determine the type of climate of the place. The program may be modified to input twelve monthly average temperatures, and calculate the average, the maximum, the minimum and the annual temperature range (see section 6F).

4E   Validation of input

There is a well-known phrase in the computer industry, which says 'Garbage In, Garbage Out'. It is often shortened to GIGO. What it means is that if the input information supplied to a program is wrong, the output

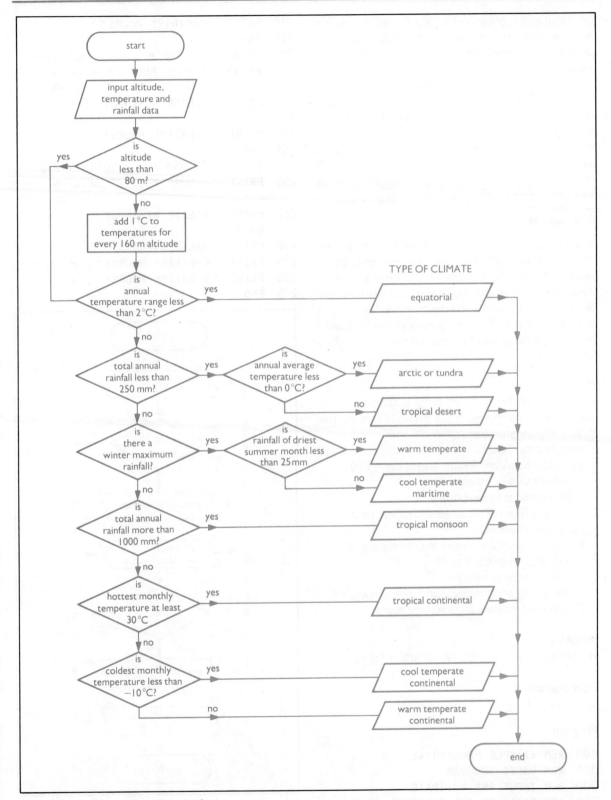

Figure 4D3 Flow diagram for climatic classification

produced by the program is wrong. For this reason it is necessary to check every item of information input to a program. This checking process is also known as **validation**.

The nature of the checks carried out in each case depend on the type of data input. For numeric data, one of the commonest checks is a **range check**, to see if the number supplied lies in a sensible range. For example, if a percentage is input, it can be checked to see if it lies in the range 0 to 100. In practice, validation checks can get extremely complicated, but even so they cannot be guaranteed to eliminate all errors.

Example 4E

A payroll program requires, amongst other things, the input of a worker's ordinary and overtime hours worked. Write the portion of the program which inputs these figures, and checks that the ordinary hours are in the range 0 to 40, and the overtime hours are in the range 0 to 10. If either figure is invalid, a suitable message is displayed, and a request is made to input the figure again.

Method

Each input variable is tested using a combination of conditions, as introduced in the previous section. The steps of the program are:

Input ordinary hours.
If ordinary hours are greater than or equal to 0
    and less than or equal to 40
    then continue to next step
    else display error messages and repeat input.
Input overtime hours.
If overtime hours are greater than or equal to 0
    and less than or equal to 10
    then continue to next step
    else display error message and repeat input.
Display valid ordinary and overtime hours.

Variables

H   ordinary hours   V   overtime hours

Flow diagram

See figure 4E1.

Program

```
100  REM EXAMPLE PROGRAM 4E
105  REM WAGES PROGRAM
200  REM INPUT AND VALIDATE
205  REM ORDINARY AND OVERTIME HOURS
```

```
210  PRINT "ORDINARY HOURS";
215  INPUT H
220  IF H >= 0 AND H <= 40 THEN 240
225  PRINT "FIGURE MUST BE BETWEEN
                    0 AND 40"
230  PRINT "PLEASE RE-INPUT";
235  GO TO 215
240  PRINT "OVERTIME HOURS";
245  INPUT V
250  IF V >= 0 AND V <= 10 THEN 270
255  PRINT "FIGURE MUST BE BETWEEN
                    0 AND 10"
260  PRINT "PLEASE RE-INPUT";
265  GO TO 245
270  PRINT "VALID INPUTS:"
275  PRINT "ORDINARY HOURS:"; H
280  PRINT "OVERTIME HOURS:"; V
285  END
```

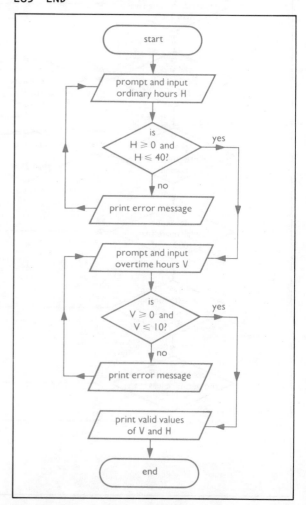

Figure 4E1   Flow diagram for example program 4E

Points to notice

- For each input, the validation condition is true if the variable is valid. If a number of tests have to be carried out, it is often necessary to test for an invalid variable, and use slightly different program logic.
- The input and validation section starts at line 200, to indicate that it is only a part of a longer program.
- The error messages are brief but informative.

Sample run

```
ORDINARY HOURS ? 42
FIGURE MUST BE BETWEEN 0 AND 40
PLEASE RE-INPUT ? 40
OVERTIME HOURS ? 12
FIGURE MUST BE BETWEEN 0 AND 10
PLEASE RE-INPUT ? 10
VALID INPUTS:
ORDINARY HOURS : 40
OVERTIME HOURS : 10
```

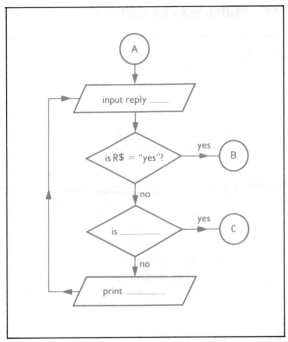

Figure 4E2   Flow diagram for exercise 4E, question 2

Exercise 4E

1 What is meant by the term validation, and why is it important?

2 Copy and complete the flow diagram and program segments for the following task:

At a certain point in a program, the user is asked a question, to which he or she can reply YES or NO. If the answer is YES, control is transferred to line 500. If the answer is NO, control is transferred to line 300. Otherwise a suitable error message is displayed, and the input is repeated.

Variable
R$ reply to question.

Flow diagram
See figure 4E2. Note that the circles are called **connectors**. They indicate a link to another part of the program, shown in a separate flow diagram.

Program

```
100  REM EXERCISE 4E QUESTION 2
105  REM VALIDATE YES/NO ANSWER
150  REM ASK QUESTION
155  INPUT _____
160  IF R$ = " YES " _____
165  IF _____
170  PRINT " _____ "
175  GO TO _____
180  REM CONTINUE
```

Draw flow diagrams and write programs for questions 3 and 4.

3 Input a pupil's name, his or her mark for a piece of work, and the total mark for the work. Calculate and output the percentage for the work, together with the pupil's name. The total mark must be

in the range 20 to 200, and the mark obtained in the range 0 to total mark. Note that the total mark must be input first.

Variables
N$	name	M mark
T	total mark	P percentage

Formula
$P = M \div T \times 100$

4 A money conversion program will either convert pounds to dollars or dollars to pounds. The user is asked to type 1 for conversion from pounds to dollars, or 2 for conversion from dollars to pounds. A sum is then input in the one currency, and checked to see if it is positive, and converted to the other currency.

Suggested variables
R   conversion rate (dollars per pound)
D   dollars   P   pounds

Formulae:
For conversion from pounds to dollars:

$D = R \times P$

For conversion from dollars to pounds:

$P = D \div R$

5 A number of programs from previous exercises can be modified to include validation of input. These include exercise 4C questions 3 and 4 (all input numbers must be positive), example 4D (percentages in range 0 to 100), exercise 4D question 3 (test results in range 0 to 10) and question 5.

4F　Multi-way branching

The previous sections of this chapter have introduced facilities for a conditional or unconditional branch to a single point in a program. A facility is also available in Basic for the conditional transfer of control to one of a number of points in a program. This operation is known as **multi-way branching**.

The Basic statement for multi-way branching contains the phrase **ON...GO TO**. An example of the use of this statement is:

```
150  ON J GO TO 200, 250, 300
```

The statement has the following effect:

if J = 1, control is transferred to line 200,
if J = 2, control is transferred to line 250,
if J = 3, control is transferred to line 300.

Variable J is called a **control variable**. In this example, its value must lie in the range 1 to 3, or a program error will occur.

Example 4F

A company sells equipment on three different sets of terms:

type 1: 10% discount, cash payable immediately,
type 2: amount payable within 30 days,
type 3: 10% surcharge, payable within 60 days.

Input a transaction number, customer name, amount and transaction type. According to the transaction type, calculate the amount payable, and print this figure together with an appropriate message.

Method

The steps of the program are as follows:

Input transaction number, customer name, amount and transaction type.
If type = 1
    then calculate discounted amount and output it with a suitable message.
If type = 2
    then output the original amount with a suitable message.
If type = 3
    then calculate amount plus surcharge, and output it with a suitable message.

Variables

T	transaction number	N$	customer name
A	amount (£)	P	transaction type
M	amount less discount or with surcharge (£)		

Formulae

A 10% discount means that the amount less discount is 90% or 0.9 of the original amount. In other words:

$$M = 0.9 \times A$$

A 10% surcharge means that the amount with the surcharge is 110% or 1.1 of the original amount. In other words:

$$M = 1.1 \times A$$

Flow diagram

See figure 4F1. Notice that several flow diagram boxes are needed for the multi-way branching.

Program

```
100  REM EXAMPLE PROGRAM 4F
105  REM TRANSACTION TYPES
110  PRINT "TRANSACTION NUMBER";
115  INPUT T
120  PRINT "CUSTOMER NAME";
125  INPUT N$
130  PRINT "AMOUNT";
135  INPUT A
140  PRINT "TRANSACTION TYPE
                   (1, 2 OR 3)";
145  INPUT P
150  ON P GO TO 155, 180, 200
155  REM TYPE 1
160  LET M = 0.9*A
165  PRINT "AMOUNT PAYABLE : £"; M
170  PRINT "TERMS : CASH ON
                   RECEIPT OF GOODS"
175  GO TO 220
180  REM TYPE 2
185  PRINT "AMOUNT PAYABLE : £"; A
190  PRINT "TERMS : PAYMENT
                   WITHIN 30 DAYS"
195  GO TO 220
200  REM TYPE 3
205  LET M = 1.1*A
210  PRINT "AMOUNT PAYABLE : £"; M
215  PRINT "TERMS : PAYMENT
                   WITHIN 60 DAYS"
220  END
```

Points to notice

● The possible values of the transaction type are included in the prompt for it.

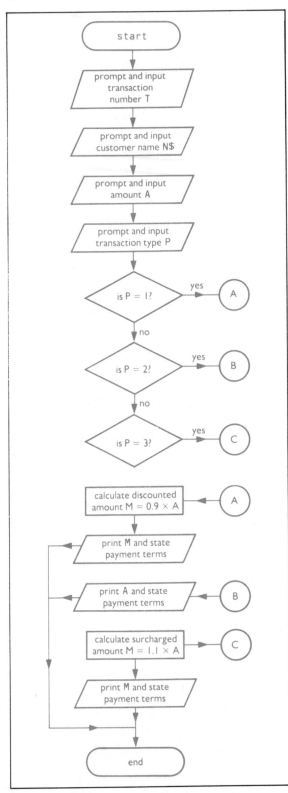

Figure 4F1   Flow diagram for example program 4F

- The segment of the program for each transaction type is identified by a **REM** statement. This is common practice in larger programs.
- Some validation of the variable P is important, as a value outside the range 1 to 3 will cause a program error. This validation has been omitted in this case to keep the program simple.

Sample run

```
TRANSACTION NUMBER ? 59268
CUSTOMER NAME ? KME ELECTRONICS
AMOUNT ? 5621.35
TRANSACTION TYPE (1,2 OR 3) ? 2
AMOUNT PAYABLE : £5621.35
TERMS : PAYMENT WITHIN 30 DAYS
```

Exercise 4F

1 Write down the meanings of the terms multi-way branch and control variable.
2 `ON K GO TO 300, 400, 500, 600.`
   a) What values can the variable K have for the above statement to work correctly?
   b) If K = 3, to which statement is control transferred?
   c) Which value of K will cause a transfer of control to line 300?

Draw flow diagrams and write programs for the tasks in questions 3 and 4. Include validation of input where appropriate.

3 A hire purchase company offers four different types of hire purchase arrangement:

   type 1 : No deposit,   24 monthly payments
   type 2 : 10% deposit, 12 monthly payments
   type 3 : 25% deposit,   6 monthly payments
   type 4 : 50% deposit,   3 monthly payments

Input an amount and arrangement type. Calculate the deposit (if there is one) and the monthly payments, and output these figures.

Suggested variables

A	amount (£)	T	arrangement type
D	deposit (£)	M	monthly payment (£)
P	percentage deposit	N	number of payments

Formulae
$$D = \frac{A \times P}{100} \qquad M = \frac{A - D}{N}$$

4 Input a single digit number and display it as a large character (say 5 character spaces by 7 lines). Note that if the digit 0 is included, then the multi-way branching statement will have to be of the form

   `ON D + 1 GO TO ...`

It is suggested that a suitable subset of the digits be chosen.

4G End-of-chapter summary

This chapter has introduced the ideas of conditional, unconditional and multi-way branching. Ways of implementing these ideas in Basic language have been demonstrated. The main points of the chapter are as follows:

- The Basic statement for a conditional branch contains the phrase **IF...THEN**. There is a condition after the word **IF** and a statement number after the word **THEN**. If the condition is true, control passes to the statement identified after the word **THEN**. If the condition is false, control passes to the statement after the **IF...THEN** statement.

- The Basic statement for unconditional branching contains the phrase **GO TO** followed by a statement number.

- Conditions can sometimes be 'turned around' to simplify the logic of a program.

- An important method of checking programs is the use of test data.

- Conditions in an **IF...THEN** statement can be combined by the words **AND** and **OR**, or negated by the word **NOT**.

- The Basic statement for multi-way branching contains the phrase **ON...GO TO**. The variable used in a multi-way branch is called a control variable.

Exercise 4G

Questions in this exercise cover various topics introduced in this or previous chapters.

1 Briefly describe the facilities provided in Basic language for various types of branching.

2 For each of the conditions below, state whether or not control will pass to line 250.

a) `IF X > 5 THEN 250`
where **X** = 5

b) `IF Y <> 7 THEN 250`
where **Y** = 6

c) `IF A < 0 OR A > 10 THEN 250`
where **A** = 9

d) `IF A$ = "A" OR A$ = "B" THEN 250`
where **A$** = "X"

e) `IF K >= 5 AND K < 10 THEN 250`
where **K** = 20

3 Each of the following **IF...THEN** statements contains an error. Rewrite the statements, correcting the errors.

a) `IF A => 4 THEN 150`

b) `IF X >< Y THEN 200`

c) `IF A$ > J THEN 250`

d) `IF X = 2 OR 3 THEN 165`

e) `IF K > "3" THEN 135`

Draw flow diagrams and write programs for questions 4 and 5.

4 A batch of metal parts produced at a factory is accepted if the average length of three samples selected from the batch is between 748 mm and 752 mm. Input a batch number and the lengths of the three samples, calculate the average length, and decide whether or not the batch is to be accepted. Pay particular attention to screen prompts for input and the layout of output. Check that the batch number is positive, and that the three lengths are in the range 740 mm to 760 mm.

5 The examination for a subject has three papers, each out of 100 marks. To pass, a candidate must get more than 30 marks in each paper, and the total mark for the three papers must exceed 100. Input a candidate name and number, and three marks. Output the total mark, together with the message **PASS** or **FAIL** as required.

6 Modify example program 4F to include a check on the transaction type. It must have a value of 1, 2 or 3.

5

More about variables, numbers, input and output

Having learned something about input, processing, and output in the previous four chapters, it is time to take a second look at some areas of Basic which have already been introduced. These areas are variable names, types of numbers, alternative forms of input and ways of controlling the layout of output. They are investigated in more detail in this chapter in preparation for later chapters of the book which introduce more substantial programs, using a number of new programming techniques. In addition, the topic of program documentation is introduced at this stage.

5A Variable names

Up to now, variable names have been restricted to a single letter, followed by a $ sign for literal variables. All versions of Basic also allow a single digit to follow the letter. Thus **A1** and **K9$** are valid variable names. Many versions allow a sequence of letters for a variable name, but this practice is not universal. and is not followed in this book.

Careful choice of variable names can make a program easier to understand. Variable names starting with the same letter are generally associated, for example **N1$** can be used for a person's first name, and **N2$** for their surname.

Example 5A

At a conference on microcomputers, it is decided to print a name badge for each person attending. A program is to be written to input the first name and surname of a person, and print a badge as follows:

```
.  MICROCON 81 MICROCON 81
.  MICROCON 81 MICROCON 81
.
.  FIRSTNAME SURNAME
.
.  MICROCON 81 MICROCON 81
```

Method
The steps of the program are:
Input a first name and surname.
Print a badge.

Variables

N1$	first name	N2$	surname
D$	"."	M$	"MICROCON 81"
S$	" "(space)		

Notice that because much of the text is duplicated, variables are used to represent characters or groups of characters.

Flow diagram
See figure 5A1.

Program

```
100  REM EXAMPLE PROGRAM 5A
105  REM PRINT CONFERENCE NAME BADGE
110  LET M$ = "MICROCON 81"
115  LET D$ = "."
```

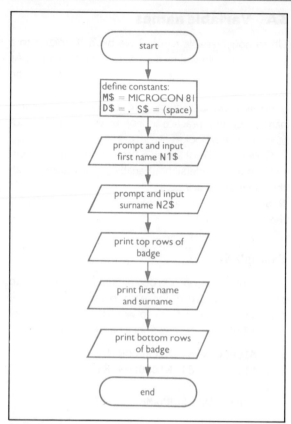

Figure 5A1 Flow diagram for example program 5A

```
120  LET S$ = " "
125  PRINT  "FIRST NAME";
130  INPUT N1$
135  PRINT  "SURNAME";
140  INPUT N2$
145  PRINT
150  PRINT
155  PRINT
160  PRINT D$; M$; S$; M$
165  PRINT D$; M$; S$; M$
170  PRINT D$
175  PRINT D$; S$; N1$; S$; N2$
180  PRINT D$
185  PRINT D$; M$; S$; M$
190  END
```

Points to notice

- The use of variables for repeated parts of the output considerably simplifies the **PRINT** statements.
- Lines 145 to 155 serve to separate the output from the prompts and input.

Sample run

```
FIRST NAME ? ALEXANDER
SURNAME ? BABBAGE

. MICROCON 81 MICROCON 81
. MICROCON 81 MICROCON 81
.
. ALEXANDER BABBAGE
.
. MICROCON 81 MICROCON 81
```

Exercise 5A

1 Identify the correct and incorrect variable names in the following list:

K3, J$4, 3A, 3$A, A21, AB7, JK$, B0

Copy and complete the flow diagram and program for question 2.

2 The average speed of a car journey is measured by recording the time of departure and distance showing on the car's mileage gauge, and the time of arrival, and the corresponding distance. The average speed is then difference in distances ÷ difference in times. A program is written to carry out this process.

Variables

D1	start distance (miles)	**D2**	end distance (miles)
T1	start time (hours)	**T2**	end time (hours)
V	speed		

Notice that times must be input as hours and decimals of an hour, thus 09.15 is 9.25 hours.

Formula

$$V = \frac{D2 - D1}{T2 - T1}$$

Flow diagram
See figure 5A2.

Program

```
100  REM EXERCISE 5A QUESTION 2
105  REM CALCULATE AVERAGE SPEED
110  REM OF CAR JOURNEY
115  PRINT  "START TIME (HOURS)";
120  INPUT _____
125  PRINT  "START MILEAGE";
130  _____
135  PRINT _____
140  _____
145  PRINT  "END MILEAGE" _____
150  _____
155  LET V = (D2 - D1) _____
160  PRINT _____
165  END
```

Draw flow diagrams and write programs for questions 3 and 4.

3 At DJS Manufacturers Limited, a label is attached to each product

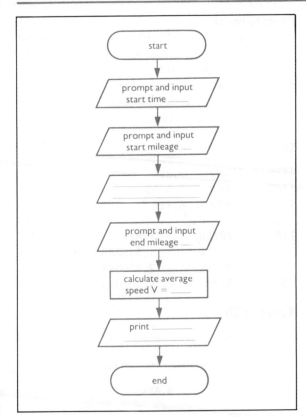

Figure 5A2   Flow diagram for exercise 5A, question 2

before it leaves the factory. The label contains the following information:

	Variables
Date	**D1**: day **D2**: month **D3**: year
Item name	**N1$**
Item reference	**N2$**
Checked by code	**C$**

Input this information, and print it on a suitably designed label.

4   Input the names and times of the first three runners finishing a race. Display this information, suitably set out, together with the difference in time between the winner and the runner-up, and between the runner-up and the person coming third. Validate the data to ensure that the three times are in ascending order.

5B   Floating point numbers

In arithmetic, very large numbers and very small fractions are often written in terms of powers of ten. For example:

3 850 000 is written as 3.85×10^6
0.000 029 is written as 2.9×10^{-5}

Numbers written in this way are known as **standard form numbers**. In Basic, there is a very similar notation for very large or very small numbers. The letter E is used to replace the 10 in the number. For example:

3 850 000 is written as 3.85E6
0.000 029 is written as 2.9E−5

Numbers written in this way are known as **floating point numbers**. The way they are stored inside the computer is very similar, although it is in base two. Numbers output by a computer in floating point form very often have the decimal point in front. Thus:

3 850 000 is output as .385E7
0.000 029 is output as .29E−4

In all cases, the power of ten is the number of places the decimal point moves from its position in the original number to its position in the standard form or floating point number.

Floating point numbers are particularly useful in scientific and engineering work, for example in dealing with very long distances, such as between planets, or very short distances such as the dimensions of atoms and molecules.

Example 5B

Three propulsion systems are proposed for a spacecraft to visit the planet Pluto, 3573 million (3.573×10^9) miles away. Their average speeds are:

type 1 : 32 000 mph (3.2×10^4)
type 2 : 147 000 mph (1.47×10^5)
type 3 : 87 500 mph (8.7×10^4)

Input the speeds of these types, and calculate and output the time (in hours) taken to reach the planet.

Method
The steps of the program are:
Input the speeds of the three types of spacecraft.
Calculate the times they each would take.
Output a table of the types, speeds and times.

Variables
S1, S2, S3 : speeds of types 1, 2 and 3
T1, T2, T3 : time for types 1, 2 and 3

Formula
The basic formula is: time = distance/speed
Thus for type 1: $T1 = 3.573 \times 10^9 \div S1$

Flow diagram
See figure 5B1.

Program

```
100  REM EXAMPLE PROGRAM 5B
105  REM SPACECRAFT TIME CALCULATIONS
110  PRINT "TYPE 1 SPEED";
115  INPUT S1
120  PRINT "TYPE 2 SPEED";
125  INPUT S2
130  PRINT "TYPE 3 SPEED";
135  INPUT S3
140  LET T1 = 3.573E9/S1
145  LET T2 = 3.573E9/S2
150  LET T3 = 3.573E9/S3
155  PRINT
160  PRINT
165  PRINT "TYPE", "SPEED", "TIME"
170  PRINT 1, S1, T1
175  PRINT 2, S2, T2
180  PRINT 3, S3, T3
185  END
```

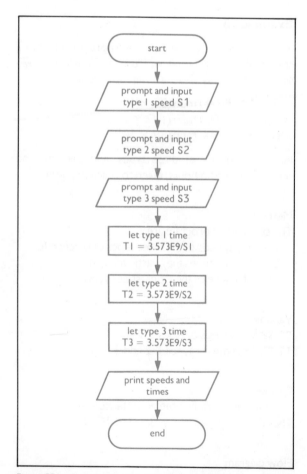

Figure 5B1　Flow diagram for example program 5B

Points to notice

- The commas in the **PRINT** statements in lines 165 to 180 cause the output to be in columns, under the headings in line 165.
- The numbers 1, 2 and 3 in lines 170 to 180 do not have to be in inverted commas. They are printed or displayed as constants.

Sample run

TYPE 1 SPEED ? <u>3.2E4</u>
TYPE 2 SPEED ? <u>1.47E5</u>
TYPE 3 SPEED ? <u>8.7E4</u>

TYPE	SPEED	TIME
1	3.2E4	1.1166E5
2	1.47E5	2.4306E4
3	8.7E4	4.1068E4

Exercise 5B

1　What is a floating point number and when are floating point numbers useful?

2　Convert the numbers below into floating point form. The first one is done as an example.
　　a)　48 000　　　　**4.8E4**
　　b)　67 000
　　c)　473 000
　　d)　831
　　e)　0.000 51
　　f)　1.8
　　g)　374.9

3　Convert the floating point numbers below into ordinary numbers. The first one is done as an example.
　　a) **6.8E3**　　　　6 800
　　b) **8.23E5**
　　c) **6.91E8**
　　d) **3.7E−4**
　　e) **2.0E−1**
　　f) **.31E6**
　　g) **.94E−7**

The number after the E of a floating point number is called the **exponent**. When carrying out arithmetic operations on floating point numbers, the rules for the exponents are:

　When multiplying, add exponents
　When dividing, subtract exponents
　When squaring, double exponents

Use these rules to dry run the programs in questions 4 to 6, using the input values given. Figure 5B2 shows a worked example using the inputs A = 80.E5 and B = 2.0E3

4　Inputs: A = 4.0E3, B = 8.0E8, C = 2.0E6

```
100  REM EXERCISE 5B QUESTION 4
105  INPUT A, B, C
110  LET D = A*C
```

```
100  REM EXERCISE 5B EXAMPLE
105  INPUT A, B                          A      B      C
110  LET C = A/B                        8.0E5  2.0E3
115  PRINT C                            8.0E5  2.0E3  4.0E2
120  END                                8.0E5  2.0E3  4.0E2
```

Figure 5B2
Dry run using floating point numbers

```
115  LET E = C/A
120  LET F = B/C
125  LET G = C↑2
130  PRINT D, E, F, G
135  END
```

5 Inputs: N1 = 2.0E7, N2 = 6.0E5, N3 = 3.0E4

```
100  REM EXERCISE 5B QUESTION 5
105  INPUT N1, N2, N3
110  LET K = N1*N2/3
115  LET L = 6*N1/N3
120  LET M = N2/N3
125  PRINT K, L, M
130  END
```

6 Inputs: I1 = 3.0E7, I2 = 2.0E−5, I3 = 8.0E3

```
100  REM EXERCISE 5B QUESTION 6
105  INPUT I1, I2, I3
110  LET J1 = I1*I2
115  LET J2 = I3/I2
120  LET J3 = I2↑2
125  PRINT J1, J2, J3
130  END
```

Draw flow diagrams and write programs for questions 7 to 9.

7 The Viking Spacecraft travelled the 204 million (2.04×10^8) miles from Earth to Mars in 320 days. Input this data, change the days to hours (multiply by 24) and calculate its average speed (speed = distance ÷ time). Use the same program with different data to calculate the average speed of the Voyager Spacecraft on their journeys to Saturn.

8 Light travels at 186 000 (1.86×10^5) miles per second. Calculate the time for light from the sun to reach the Earth, 93 million (9.3×10^7) miles away (time = distance ÷ speed).

9 A proton is a particle found in the centre of atoms. It has mass 1.67×10^{-24} kg, radius 2.3×10^{-13} metres. Calculate its volume and density.
  volume = $\frac{4}{3} \times 3.14159 \times$ radius^3 (m^3)
  density = mass ÷ volume (kg/m^3)

5C The READ statement

The **READ** statement provides an alternative method of input to the **INPUT** statement. The **INPUT** statement is interactive, allowing values of variables to be entered at the keyboard while a program is running. By contrast, the **READ** statement uses data which is loaded together with the program. It is used for the input of data which does not change from one run of the program to the next, particularly for tables of reference data which would be very tedious to key in every time a program is run.

Data for **READ** statements is supplied by means of **DATA** statements. **DATA** statements are generally placed directly after the **READ** statements to which they refer, or at the end of the program. The action of a **READ** and a **DATA** statement is illustrated in the following example:

```
135  READ C$, R1, R2
140  DATA "DOLLARS", 2.40, 0.42
```

The variables are read in order, thus C$ takes the value DOLLARS, R1 takes the value 2.40 and R2 takes the value 0.42. Notice that commas are used as separaters in both **READ** and **DATA** statements, and that there must be the same number of variables in the **READ** statement as values in the **DATA** statement. However, a **READ** statement can use more than one **DATA** statement, and vice versa. For example, the following statements have the same effect as the previous two:

```
135  READ C$, R1
140  READ R2
145  DATA "DOLLARS"
150  DATA 2.40, 0.42
```

Notice also that literal data must be in inverted commas.

Example 5C

The program below converts from pounds sterling to dollars using a conversion rate which is read as data. This enables the conversion rate to be changed fairly easily, without having to be input every time the program is run.

Method
The steps of the program are:
  Read the conversion rate from stored data.

Input the amount in pounds sterling.
Calculate the equivalent amount in dollars.
Output the amount in dollars.

Variables
P   pounds   D   dollars
R   conversion rate

Formula
$D = P \times R$

Flow diagram
See figure 5C1.

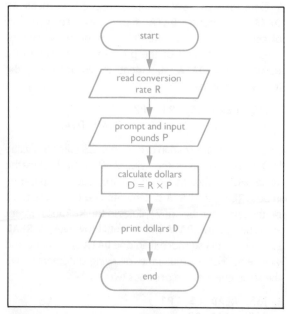

Figure 5C1   Flow diagram for example program 5C

Program

```
100  REM EXAMPLE PROGRAM 5C
105  REM CURRENCY CONVERSION
110  READ R
115  DATA 1.83
120  PRINT "POUNDS";
125  INPUT P
130  LET D = R*P
135  PRINT "DOLLARS: $"; D
140  END
```

Points to notice
● In this example, the **DATA** statement follows the
  READ statement to which it refers. It is also

common practice to place **DATA** statements at the
end of a program.

Sample run

```
POUNDS ?  10.00
DOLLARS $ 18.30
```

Exercise 5C

1 Briefly compare and contrast the **INPUT** and **READ** statements.
2 Write down the values of each variable after the following
   sequence of statements.

```
150  READ A, B
155  DATA 37, −6.9E8
160  READ N1$, C1$, N2$, C2$
165  DATA "JAPAN", "TOKYO"
170  DATA "CHINA", "PEKING"
175  READ J
180  READ K
185  DATA −6.3, 4.9E8
```

Copy and complete the flow diagram and program for question 3.

3 A cinema complex has three studios. A simple information
   retrieval program enables a user to key in the number of a studio
   (1, 2 or 3) whereupon the title of the film at that theatre and the
   showing times are displayed.

Method
The titles of the films and showing times are read from data
stored with the program. The studio number is input and
validated, and an **ON...GO TO** statement is used to output the
required information.

Variables
F1$, F2$, F3$ names of films
T1$, T2$, T3$ times
N   studio number

Flow diagram
See figure 5C2.

Program

```
100  REM EXERCISE 5C QUESTION 3
105  REM FILM STUDIO DATA RETRIEVAL
110  REM SYSTEM
115  READ F1$, T1$
120  READ F2$, ___
125  _____
130  PRINT "STUDIO NUMBER";
135  _____ N
140  IF N = 1 OR N = 2 OR _____ THEN _____
145  PRINT _____
150  GO TO 135
155  ON N GO TO 160, _____, _____
160  PRINT F1$
165  PRINT "SHOWING AT"; T1$
170  GO TO ____
175  PRINT ____
```

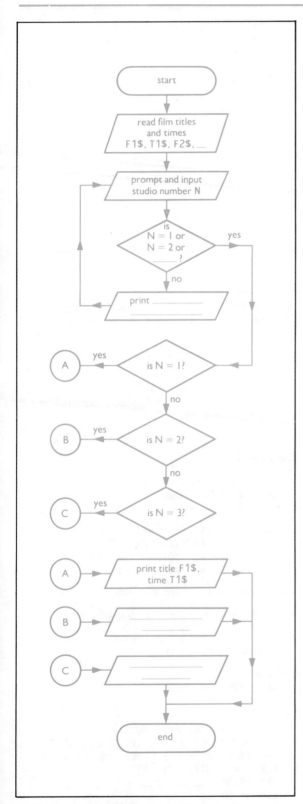

Figure 5C2   Flow diagram for exercise 5C, question 3

```
180  PRINT _____
185  _____
190  PRINT _____
195  PRINT _____
200  DATA  " CAVEMAN " ,  " 7.30PM "
205  DATA _____
210  _____
215  END
```

Draw flow diagrams and write programs for questions 4 and 5.

4 A garage sells five different models of a certain type of car. To record a sale, an invoice is produced. The customer's name and address are input, together with the model number (from 1 to 5). The name and address, together with the name and price of the car are then printed on a suitably laid out invoice. The names and prices of the five cars are read from data.

5 Extend example program 5C to convert from pounds to one of three different foreign currencies. The names and conversion rates are read from data. At the start of the program, the user is prompted to type 1, 2 or 3 depending on the foreign currency required.

5D   Tabulating output

Two methods of controlling the spacing of output in **PRINT** statements have so far been introduced, namely the use of columns and of semicolons. Commas cause the output to be spaced in columns. The number of columns and width of a column unfortunately depends on the type of computer. Semicolons cause close spacing of output. Literal variables are immediately adjacent to each other, numeric variables are generally preceded by a space which may contain a minus sign. These methods of controlling the layout of output are sufficient for many purposes, but they do have limitations.

Much more precise control of the layout of output is achieved by means of the **TAB** function. The **TAB** function, derived from a tab stop on a typewriter, determines the number of spaces from the start of the line to the start of the next output. For example:

```
175  PRINT TAB (10); " DATE " ; TAB (20); D$
```

causes the word **DATE** to be printed after 10 spaces and the value of variable **D$** to be printed after 20 spaces. Notice that the number of spaces is always counted from the start of the line, and not from the previous output.

The **TAB** function may contain a numeric variable. For example:

```
150  PRINT TAB (X);  " * "
```

prints an asterisk after **X** spaces. This aspect of the **TAB** function is discussed in more detail in section 11B.

Tabs must be in ascending order in a **PRINT** statement. Thus the following statement is wrong:

```
185  PRINT TAB (30); X$; TAB (10); Y$
```

Example 5D

The program below produces a simple block diagram of the main parts of a computer, produced using the **TAB** function to make the layout easier.

Method
Values of a number of variables are read from data, and used as 'building blocks' to make up the diagram. The diagram is displayed line by line. It is not necessary to draw a flow diagram of the process.

Variables

I$	INPUT	P$	PROCESSOR
O$	OUTPUT	R$	OPERATORS
C$	CONSOLE	B$	BACKING
S$	STORE	D$	.
L$	-----------	A$	- .

Program

```
100  REM EXAMPLE PROGRAM 5D
105  REM DISPLAY BLOCK DIAGRAM
110  REM OF COMPUTER
115  READ I$, P$, O$
120  READ R$, C$, B$, S$
125  READ D$, L$, A$
130  PRINT
135  PRINT
140  PRINT TAB (15);L$
145  PRINT TAB (15);D$;R$;D$
150  PRINT TAB (15);D$;" ";C$;"  ";D$
155  PRINT TAB (15);L$
160  PRINT TAB (20);D$
165  PRINT TAB (20);D$
170  PRINT TAB (2);L$;TAB (15);L$;TAB (28);L$
175  PRINT TAB (2);D$;" ";I$;" ";D$;A$;
180  PRINT D$;P$;D$;A$;D$;" ";O$;" ";D$
185  PRINT TAB (2);L$;TAB (15);L$;TAB (28);L$
190  PRINT TAB (20);D$
195  PRINT TAB (20);D$
200  PRINT TAB (15);L$
205  PRINT TAB (15);D$;" ";B$;"  ";D$
210  PRINT TAB (15);D$;" ";S$;"  ";D$
215  PRINT TAB (15);L$
220  PRINT
225  PRINT
230  DATA  "INPUT",  "PROCESSOR",  "OUTPUT"
235  DATA  "OPERATORS",  "CONSOLE"
240  DATA  "BACKING",  "STORE"
```

```
245  DATA  ".",  "-----------",  "->"
250  END
```

Sample run
The output produced by the program is shown below:

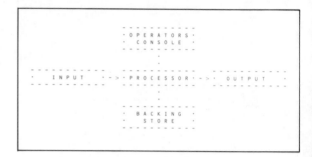

Points to notice
- The semicolon at the end of statement 175 means that statement 180 continues on the same line of output.
- The use of variables as 'building blocks' of a diagram makes the program more concise, but somewhat more difficult to read.
- Commas are not generally used in conjunction with the **TAB** function.

Exercise 5D

1 Briefly describe the three methods of controlling the spacing of output in **PRINT** statements.

2 Correct the errors in the following **PRINT** statements:

```
100  PRINT TAB (20) A$
105  PRINT TAB (K$); J$
110  PRINT TAB (30);X; TAB (20); Y
115  PRINT J$, TAB (7); K$
```

Copy and complete the program for question 3.

3 Input the names of nine people, and display then in three columns, under the headings GROUP 1, GROUP 2 and GROUP 3, which are suitably underlined. The names are input in the order: Group 1, Group 2, Group 3.

Variables
N1$** to **N9$ names of people.

Program

```
100  REM EXERCISE 5D QUESTION 3
115  REM NAMES OF PEOPLE IN GROUPS
120  PRINT "TYPE 3 NAMES FOR GROUP 1"
125  INPUT N1$, N2$, N3$
130  PRINT _____
135  INPUT _____
140  _____
```

```
145  _____
150  PRINT
155  PRINT
160  PRINT TAB (2); "GROUP 1"; TAB (15);
                                "GROUP 2";
165  PRINT TAB (28); "_____"
170  PRINT TAB (2); "_____";
                         TAB (15); _____;
175  _____
180  PRINT TAB (2); N1$; TAB(15); N4$;
                         TAB(28); N7$
185  _____
190  _____
195  END
```

Notice how the order of input is not the same as the order of output.

Write programs for the tasks in questions 4 and 5, drawing flow diagrams if necessary.

4 Decide on a suitable layout for personal letterhead notepaper for yourself, showing your name, address and telephone number. Write a program to produce the paper.

5 Design a simple diagram, similar to that produced by example program 5D, and write a program to produce the diagram. It is very useful to draw the diagram on squared paper before writing the program.

5E Documenting programs

One of the most important, but most neglected, areas of programming is **documentation**. Documentation is a written description of a program, and is generally of two types – **user documentation** and **programmer's documentation**.

User documentation is a guide to the use of the program. It does not contain any details about how the program works; it simply states what the program does, and what a user must do to run it. The style of user documentation must be suited to the type of people for whom the program is written.

Programmer's documentation is a written description of how a program works. It is written for someone who needs to understand the workings of a program, so that they can modify the program or locate and correct errors in it. It is safe to assume that the person reading programmer's documentation has some knowledge of programming.

In both types of documentation, the use of clear, concise English is essential. Documentation should be planned carefully, and set out in an orderly way. Remember that documentation is intended to be read and understood by someone other than the person writing it.

This section provides a brief introduction to program documentation. An example is given of the two types of documentation, followed by an exercise giving practice in various aspects of documentation. It is intended that the skills learned in this section be put into practice throughout the rest of this book, and indeed whenever any programming is done. Documentation is not an optional extra; it is an essential part of programming.

Example 5E

A complete set of program documentation is written below for example program 4F. For completeness the specification of the program is repeated here.

Program specification

A company sells equipment on three different sets of terms:

> type 1: 10% discount, cash payable immediately.
> type 2: Amount payable within 30 days.
> type 3: 10% surcharge, payable within 60 days.

Input a transaction number, customer name, amount and transaction type. According to the transaction type, calculate the amount payable, and print this figure, together with an appropriate message.

Programmer's documentation

The main steps of the program are as follows:
> Prompt and input transaction number.
> Prompt and input customer name.
> Prompt and input amount.
> Prompt and input transaction type.
> Depending on transaction type, branch to one of the following:

Type 1: Calculate the amount less 10% discount, and display the message

TERMS: CASH ON RECEIPT OF GOODS

Type 2: Display the amount payable, and the message

TERMS: CASH WITHIN 30 DAYS

Type 3: Calculate the amount plus 10% surcharge, and display the message

TERMS: PAYMENT WITHIN 60 DAYS

Variables

T transaction number   N$ customer name
A amount (£)   P   transaction type
M amount less discount or with surcharge

Formulae

Amount less 10% discount:

$$M = 0.9 \times A$$

Amount with 10% surcharge:

$$M = 1.1 \times A$$

Points to notice

- The first part of the documentation is a brief, informal description of the overall structure and working of the program.
- The second part of the documentation is more technical, containing variable names and formulae.
- Documenting a program at two levels, in this way, is quite a common practice, but by no means the only approach to programmer's documentation.
- If a flow diagram of the logic of the program is drawn, it forms a useful addition to documentation of this type.

User documentation

Purpose of the program:
The program processes the information for three types of sales:

type 1: 10% discount, cash payable immediately.
type 2: Amount payable within 30 days.
type 3: 10% surcharge, payable within 60 days.

A transaction number, customer name, amount and transaction type are typed in, and the program calculates the amount payable and displays it together with the payment terms.

How to use the program:
When the program is run, prompts are displayed for various items of information, as follows:

`TRANSACTION NUMBER`

Type a transaction number in the proper form. It must not contain any alphabetic characters.

`CUSTOMER NAME`

Type the initials and surname of the customer.

`AMOUNT`

Type the amount of the transaction. Do not type a **£** sign, just the figure.

`TRANSACTION TYPE (1, 2 OR 3)`

Type the transaction type. It must be either 1 or 2 or 3. Any other number will cause the program to fail. Depending on the transaction type, the amount payable and the terms are displayed.

Worked example

Input from the keyboard is underlined.

```
TRANSACTION NUMBER 4621
CUSTOMER NAME F. J. ALLINSON
AMOUNT 467.95
TRANSACTION TYPE (1, 2, OR 3) 2
AMOUNT PAYABLE: £467.95
TERMS: PAYMENT WITHIN 30 DAYS
```

Points to notice

- The user documentation is in three parts, namely a brief statement of what the program does, a step-by-step explanation of how to use it, and a worked example.
- The documentation is written in clear, concise English. No technical terms are used.

Exercise 5E

1 Briefly describe the two types of documentation commonly written for programs.
2 Find out what other types of program documentation are occasionally written.
3 Below is a set of programmer's documentation and user documentation for example program 3C. Read it carefully, and then rewrite it, correcting it in accordance with the recommendations in this chapter.

Program specification
The program inputs a sum of money, interest rate and time, calculates the interest, and outputs all the information with suitable headings and units.

Programmer's documentation
The program calculates the interest on a sum of money, which is input. The formula is:

$$I = \frac{PRT}{100}$$

The rate and time are also input, and the variables are:

P sum of money   R interest rate

T time saved   I interest

Everything is output.

User documentation

When it says SUM OF MONEY input the money. Also input the interest rate when it says INTEREST RATE and input the time when it says TIME. Do not input any alphabetic or special characters.

The interest is calculated on the money you have input and everything is output.

4 Write programmer's documentation and user documentation for example program 4D.

5 Write suitable documentation for some of the programs you have written as answers to exercises. Particularly suitable are exercise 4D question 5 and exercise 4E question 4.

5F End-of-chapter summary

This chapter has taken a second look at some important areas of programming, namely variable names, types of number, alternative forms of input and ways of controlling the layout of output. In addition, the topic of program documentation has been introduced. The main points of the chapter are as follows:

- A Basic variable name consists of a letter, optionally followed by a single digit, followed by a $ symbol for literal variables.

- Very large and very small numbers may be written as standard form numbers. In programming, these numbers are written in a similar way, called floating point numbers.

- The **READ** statement inputs data which has been loaded with the program in **DATA** statements.

- **READ** statements are very useful for data which does not usually change from one run of a program to the next, particularly tables of reference information.

- The **TAB** function controls the layout of output. It determines the number of spaces from the start of a line to the start of the next output.

- Documentation is a written description of the working of a program, and how it is used. Programmer's documentation is a description of how a program works; user documentation is a guide to the use of the program.

- Documentation should be carefully planned, and written in clear, concise English.

Exercise 5F

Questions in this exercise cover various topics introduced in this or previous chapters.

1 Correct the errors in each of the following statements. The statements do not form a complete program.

a) `LET X13 = 3.5E9.0*A1`

b) `READ A1$; B$2, C`
   `DATA MAY, JUNE, JULY`

c) `PRINT TAB (30); "PRICE", TAB (5); VAT`

d) `IF 3X < 1.E-56, THEN 521`

e) `ON K$, GO TO 300, 400 500`

Dry run the programs in questions 2 and 3 using the data values given.

2 Data values: $M1 = 5E3$, $M2 = 2.5E6$, $M3 = 4E-2$

```
100  REM EXERCISE 5F QUESTION 2
105  INPUT M1, M2, M3
110  LET H1 = M1/M2
115  LET H2 = M1*M3
120  LET H3 = M2*M3
125  LET H4 = H1/H2
130  PRINT H1, H2, H3, H4
135  END
```

3
```
100  REM EXERCISE 5F QUESTION 3
105  READ X, Y, Z
110  LET V = X*Y
115  LET W = X/Y
120  LET U = X*Z
125  LET T = X*Y/Z
130  PRINT T, U, V, W
135  DATA 1E10, 5E3, 25
140  END
```

Draw flow diagrams, write programs and write user and programmer's documentation for the tasks in questions 4 to 6.

4 Produce a cartoon picture of a face, which can have one of three expressions selected by the user, and a caption which is typed by the user when the program is run. Validate input where necessary.

5 Design a suitable form to be displayed on the screen and filled in by someone joining a sports club or youth club. The information requested should include name, age, interests etc. Validation should be included on items such as age, and on any questions which require a YES/NO answer. When all the information has been correctly input, the complete form is displayed or printed in a suitable layout.

Note that this program can later form part of a larger program to keep club records. See exercise 12E.

6 The speed of light is $1.86 = 10^5$ miles per second, or $2.99 = 10^8$ metres per second. Input a distance in the units you choose to use, and calculate the time taken by light to travel the distance.

6
Program Loops

A major advantage of computers over previous calculating devices is their ability to perform calculations and other operations repeatedly. This is achieved by certain instructions which cause sections of a program to be carried out more than once. A section of a program which is performed repeatedly is called a **loop**.

The number of times a loop is repeated can be controlled in several ways. This chapter introduces the use of counters to control the repetition; the next chapter shows how conditions can be used to control loops.

6A   Counters

One of the simplest ways of controlling a loop is to instruct the computer to perform the loop a certain number of times. A variable, called a **counter**, is used to record the number of times the loop has been repeated.

The counter:
- Starts at a certain value (usually 1).
- Ends at a certain value (usually the number of times the loop is repeated).
- Is increased by a certain amount (the *step*, usually 1) each time the loop is performed.

There is a statement to mark the start of a loop, and one to mark the end. These statements are introduced in the example below.

Example 6A

Part of a program is to be repeated ten times. Counter K goes from 1 to 10 in steps of 1.

Flow diagram
See figure 6A1.

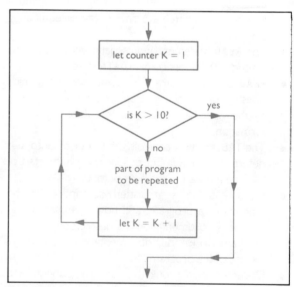

Figure 6A1   Flow diagram for **FOR...NEXT** loop

Program

```
150  FOR  K  =  1  TO  10  STEP  1
```

...part of program to be repeated

```
195  NEXT  K
```

Points to notice

- A loop starts with a **FOR...TO** statement, containing:
    the loop counter (here K),
    the starting value of the counter (here 1),
    the final value of the counter (here 10),
    the step size (here 1).
- A loop ends with a **NEXT** statement. This statement also contains the loop counter.
- The value of the loop counter changes after each repetition of the loop.
- The word **STEP** may be left out if the step is **1**. For example:
    ```
    FOR K = 1 TO 10
    ```
    means the same as
    ```
    FOR K = 1 TO 10 STEP 1.
    ```
- Two flow diagram boxes correspond to the **FOR ...TO** statement.
- In some versions of Basic, the counter may be left out of a **NEXT** statement. This practice is not recommended, and is not used in this book.

Exercise 6A

Draw the parts of flow diagrams and write **FOR...TO** and **NEXT** statements for the following loops:

1 A loop is to be repeated for counter L from 1 to 8 in steps of 1.
2 A part of a program is to be repeated twelve times, using counter A.
3 Part of a program is to be repeated for values of B from 0 to 100 in steps of 5. (How many times will this loop be repeated?)
4 A loop is to be repeated with variable M starting at 1.5 and going up in steps of 0.5 until it reaches 6.5.
5 A loop is to be repeated with variable Q starting at 20 and going down in steps of − 1 until it reaches 1.
6 A loop is to be repeated for counter K going from A to B in steps of C. Values of A, B and C are input before the loop starts.

6B Using program loops

This section introduces some simple examples of program loops.

Example 6B

Each working day at a factory, a record is made of the production of the eight machines. For each machine, its reference code, number of items produced and number of running hours are input. The production rate (number of items produced per hour) is calculated and output. The date is input at the start of the program.

Method

The overall steps of the program are as follows:
    Display a suitable heading.
    Prompt and input the date.
    Repeat, for counter L from 1 to 8 in steps of 1:
        prompt and input the machine reference code,
        prompt and input the number of items produced,
        prompt and input the number of running hours,
        calculate and output the production rate.

Variables

M$ machine reference code
P number of items produced
T hours running
R production rate
D$ date

Formula

$R = P \div T$

Flow diagram

See figure 6B1.

Program

```
100  REM EXAMPLE PROGRAM 6B
105  REM MACHINE PRODUCTIVITY
                          CALCULATIONS
110  PRINT "DAILY MACHINE
                    PRODUCTIVITY RECORD"
115  PRINT "----- -------
                    ------------ ------"
120  PRINT
125  PRINT "DATE"
130  INPUT D$
135  PRINT
140  FOR L = 1 TO 8 STEP 1
145  PRINT "MACHINE REFERENCE CODE";
150  INPUT M$
155  PRINT "NUMBER OF ITEMS PRODUCED";
160  INPUT P
165  PRINT "RUNNING HOURS";
170  INPUT T
175  LET R = P/T
180  PRINT "PRODUCTIVITY:"; R;
                    "ITEMS PER HOUR"
185  PRINT
190  NEXT L
195  END
```

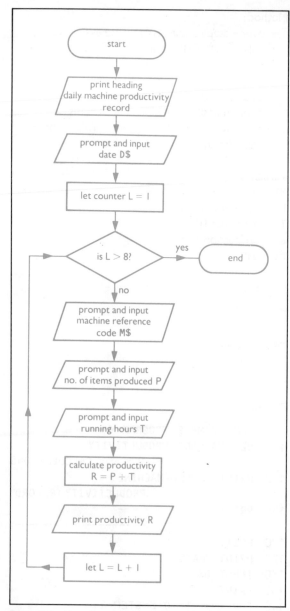

Figure 6B1   Flow diagram for example program 6B

Points to notice

- Lines 110 to 120 print an overall heading for the program.
- Lines 140 to 190 are repeated 8 times.
- Line 185 separates the output for one machine from that for the next.

Sample run

```
DAILY MACHINE PRODUCTIVITY RECORD
----- ------- ------------- ------
```

```
DATE  ?  02/10/81
MACHINE  REFERENCE  CODE  ?  K13
NUMBER  OF  ITEMS  PRODUCED  ?  8427
RUNNING  HOURS  ?  9.4
PRODUCTIVITY :  896.5  ITEMS  PER  HOUR

MACHINE  REFERENCE  CODE  ?  J3
NUMBER  OF  ITEMS  PRODUCED  ?  3624
RUNNING  HOURS  ?  6.9
PRODUCTIVITY :  525.2  ITEMS  PER  HOUR
```

. . . repeated a total of eight times.

Exercise 6B

1   Briefly define the terms loop and counter.
2   Identify and, where possible, correct the errors in the following pairs of **FOR . . . TO** and **NEXT** statements:
   a) `FOR K = 1 TO 5`
      `NEXT J`
   b) `FOR M = 1 TO 10 STEP -1`
      `NEXT M`
   c) `FOR A$ = 1 TO 5 STEP 2`
      `NEXT A$`
   d) `FOR J = J TO 10`
      `NEXT J`
   e) `FOR D = 1 TO D`
      `NEXT D`
   f) `LET K = 1 TO 100`
      `NEXT K`

Copy and complete the flow diagram and program for question 3.

3   Input the name, mass and volume of each of five substances and calculate the density of each. Display suitable prompts, and label the output.

Variables

M	mass (kg)	V	volume (m³)
D	density (kg/m³)	J	loop counter
N$	name of substance		

M   mass (kg)   V   volume (m^3)
D   density (kg/m^3)   J   loop counter
N$ name of substance

Formula
$D = M \div V$

Flow diagram
See figure 6B2.

Program

```
100  REM EXERCISE 6B QUESTION 3
105  REM DENSITY CALCULATIONS
110  FOR J = _____
115  PRINT "SUBSTANCE";
120  INPUT _____
125  PRINT _____
130  INPUT M
135  _____
140  _____
145  LET D = _____
```

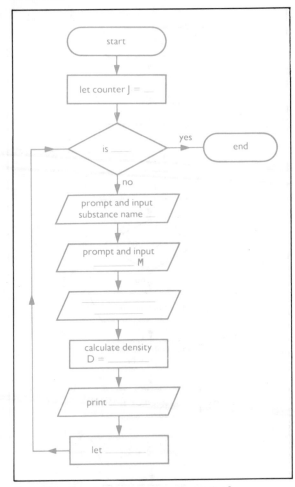

Figure 6B2 Flow diagram for exercise 6B, question 3

```
150  PRINT_____
155  _____
160  NEXT__
165  END
```

Draw flow diagrams and write programs for the tasks in questions 4 to 7.

4   The five members of a rock band agree on what percentage of their year's income each should get. Input the name of the group and their year's income. For each member, input his or her name and percentage of the total. Calculate and output his or her share. Note that the percentages input must add up to 100.

Variables

B$	name of band	N$	name of member
I	year's income (£)	P	percentage
S	share (£)		

Formula

$$S = \frac{P \times I}{100}$$

5   The average weekly earnings (£) of workers in the UK from 1970 to 1974 were:

Year	Men	Women
1970	28.05	13.99
1971	30.93	15.80
1972	35.82	18.30
1973	40.92	21.16
1974	48.63	27.01

Input this information, or more up-to-date figures, and, for each year, calculate the difference between the men's wage and the women's wage.

Variables

M	men's wage	W	women's wage
D	difference	Y	year (can be used as loop counter)

Formula

$D = M - W$

6   The number of cars in EEC countries in 1972 was as follows:

Country	Cars (millions) 1972	% increase 1961 to 1972
UK	13.2	105
Belgium	2.3	172
Denmark	1.2	145
France	13.4	118
West Germany	15.6	202
Ireland	0.4	134
Italy	12.5	409
Luxembourg	0.1	165
Netherlands	2.8	355

For each country, input the above information, and estimate the number of cars in 1983 if the 1961 to 1972 percentage increase were to continue.

Variables

C$	name of country	N	cars in 1972
P	% increase	M	cars in 1983

Formula

$$M = N \times \left(1 + \frac{P}{100}\right)$$

7   Program loops can be used to display a number of shapes on the screen very easily. For example, to display a large rectangle, the following segment of program can be used:

```
100  REM EXERCISE 6B QUESTION 7
105  REM DISPLAY LARGE RECTANGLE
110  PRINT TAB (10); "*";
115  FOR K = 11 TO 30
120  PRINT "*";
125  NEXT K
130  PRINT
135  FOR L = 1 TO 15
140  PRINT TAB (10); "*"; TAB (30); "*"
145  NEXT L
```

```
150  PRINT TAB (10); "*";
155  FOR M = 11 TO 30
160  PRINT "*";
165  NEXT M
170  PRINT
175  END
```

Combine this technique with the method discussed in question 6 of exercise 2C to produce interesting shapes on the screen.

6C Adding up totals in loops

A large number of programming tasks require the total of a set of numbers. Adding up a total is best done in a loop. The method is introduced in example 6C below.

Example 6C
Input 20 numbers. Calculate and output their total and average.

Method
The steps of the program are:
  The total (variable **T**) is set to zero before the loop starts.
  Inside the loop, a number (variable **N**) is input and added to the total ($T = T + N$).
  After the loop, variable **T** is the total of all the numbers. It is divided by 20 to find the average.
Notice that the value of variable **T** changes inside the loop as each number is added.

Flow diagram
See figure 6C1.

Program

```
100  REM EXAMPLE PROGRAM 6C
105  REM CALCULATE AVERAGE OF
110  REM TWENTY NUMBERS
115  PRINT "TYPE 20 NUMBERS."
120  PRINT "THIS PROGRAM WILL CALCULATE"
125  PRINT "THEIR AVERAGE"
130  PRINT
135  LET T = 0
140  FOR K = 1 TO 20
145  INPUT N
150  LET T = T + N
155  NEXT K
160  PRINT "TOTAL:"; T
165  LET A = T/20
170  PRINT "AVERAGE:"; A
175  END
```

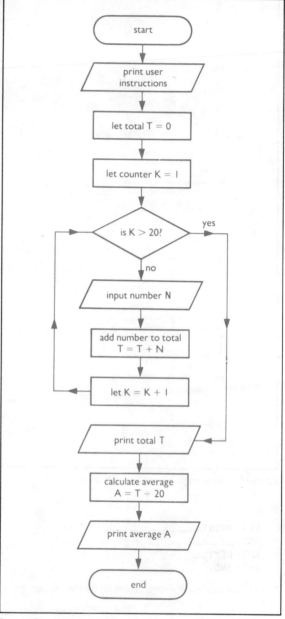

Figure 6C1 Flow diagram for example program 6C

Points to notice
● Notice carefully which operations are done inside the loop, and which are done before or after it.

Sample run

```
TYPE 20 NUMBERS
THIS PROGRAM WILL CALCULATE
THEIR AVERAGE
```

? 17
? 19
? 23
? 5
? 30
? 11
? 20
? 22
? 16
? 18
? 9
? 22
? 20
? 18
? 25
? 15
? 19
? 26
? 24
? 20
TOTAL : 379
AVERAGE : 18.95

Exercise 6C

1 Briefly describe the method for adding up a total using a loop.

Copy and complete the flow diagram and program for question 2.

2 On a cable laying ship, a daily record is kept of the number of hours worked and the number of metres laid. Input this information for ten days, together with the dates, and calculate the total hours worked and total metres laid. From the two totals, calculate the average number of metres laid per hour.

Variables

D$	date	L	metres laid
H	hours worked	T1	total metres laid
T2	total hours worked	A	average metres per hour
J	loop counter		

Formula
$A = T1 \div T2$

Flow diagram
See figure 6C2.

Program

```
100  REM EXERCISE 6C QUESTION 2
105  REM CABLE LAYING SHIP RECORDS
110  PRINT "FOR EACH OF TEN DAYS"
115  PRINT "INPUT DATE, HOURS WORKED,"
120  PRINT "AND METRES LAID"
125  PRINT
130  LET T1 = ___
135  LET _____
140  FOR J = _____
```

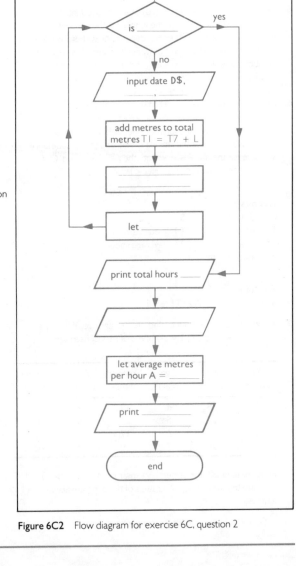

Figure 6C2 Flow diagram for exercise 6C, question 2

```
145  INPUT D$, ___, ___
150  LET T1 = T1 + L
155  LET _____
160  NEXT _____
165  PRINT "TOTAL HOURS:"; _____
170  PRINT _____
175  LET A = _____
180  PRINT _____
185  END
```

Draw flow diagrams and write programs for the tasks in questions 3 to 9. Include validation of input where appropriate, and pay attention to the layout of output. Use suitable test data to check the workings of the programs.

3   Calculate the average of 10 numbers.

4   A school orders sets of eight different text books from a bookseller. Input the name of the school, and the title, quantity and price of each book. Calculate the cost of each (cost = quantity × price) and the total cost. Output the cost and the total in a suitable layout.

5   Write a program to keep records of a bank account. The account number, person's name and the amount in the account (the balance) are first input. Then ten deposits or withdrawals are input, each with a date. Withdrawals are entered as negative numbers, so both deposits and withdrawals are added to the existing balance to get the new balance. Output the balance after each transaction.

6   Each section of a railway line can be taken at a certain speed, depending on the gradient, curvature etc. Input the distances and speed limits of seven sections of a line. Calculate the time to cover each section, at the limiting speed, and the total distance and time for the line. Also calculate the average speed. Output all the quantities calculated in a suitable layout.

Variables

D	distance	S	speed
T	time	T1	total distance
T2	total time	A	average speed
P	loop counter		

Formulae

$$T = D \div S \qquad A = T1 \div T2$$

7   A survey was carried out to find the average age of the cars passing a certain place. The numbers of cars of each age were:

Age (years)	Number of cars	Age (years)	Number of cars	Age (years)	Number of cars
0	9	4	19	8	3
1	22	5	22	9	0
2	35	6	17	10	1
3	28	7	9	11	0

Input these results (or preferably similar ones of your own) and calculate the average age. The steps of the program are as follows:

Set the total age and total cars to zero.

Use a loop to input the information. Add the number of cars to the total cars. Multiply the number of cars by the age and add the answer to the total age.

After the loop, calculate the average age:

$$\text{average age} = \frac{\text{total age}}{\text{total cars}}$$

8   The table below shows the populations and areas of the EEC countries. Input this data and calculate the population density (the number of people per square kilometre) of the country, and the average population density.

Variables

C$	name of country
P	population (millions)
A	area (thousands of square kilometres)
D	population density (people per square kilometre)
U	total area (thousands of square kilometres)
T	total population (millions)
E	average population density (people per square kilometre)
F	loop counter

Formulae

$$D = \frac{P \times 1000}{A} \qquad\qquad E = \frac{T \times 1000}{U}$$

Country	Population (millions)	Area (thousands of square kilometres)
UK	55.93	244.0
Belgium	9.76	30.5
Denmark	5.03	43.1
France	52.13	547.0
West Germany	61.97	248.6
Ireland	3.03	70.3
Italy	54.89	301.2
Luxembourg	0.35	2.6
Netherlands	13.44	40.8

9   Examination marks at a school are graded as follows:

80% or more	grade A
60% to 79%	grade B
35% to 59%	grade C
Less than 35%	grade F

Input the names and percentages of (say) 15 pupils. For each pupil, determine the grade. Calculate the number of pupils obtaining each grade, and also the average percentage.

Suggested method
Use four totals, one for each grade. Start by setting the totals all to zero. Within the loop, when the grade for a pupil has been determined, add 1 to the total for that grade.

6D   Conversion tables

A common use of program loops is to produce tables of various kinds, particularly conversion tables. These loops are generally controlled by **FOR...TO** and **NEXT** statements. In most cases the loop counter is used in the calculation.

Example 6D

Print a conversion table from inches to centimetres, over the range 1 inch to 12 inches (1 inch = 2.54 centimetres).

Method

The loop counter I is also the variable for inches. It is used inside the loop to calculate the centimetres (variable C) from the formula:

$$C = 2.54 \times I$$

The values of I and C are printed under suitable headings.

Flow diagram

See figure 6D1.

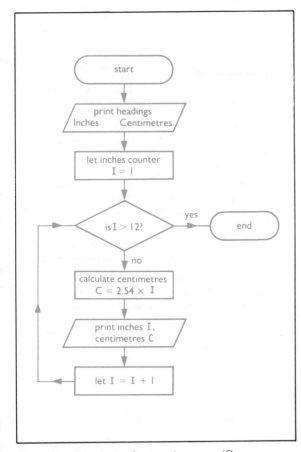

Figure 6D1 Flow diagram for example program 6D

Program

```
100  REM EXAMPLE PROGRAM 6D
105  REM INCHES TO CENTIMETRES
110  REM CONVERSION TABLE
115  PRINT TAB (10); "INCHES";
120  PRINT TAB (25); "CENTIMETRES"
125  PRINT
130  FOR I = 1 TO 12
135  LET C = 2.54*I
140  PRINT TAB (10); I; TAB (25); C
145  NEXT I
150  END
```

Points to notice

● There are no **INPUT** statements
● The loop counter I is used in the calculation.
● The **TAB** function is used to line up the headings with the figures.

Sample run

INCHES	CENTIMETRES
1	2.54
2	5.08
3	7.62
4	10.16
5	12.7
6	15.24
7	17.78
8	20.32
9	22.86
10	25.4
11	27.94
12	30.48

Exercise 6D

1 Briefly describe the general method used to produce conversion tables in Basic language.

Copy and complete the flow diagram and program for the task in question 2.

2 Print a table of the VAT to be paid on prices from 5p to £1.00 in intervals of 5p, and the price plus VAT. Input the VAT rate.

Variables
P   price (pence)   R   VAT rate (%)
V   VAT (pence)   T   price + VAT (pence)

Formulae
$$V = \frac{P \times R}{100} \qquad T = P + V$$

Method

The steps of the program are as follows:

The VAT rate is input.

Headings are printed.

The price is used as a loop counter, from 5 to 100 in steps of 5. Inside the loop, the VAT and price plus VAT are calculated and printed.

Flow diagram

See figure 6D2.

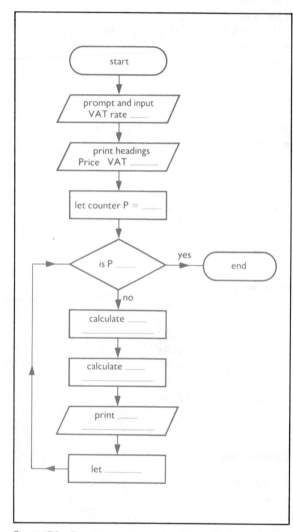

Figure 6D2 Flow diagram for exercise 6D, question 2

Program

```
100  REM EXERCISE 6D QUESTION 2
105  REM VAT CALCULATIONS
110  PRINT "VAT RATE";
115  INPUT ____
120  PRINT
125  PRINT TAB (5); "PRICE";
130  PRINT TAB (15); "VAT" ____
135  PRINT TAB (25); _____
140  PRINT
145  FOR P = ____ TO ____ STEP ____
150  LET _____
155  LET _____
160  PRINT TAB (__); __; TAB (__); __;
              TAB (__); ____
165  NEXT ____
170  END
```

Draw flow diagrams and write programs for the tasks in questions 3 to 7. Validate input where necessary, and pay attention to the layout of output. Choose suitable test data to check the workings of the programs.

3 Print a table of the squares, cubes, square roots and reciprocals of the (whole) numbers from 1 to 25. Pay particular attention to the layout of the output.

Variables

N	number, also loop counter	**S**	square
C	cube	**R**	square root
P	reciprocal		

Formulae

$$S = N \times N \qquad\qquad C = N \times N \times N$$
$$R = N^{0.5}$$
$$P = \frac{1}{N}$$

4 Print one or more of the following conversion tables, over a suitable range of values

a) Kilograms to pounds: $P = 2.2 \times K$
   P pounds **K** kilograms

b) Pounds to grams: $G = 453.6 \times P$
   G grams **P** pounds

c) Miles to kilometres: $K = 1.609 \times M$
   K kilometres **M** miles

d) Pints to litres: $L = 0.568 \times P$
   L litres **P** pints

5 When an object is dropped, it falls under the influence of gravity, accelerating all the time. Its speed, and the distance it has fallen at a certain time after being dropped are calculated from the following formulae:

$$V = 9.8 \times T \qquad\qquad D = 4.9 \times T \times T$$
V speed (metres/second) **D** distance (metres)
T time taken (seconds)

Note that these formulae ignore the effects of air resistance. Print a table of speeds and distances of the falling object for times up to 25 seconds.

6 A sum of money is invested at a certain rate of compound interest. Every year, interest is added to the sum, the formula for the total amount being:

$$A = P \times \left(1 + \frac{R}{100}\right)^{T}$$

A amount (£) **P** sum invested (£)
R interest rate (%) **T** time (years)

Input the sum invested and the interest rate. Print a table of amounts over times from 1 to 20 years.

7 Find out the current conversion rates for pounds sterling to a number of foreign currencies, such as USA dollars, German marks, French francs, Swiss francs, Italian lire. Input the names of (say) four foreign currencies, and their conversion rates. Print a table of conversions from sterling to the foreign currencies, over the range £1 to £50. Validate the conversion rates, checking that they are not zero or negative.

Variables

P	pounds, also loop counter
C1$ to C4$	names of four foreign currencies
R1 to R4	conversion rates for the four foreign currencies
M1 to M4	amounts in the four foreign currencies

Formula
M1 = R1 × P
Formulae for M2 to M4 are similar.

6E Loops of variable length

In many cases it is convenient to repeat a section of a program a variable number of times. This is quite easily achieved, as the following example shows.

Example 6E

The program below stores a simple pattern, and displays it repeatedly across the screen. The number of repetitions is variable, and is input by the user at the start of the program.

Method

The pattern is five character spaces wide and four lines deep. Thus for a forty character wide screen, there can be a maximum of eight repetitions of the pattern. The pattern is stored as four literal variables, with values read from **DATA** statements. In this way the pattern can easily be changed.

Four loops are used, one for each line of output. In each loop, a line of the pattern is displayed, repeated the specified number of times.

Variables

N	number of repetitions of the pattern
J	loop counter
P1$ to P4$	lines of the pattern

Flow diagram
See figure 6E1.

Program

```
100  REM EXAMPLE PROGRAM 6E
105  REM DISPLAY REPEATED PATTERN
110  READ P1$, P2$, P3$, P4$
115  DATA " O "
120  DATA " -I- "
125  DATA " I "
130  DATA " I I "
135  PRINT "HOW MANY REPETITIONS";
140  INPUT N
145  IF N >= 1 AND N <= 8 THEN 160
150  PRINT "MUST BE BETWEEN 1 AND 8"
155  GO TO 135
160  PRINT
165  PRINT
170  REM FIRST LINE
175  FOR J = 1 TO N
180  PRINT P1$;
185  NEXT J
190  PRINT
195  REM SECOND LINE
200  FOR J = 1 TO N
205  PRINT P2$;
210  NEXT J
215  PRINT
220  REM THIRD LINE
225  FOR J = 1 TO N
230  PRINT P3$;
235  NEXT J
240  PRINT
245  REM FOURTH LINE
250  FOR J = 1 TO N
255  PRINT P4$;
260  NEXT J
265  PRINT
270  PRINT
275  PRINT
280  END
```

Points to notice

- The same loop counter is used in all four loops.
- The **PRINT** statements after each loop do not produce a blank line; they simply start the next output on a new line.
- Changing the data in lines 115 to 130 enables a different pattern to be produced.
- It is possible to write this program using fewer statements, by means of a technique introduced in section 6G.

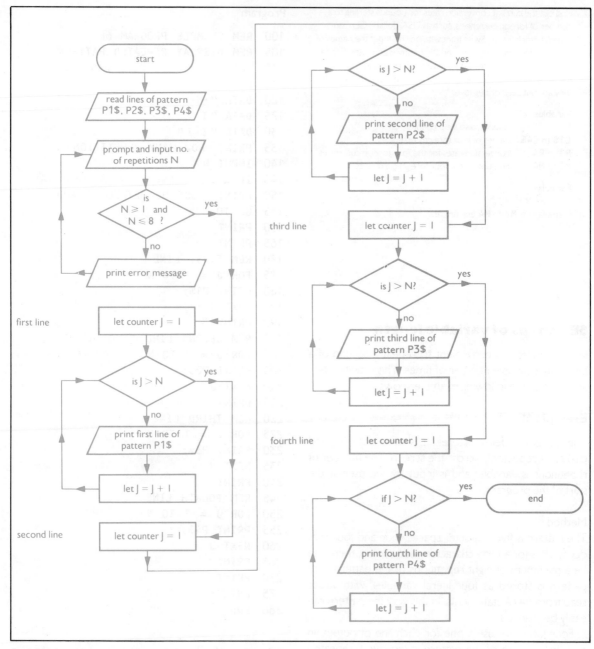

Figure 6E1 Flow diagram for example program 6E

Sample run

A sample run of the program is shown below. Input from the keyboard is underlined.

```
HOW MANY REPETITIONS ? 3
  0     0     0
 -I-   -I-   -I-
  I     I     I
 I I   I I   I I
```

Exercise 6E

1 Alter example program 6E to produce a different pattern. Use graphics symbols if your computer has them.

Copy and complete the flow diagram and program for the task in question 2.

2 a) Input the name, fuel consumption (miles per gallon) and the price per gallon of the fuel used, for a number of cars. For each car calculate the number of gallons needed to travel 100 miles.

and the cost of the fuel. At the start of the program, input the number of cars to follow.

Variables

R	number of cars	N$	name of a car
F	fuel consumption (mpg)	X	loop counter
P	petrol price (£ per gallon)		
C	cost (£) of petrol for 100 miles		
G	number of gallons for 100 miles		

Formulae

$$N = \frac{100}{F} \qquad C = N \times P$$

Flow diagram

See figure 6E2.

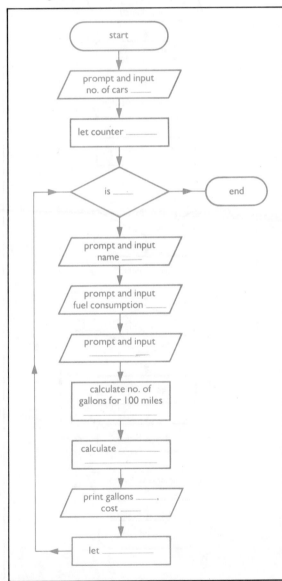

Figure 6E2   Flow diagram for exercise 6E, question 2

Program

```
100  REM EXERCISE 6E QUESTION 2
105  REM FUEL CONSUMPTION AND COST
110  REM CALCULATIONS FOR DIFFERENT CARS
115  PRINT "NUMBER OF CARS";
120  INPUT _____
125  PRINT
130  FOR _____ = 1 TO _____
135  PRINT "NAME";
140  INPUT _____
145  PRINT "FUEL CONSUMPTION";
150  _____
155  PRINT _____
160  INPUT _____
165  LET N = _____
170  LET _____
175  PRINT "USES"; ____;
                   "GALLONS FOR 100 MILES"
180  PRINT "COST £"; _____
185  _____
190  END
```

b) Modify the program to validate the number of cars input. This number should be in the range 1 to 20.

Draw flow diagrams and write programs for questions 3 to 6. Validate input data where necessary. Choose suitable data to test the working of the programs.

3 a) At the end of a term, the marks for the various pieces of work done by each pupil in a class are added up. Each total is out of a different amount, as some pupils have been absent for some pieces of work. Input the number of pupils in the class, and then, for each pupil, input a name, mark and what the mark is out of. Calculate and output the pupil's percentage.

Variables

N	number of pupils in the class	P	percentage
P$	pupil name	M	mark
F	total possible mark (mark out of)		

Formula

$$P = \frac{M \times 100}{F}$$

b) Modify the program to calculate the total mark for all the pupils, and the total of the possible marks. Use these totals to calculate the average percentage for the class.

4 Input a number, and calculate the sum of the squares of the whole numbers up to this number. For example, if the number input is 4, then the sum is

$$1^2 + 2^2 + 3^2 + 4^2 = 1 + 4 + 9 + 16 = 30$$

Validate the number input, checking that it is in the range 0 to 1000.

5 The floor of a house is to be covered with carpet tiles, each of area 0.25 square metres. Input the number of rooms in the house, and then the length and breadth (in metres) of each room. Calculate the area of the room, and the number of carpet tiles needed. Also calculate the total area, and the total number of carpet tiles.

Variables

R	number of rooms	L	length of room (metres)
N	number of tiles in a room	A	area of room (square
T1	total floor area (square		metres)
	metres)	B	breadth of room (metres)
T2	total number of tiles		

Formulae

$$A = L \times B \qquad N = T \div 0.25$$

6   Input the pass mark for an examination, and then a set of pupils' names and their marks. For each pupil, display the word PASS or FAIL according to their mark. Also calculate the total who pass and the total who fail. Output these totals suitably labelled. At the start of the program, input the number of pupils in the class.

A number of programs in previous exercises can be modified to allow the loop to be repeated a variable number of times. Especially suitable are:
    exercise 6B: questions 3 and 7,
    exercise 6C: questions 2, 3, 4, 5, 6 and 9,
    exercise 6D: questions 2, 3, 4, 5, 6 and 7.

6F   Finding the largest number

A great many programming tasks require the computer to select the largest (or the smallest) of a set of numbers. A method of finding the largest of a set of numbers is introduced in this section.

Example 6F

Input a set of numbers, and output the largest one.

Method

A loop of variable length is used, as introduced in the previous section. The steps of the task are as follows:
    The largest number is set to a very small value, say −999999.
    For each number input:
        The current value of the largest number is compared with the input number.
        If the input number is larger, the current value of the largest number is made equal to it.
In this way, the value of the largest number is retained after all the numbers have been input.
    For example, if the input numbers are 5, 7, 9, 4 and 8, and variable M represents the largest number, then the steps are as follows:

	Old value of M	Number	New value of M
Start	−999999	5	5
	5	7	7
	7	9	9
	9	4	9
	9	8	9

M ends with the value 9, the largest number in the set.

Variables

T	number of numbers in the set	M	largest number
N	number	K	loop counter

Flow diagram
See figure 6F1.

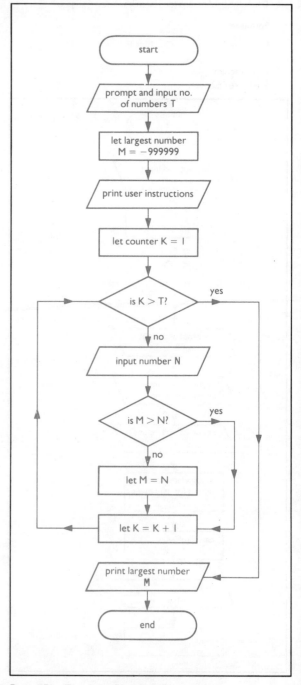

Figure 6F1   Flow diagram for example program 6F

Program

```
100  REM EXAMPLE PROGRAM 6F
105  REM DETERMINE THE LARGEST
110  REM NUMBER IN A SET
115  PRINT "NUMBER OF NUMBERS IN SET";
120  INPUT T
125  LET M = -999999
130  PRINT "TYPE THE NUMBERS
                        ONE AT A TIME"
135  FOR K = 1 TO T
140  INPUT N
145  IF M > N THEN 155
150  LET M = N
155  NEXT K
160  PRINT "LARGEST NUMBER:"; M
165  END
```

Points to notice

- The condition in line 145 has been 'turned around' to simplify the program structure. The condition is the one for taking no action, i.e. the current value of the maximum is larger than the number input.
- The initial value of the maximum (−999999) is chosen so that it is smaller than any numbers likely to be input.
- This method can easily be modified to find the smallest number in a set.

Sample run

```
NUMBER OF NUMBERS IN SET ? 5
TYPE NUMBERS ONE AT A TIME
? 5
? 7
? 9
? 4
? 8
LARGEST NUMBER : 9
```

Exercise 6F

1 By suitable modification to the method used in example program 6F, outline a method determining the smallest number in a set.

Copy and complete the flow diagram and program for question 2.

2 A firm has six branches. At the end of each month, a sales analysis program inputs the name of each branch, and the four weekly sales figures for the branch. The total sales figure is calculated and displayed. After the input is complete, the highest total sales figure is displayed, together with the name of the branch having the highest figure.

Method

In addition to a variable for the highest total sales, there is one for the name of the branch with the highest total. The method of determining the maximum sales total is the same as in example program 6F, but every time the maximum is changed, so is the name of the branch having the maximum.

Variables

B$	branch name	**S1** to **S4**	weekly sales figures (£)
		J	loop counter
M	highest sales total (£)		
T	total sales figure (£)		
H$	branch with highest sales total		

Formula

$T = S1 + S2 + S3 + S4$

Flow diagram

See figure 6F2.

Program

```
100  REM EXERCISE 6F QUESTION 2
105  REM MONTHLY SALES ANALYSIS
110  LET M = _____
115  LET H$ = "XXXX"
120  FOR J = ___ TO ___
125  PRINT "BRANCH NAME";
130  _____
135  PRINT "FOUR SALES FIGURES";
140  _____
145  LET T = _____
150  IF M ___ T THEN _____
155  LET M = _____
160  LET H$ = _____
165  NEXT ___
170  PRINT
175  PRINT "BRANCH WITH HIGHEST
                        TOTAL"; ___
180  PRINT _____
185  END
```

Draw flow diagrams and write programs for questions 3 to 6. Validate input data where necessary and set out the output carefully. Choose suitable test data to check the working of the program.

3 At a shop, the price of tins of fruit was varied to see which price gave the maximum income. A record was kept of the price and the number sold in a week at that price.

Price (pence)	Number sold
15	1462
16	1438
17	1406
17.5	1395
18	1321
19	1143
20	1021

Input this data and calculate the income (income = number sold × price) at each price. Output the income, the maximum income and the price at which the maximum income occurred.

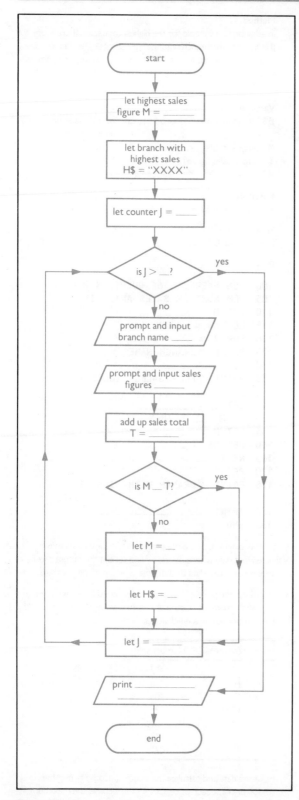

Figure 6F2   Flow diagram for exercise 6F, question 2

4   Input a set of numbers and output the smallest in the set.
5   Input a set of numbers, and calculate the range of the numbers (largest – smallest).
6   The height of a rocket a certain number of seconds after launching is given by the formula:
$$h = 1550t - 5t^2$$
h   height (metres)   t   time from launch (seconds)
Display the height of the rocket each second after launch until it lands again (after 310 seconds), and also display the maximum height, and the time taken to reach this height.

6G   Nested loops

The idea of repetition can be extended to include the situation where one loop is enclosed inside another loop. Loops which are used in this way are known as **nested loops**. For example, if a table of data is set out in rows and columns, processing the data is generally done as follows:
> Repeat, for every row of the table
> > Repeat, for every column in the row
> > > Process data item
> > End column repetition
> End row repetition

Basic language can, in fact, accommodate several layers of nested loops. However, examples and exercises in this chapter are restricted to two layers, as this is sufficient to establish the principle. More than three layers of nested loops are very rare in well-written programs.

Example 6G

Produce a set of multiplication tables up to the ten times table, arranged in columns and rows.

Method

Nested loops are used, the outer one being for each table, and the inner one being for each number in a particular table. The overall steps are as follows:
> Display heading
> Repeat, for each table
> > Repeat, for each number in the table
> > > Calculate product
> > > Display product
> > End number repetition
> End table repetition

Variables

T   table (outer loop counter)   P   product
N   number in table (inner loop counter)

Formula

$P = N \times T$

Flow diagram

See figure 6G1. Note how the outer loop 'encloses' the inner loop.

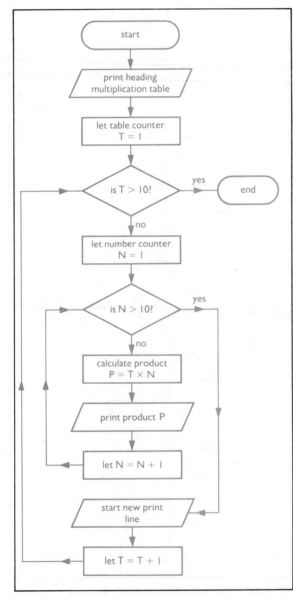

Figure 6G1   Flow diagram for example program 6G

Program

```
100  REM EXAMPLE PROGRAM 6G
105  REM MULTIPLICATION TABLE
110  PRINT
115  PRINT TAB (10); "MULTIPLICATION TABLE"
120  PRINT TAB (10); "--------------- ----- "
125  PRINT
130  REM OUTER LOOP
135  FOR T = 1 TO 10
140  REM INNER LOOP
145  FOR N = 1 TO 10
150  LET P = T*N
155  PRINT TAB (3*N+2); P;
160  NEXT N
165  REM END OF INNER LOOP
170  PRINT
175  NEXT T
180  REM END OF OUTER LOOP
185  END
```

Points to notice

- The **TAB** function in line 155 outputs the products at intervals of three spaces, starting after five spaces.
- The semicolon on the end of line 155 means that successive figures are output on the same line. The **PRINT** statement in line 170 starts a new line.
- Instructions in the inner loop are repeated a total of 100 times.

Sample run

MULTIPLICATION TABLE

1	2	3	4	5	6	7	8	9	10
2	4	6	8	10	12	14	16	18	20
3	6	9	12	15	18	21	24	27	30
4	8	12	16	20	24	28	32	36	40
5	10	15	20	25	30	35	40	45	50
6	12	18	24	30	36	42	48	54	60
7	14	21	28	35	42	49	56	63	70
8	16	24	32	40	48	56	64	72	80
9	18	27	36	45	54	63	72	81	90
10	20	30	40	50	60	70	80	90	100

Exercise 6G

1   Briefly explain the meaning the term nested loop.

Copy and complete the flow diagram and program for question 2.

2   The following credit terms are offered by a shop:
        a deposit of 15% of the cash price,
        the rest paid in equal monthly instalments over 6, 9 or 12 months.
Print a table of cash price, deposit and monthly instalments over the three repayment periods, for cash prices from £5 to £100 in steps of £5.

Method

The price is used as a loop counter from 5 to 100 in steps of 5. In this loop the deposit is calculated and the price and deposit printed.

The number of monthly instalments is used as a counter in a nested loop, from 6 to 12 in steps of 3. In this loop the monthly instalments are calculated and printed.

Variables

P   cash price (£)   D   deposit (£)
M   monthly instalments (£)   N   number of monthly
                                 instalments

Formulae

$D = 0.15 \times P$ $M = (P-D) \div N$

Flow diagram
See figure 6G2.

Program

```
100  REM EXERCISE 6G QUESTION 2
105  REM TABLE OF MONTHLY INSTALMENT
110  REM PAYMENTS
115  PRINT TAB (16); "MONTHLY PAYMENTS"
120  PRINT
125  PRINT "PRICE"; TAB (8); "DEPOSIT";
130  PRINT TAB (16); "6 MTHS";
                    TAB (__); "9 MTHS"__
135  PRINT TAB (__); _____
140  PRINT
145  FOR P = _____
150  LET D = _____
155  PRINT P; TAB(__); __;
160  FOR __ = __ TO _____
165  LET M = _____
170  PRINT TAB (8 + N/6*8); __;
175  NEXT __
180  PRINT
185  NEXT __
190  END
```

Draw flow diagrams and write programs for questions 3 to 7. Validate input data where necessary, and pay attention to the layout of output. Choose suitable test data to check the working of the programs.

3 Print a table of the discount at 5%, 10%, 15% and 20% on amounts from £1 to £25 in steps of £1.

Variables

A   amount (£)   R   discount rate (%)
D   discount (£)

Formula

$$D = \frac{R \times A}{100}$$

4 Workers assembling radio sets are paid by the number of sets they assemble. Input the name and works number of a number of workers, together with their five production figures for each day of the week. Calculate and output the total for each worker, and their wage, based on the formula:

$$W = 35 + 0.37 \times T$$

where W is their wage (£) and T the total number of sets assembled.

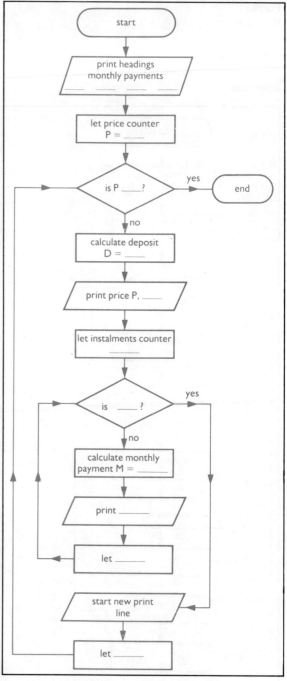

Figure 6G2   Flow diagram for exercise 6G, question 2

5 Write a program to shade in a rectangular portion of the screen, using a certain character. The program accepts as input the width (number of character spaces) and depth (number of lines) of the rectangle, the distance of the left-hand edge of the rectangle from the left-hand edge of the screen, and the character to be used as shading.

6 Print a table of the square, cube, fourth and fifth roots of the whole numbers from 1 to 100.

Variables

N number   R root
K order of root (K = 2 for square roots, 3 for cube roots etc.)

Formula
$R = N^{1/K}$

7 Print a table of the interest gained by a sum of money saved at rates of 6%, 8%, 10% and 12% over times from 1 year to 25 years in steps of 1 year. Input the sum of money saved. Either use the simple interest formula, or the compound interest formula, given below.

Variables

P   sum of money saved (£)   R   interest rate (%)
T   time (years)   I   interest (£)
A   amount (= sum plus interest)

Formulae

simple interest $I = \dfrac{P \times R \times T}{100}$

compound interest $A = P \times \left(1 + \dfrac{R}{100}\right)^{T}$

6H Branching out of loops

In some situations, a program loop must be repeated a certain number of times unless some condition is satisfied in the meantime. In the latter case, control must be transferred out of the loop.

At first sight, the obvious method of transferring control out of a loop is to use an **IF...THEN** or **GO TO** statement which branches past the end of the loop. For a number of reasons, however, this approach is not recommended. On some computers it will cause an error, and on most computers the current value of the loop counter will be retained in working memory until the end of the program, thus 'clogging' the main store of the computer.

A method of transferring control out of a loop before it has finished is introduced in this section, which does not suffer from the drawbacks mentioned above. It is recommended that this method is used instead of a direct jump out of the loop.

It is worth mentioning at this point that a branch into a loop is to be avoided at all times. On some computers it will cause an error, on others the results will be unpredictable. If a program is properly designed, the situation should never arise where branching into a loop is necessary.

Example 6H

The program below is the outline of a simple general knowledge quiz, which can be adapted for a variety of purposes. The questions and correct answers are stored in **DATA** statements, and read by the program as it proceeds. A question is displayed, and the user is given three attempts to answer it correctly. A correct first attempt scores 4 points, a correct second attempt 2 points and a correct third attempt 1 point. If all the attempts are wrong, the correct answer is displayed, and no points are scored. A running total of the score is kept, which is displayed after each question, and after all the questions.

Method

Suitable user instructions are displayed and the total score is set to zero. A loop is used to work through the questions. A question is read from data and displayed. A second nested loop is used to count the answers. If no answer is correct, this loop is repeated three times before the correct answer is displayed. If one of the answers is correct, control is transferred out of the loop. A message is displayed and the score is updated. The next question is then displayed.

Variables

Q$ question
A$ answer
T   total score
K   loop counter for answers
C$ correct answer
N   loop counter for questions
S   score for a question
C   check for correct answers

Flow diagram
See figure 6H1.

Program

```
100  REM EXAMPLE PROGRAM 6H
105  REM GENERAL KNOWLEDGE QUIZ
110  REM
200  REM DISPLAY USER INSTRUCTIONS
205  PRINT "GENERAL KNOWLEDGE QUIZ"
210  PRINT "----------------------"
215  PRINT
220  PRINT "WHEN A QUESTION IS DISPLAYED,"
225  PRINT "YOU HAVE UP TO THREE TRIES"
230  PRINT "TO ANSWER IT CORRECTLY"
235  PRINT
240  PRINT "YOU SCORE 4 POINTS IF YOU"
```

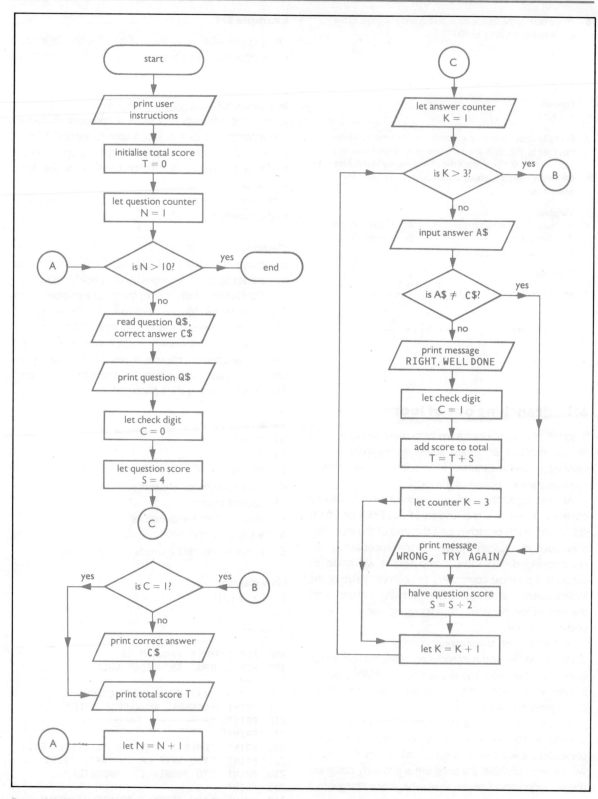

Figure 6H1 Flow diagram for example program 6H

```
245 PRINT "ARE RIGHT FIRST TIME, 2"
250 PRINT "POINTS IF YOU ARE RIGHT"
255 PRINT "SECOND TIME AND 1 POINT"
260 PRINT "IF YOU ARE RIGHT THIRD TIME"
265 PRINT
270 PRINT "HERE IS YOUR FIRST QUESTION"
275 PRINT
280 PRINT
300 REM INITIALISE SCORE AND
305 REM START OUTER LOOP
310 LET T = 0
315 FOR N = 1 TO 10
320 READ Q$, C$
325 PRINT QS;
330 LET S = 4
335 LET C = 0
400 REM INNER LOOP INPUTS AND
405 REM COMPARES ANSWERS
410 FOR K = 1 TO 3
415 INPUT A$
420 IF A$ <> C$ THEN 455
425 REM ANSWER CORRECT
430 PRINT "RIGHT. WELL DONE"
435 LET C = 1
440 LET T = T + S
445 LET K = 3
450 GO TO 470
455 REM ANSWER INCORRECT
460 PRINT "WRONG. TRY AGAIN";
465 LET S = S/2
470 NEXT K
500 REM DISPLAY CORRECT ANSWER IF NECESSARY
505 IF C = 1 THEN 515
510 PRINT "THE CORRECT ANSWER IS"; C$
515 PRINT
520 PRINT "YOUR SCORE IS"; T
525 PRINT
530 NEXT N
600 REM FINISH OFF PROGRAM
605 PRINT "YOUR FINAL SCORE IS"; T
610 PRINT "OUT OF A MAXIMUM OF 40"
615 PRINT
620 PRINT
700 REM QUESTIONS AND ANSWERS
705 DATA "THE HIGHEST MOUNTAIN
                    IN THE WORLD IS MOUNT"
710 DATA "EVEREST"
715 DATA "THE SURNAME OF
              THE FIRST MAN ON THE MOON IS"
720 DATA "ARMSTRONG"
725 DATA "HOW MANY YARDS
                    ARE THERE IN A MILE"
730 DATA "1760"
735 REM DATA FOR SEVEN MORE QUESTIONS
900 END
```

Points to notice

- The statements which transfer control out of the inner nested loop are lines 445 and 450. In these statements, the loop counter is set to its maximum value (here 3) and the program branches to the **NEXT** statement (line 470). This is the recommended method for transferring control out of a loop.

- Because it is a fairly long program, the code is written as a number of short segments. Each segment performs one task, and starts on a line which is a multiple of 100. A **REM** statement at the start of each segment indicates what the segment does.

- The check variable C is set to zero before any answers to a question are input, and then changed to 1 if an answer is correct. It is used in line 505 to determine whether or not a correct answer has been input.

- This program can be modified in a number of ways to be useful in a variety of situations.

Sample run

```
GENERAL KNOWLEDGE QUIZ
----------------------

WHEN A QUESTION IS DISPLAYED,
YOU HAVE UP TO THREE TRIES
TO ANSWER IT CORRECTLY

YOU SCORE 4 POINTS IF YOU
ARE RIGHT FIRST TIME, 2
POINTS IF YOU ARE RIGHT
SECOND TIME AND 1 POINT
IF YOU ARE RIGHT THIRD TIME

HERE IS YOUR FIRST QUESTION

THE HIGHEST MOUNTAIN IN THE WORLD IS
MOUNT ? SNOWDON
WRONG. TRY AGAIN ? KILIMANJARO
WRONG. TRY AGAIN ? EVEREST
RIGHT. WELL DONE
YOUR SCORE IS 1

THE SURNAME OF THE FIRST MAN ON THE
MOON IS ? ARMSTRONG
RIGHT. WELL DONE
YOUR SCORE IS 5
```

... for a total of ten questions.

Exercise 6H

1 Briefly describe, in general terms, the method for transferring control out of a loop introduced in example program 6H.
2 The lines of program shown below attempt to transfer control out of a loop of variable length. The condition for branching out of the loop is that variable A has the value 100.

```
200  INPUT N
205  FOR K = 1 TO N
       .
       .
250  IF A <> 100 THEN 265
255  LET N = K
260  GO TO 280
265  REM CONTINUE
       .
       .
270  NEXT K
```

Correct the error in one of these program lines so that the method introduced in example program 6H is followed. The incorrect method shown in these lines should never be used to transfer control out of a loop.

Draw flow diagrams and write programs for questions 3 to 5. Validate input data where necessary, and pay attention to the layout of output. Choose suitable test data to check the working of the program.

3 Input a set of numbers, of any length, and calculate their average. The number of numbers in the set is input first. However, the number 0 can be entered at any stage, indicating that an error has been noticed during input. If this occurs, the program halts without calculating the average.
4 Modify example program 6H so that the user can 'give up' at any stage of answering a question by typing GIVE UP. In this case, the correct answer is displayed, and nothing is added to the score.
5 A general-purpose cargo ship can carry a variety of types of cargo. Input the total carrying capacity of the ship (in tonnes) and then the names and tonnages of a number of consignments. If, however, a particular consignment will take the total tonnage over the capacity of the ship, display the message REJECTED, and do not accept any further input. Display the total tonnage of the accepted consignments.

6I End-of-chapter summary

This chapter has introduced a technique for repeating a portion of a program a certain number of times. A variety of applications of the technique have been demonstrated. As will be seen in the next chapter, the method of using **FOR...TO** and **NEXT** statements to control program loops is not the only one which can be used.

The main points introduced in this chapter are as follows:

- One of the simplest ways of controlling a loop is by means of a counter, which records the number of repetitions.

- A loop controlled by a counter starts with a **FOR...TO** statement and ends with a **NEXT** statement.
- A total can easily be added up in a loop, by setting the total to zero before the loop starts, and adding each successive item to the total inside the loop.
- The value of a loop counter may be used in calculations inside the loop. This is particularly useful in preparing tables of information, such as conversion tables.
- The largest number in a set may be found by comparing each number in turn with the current maximum and, if the number is larger, assigning its value to the current maximum.
- Two or more loops may be nested inside each other.
- Control may be transferred out of a loop before it is complete, by altering the value of the loop number to its limiting value, and branching to the end of the loop.

Exercise 6I

Questions in this exercise cover topics introduced in this or previous chapters.

1 The general form of the **FOR...NEXT** statement is

$$\text{FOR K = A TO B STEP C}$$

In each of the following cases, say how many times the loop will be repeated.

Example: A = 1, B = 10, C = 1
           loop repeated 10 times.

a) A = 1, B = 20, C = 1
b) A = 2, B = 8, C = 2
c) A = 0, B = 7, C = 1
d) A = 5, B = 1, C = −2
e) A = 1, B = 10, C = 3

Draw flow diagrams and write programs for questions 2 to 5. Validate input data where necessary, and pay attention to the layout of output. Choose suitable test data to check the workings of the program. Document the programs for both users and programmers.

2 Input the names and prices of a number of food items, and the prices of the same items some time ago. For each item, calculate the percentage change (generally increase) in price. Also calculate the total current price, the total previous price and the percentage change in the totals.

Variables

C	current price (£)	R	previous price (£)
P	percentage increase	N$	name of item
N	number of items	T1	total current price (£)
T2	total previous price (£)	F	loop counter

Formulae

$$P = \frac{(C - R) \times 100}{R} \qquad P = \frac{(T1 - T2) \times 100}{T1}$$

3 The factorial of a whole number N (written N!) is
$1 \times 2 \times 3 \times \ldots \times N$. For example $4! = 1 \times 2 \times 3 \times 4 = 24$.
Write a program to calculate N! for any positive input N. Check
that the number input is positive, and less than some suitable
upper limit.

☐ **4** When a house is bought on a mortgage, repayments are made
(usually once a month) so that at the end of a certain period of
time (usually 20 or 25 years) the money borrowed and the
interest charged have been paid back. The formula for the
amount paid back per year is:

$$A = P \times K^N \times \frac{(1 - K)}{1 - K^N}$$

where

$$K = 1 + \frac{R}{100}$$

P amount borrowed (£)
N number of years of repayment
A amount paid back per year
R interest rate (%)

The amount paid back per month is:

$$M = \frac{A}{12}$$

M amount paid back per month (£)

The total amount paid back is:

$$T = N \times A$$

T total amount repaid (£)
Input an amount borrowed and a period of repayment.
Calculate and output the amounts paid back per year and per
month and the total amount paid back, for interest rates from
10% to 20% in steps of 0.5%. Display or print the information
in a suitable table.

☐ **5** Input a year, the day of the week of January 1st of that year,
and whether or not the year is a leap year. Display or print a
calendar for the year, showing the day of the week for each
date.

6 Write a suitable user guide for example program 6H, assuming
that the intended users are fairly young children.

7

Using Conditions to form Loops

The previous chapter introduced the idea of a program loop, and demonstrated how a loop can be controlled by a counter. Using a counter means that a loop is repeated a certain number of times. This chapter considers the control of a loop in a slightly different way. The repetition of the loop is controlled by a condition. Repetition continues until a certain condition becomes true, or while a certain condition remains true. No new Basic statements are introduced in this chapter; loops are controlled by IF...THEN and GO TO statements.

7A The idea of conditional repetition

The general idea of a loop controlled by a condition is shown in figure 7A1. Somewhere within the loop there is a condition, which, if true, transfers control out of the loop.

Although a program for a loop of this type is quite easy to write, it is not a very common practice. It is far more usual to place the condition for repetition either at the start of the loop, or at the end. These two cases are discussed in the next two sections.

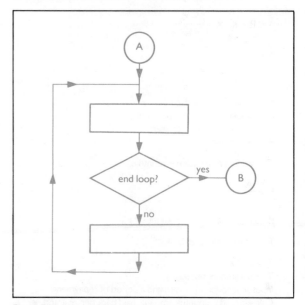

Figure 7A1   A loop controlled by a condition

7B Repeat while

A loop with the condition for repetition at the front is known as a **'repeat while'** loop, because repetition continues while the condition remains true. An important property of a 'repeat while' loop is that, if the condition for repetition is false at the start, the loop is not repeated at all. Thus a 'repeat while' loop is carried out zero or more times. A number of programming languages, including some versions of Basic, have a special statement to control a 'repeat while' loop.

Figure 7B1 illustrates the general idea of a 'repeat while' loop. Notice that the condition in the decision box must be written as one for ending the repetition. It is the 'repeat while' condition turned around, as explained in section 4B. Figure 7B1 clearly shows how it is possible for the loop not to be repeated at all.

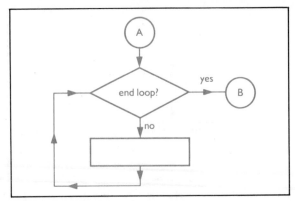

Figure 7B1   A 'repeat while' loop

Example 7B

You will probably remember being taught that division of whole numbers is a process of repeated subtraction. For example, to divide 20 by 3, subtract 3 from 20 repeatedly. The number of subtractions (6) is the quotient, and the amount left over (2) is the remainder. Using this method to divide 4 by 7, you will see that the quotient is 0 (no subtractions are possible), and the remainder is 4.

A program to illustrate the method of division by repeated subtraction requires a loop which is repeated zero or more times, in other words, a 'repeat while' loop.

Method
The steps of the program are as follows:
To divide a number X by a number Y:
   Start with quotient = 0 and remainder = X.
   While remainder is greater than or equal to Y, repeat.
      Subtract Y from remainder,
      Add 1 to quotient.

Variables
X number divided (dividend)   **Q** quotient
Y number of parts (divisor)   **R** remainder

Flow diagram
See figure 7B2. Note that the condition is one for ending the loop. The 'repeat while' condition is turned around in the decision box.

Program

```
100  REM EXAMPLE PROGRAM 7B
105  REM DIVISION BY REPEATED SUBTRACTION
```

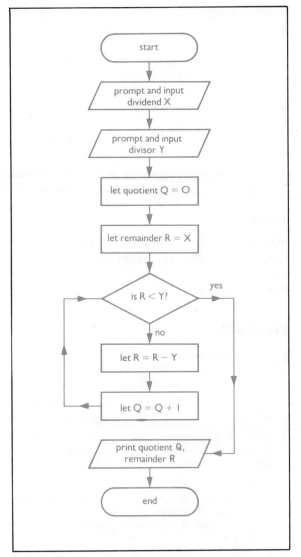

Figure 7B2   Flow diagram for example program 7B

```
110  PRINT "NUMBER DIVIDED (DIVIDEND)";
115  INPUT X
120  PRINT "NUMBER OF PARTS (DIVISOR)";
125  INPUT Y
130  LET Q = 0
135  LET R = X
140  IF R < Y THEN 160
145  LET R = R-Y
150  LET Q = Q+1
155  GO TO 140
160  PRINT "QUOTIENT :"; Q
165  PRINT "REMAINDER :"; R
170  END
```

Points to notice

- The condition for repetition (line 140) is at the start of the loop.
- The end of the loop (line 155) is a **GO TO** statement which transfers control back to the start of the loop.
- It is quite possible that the loop is not repeated at all.
- The values of variables Q and R are changed in the loop.
- Care must be taken to avoid putting the computer into an endless loop with this type of program.

Sample run

```
NUMBER DIVIDED (DIVIDEND) ? 20
NUMBER OF PARTS (DIVISOR) ? 3
QUOTIENT : 6
REMAINDER : 2
```

Exercise 7B

1 a) Briefly describe how a 'repeat while' loop works.
   b) How is a 'repeat while' loop constructed in Basic?
   c) Mention one difficulty with 'repeat while' loops in Basic.

Copy and complete the flow diagram and program for the task in question 2.

2 Input a worker's name and the number of components he or she has assembled in a shift. Output a ★ symbol for every 15 components assembled.

Method
If the number of components is N, the steps of the program are:
   Input name and number of components N.
   While N is greater than or equal to 15, repeat
      Print ★.
      Subtract 15 from N.

Variables
A$ name   **N** number of components

Flow diagram
See figure 7B3.

Program

```
100  REM EXERCISE 7B QUESTION 2
105  REM PRODUCTIVITY RECORD DISPLAY
110  PRINT "NAME";
115  INPUT _____
120  PRINT _____
125  INPUT _____
130  IF N ___ 15 THEN ___
135  PRINT "*" ___
140  LET N = _____
145  GO TO _____
150  END
```

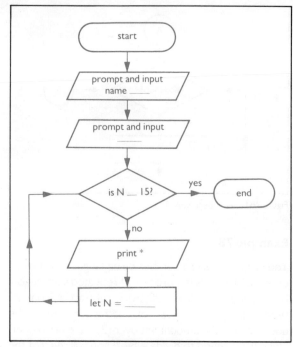

Figure 7B3   Flow diagram for exercise 7B, question 2

Draw flow diagrams and write programs for the tasks in questions 3 to 5. Validate input data where necessary, and choose suitable test data to check the working of the programs. Include test data to cause the loop to be carried out zero times.

3 Input the name of a pupil, and a set of marks he or she has obtained for a number of pieces of work. Calculate and output the total mark. At the start of the set, input the number of marks in the set, which may be zero.

4 The idea of a factorial has already been introduced, and a program to calculate factorials using a **FOR...NEXT** loop has been discussed. A more precise definition of the factorial of a positive whole number is as follows (the factorial of a number N is written as N!):

if $N = 0$, then $N! = 1$
if $N > 0$, then $N! = N \times (N-1) \times (N-2) \times \ldots \times 2 \times 1$.

Use this definition to write a program to calculate and output the factorial of a given positive whole number N.

☐ 5 Simulate the operation of a slot machine which sells bus or train tickets, as follows:
   Input the value of the ticket.
   Set the total value of coins inserted to zero.
   Input the value of a coin inserted, and add it to the total value.
   While the total value of the coin(s) inserted is less than the value of the ticket, repeat:
      Display the total value of the coins inserted.
      Display the amount still to be inserted.
      Input the value of a coin inserted, and add it to the total value.
   Print the ticket and the value of any change to be issued.

Note that this program can be enhanced in a number of ways.

7C Repeat until

A loop with the condition for repetition at the end is known as a **'repeat until'** loop, because repetition continues until the condition becomes true. An important property of a 'repeat until' loop is that it is always repeated at least once, even if the condition for ending the repetition is true at the start. A 'repeat until' loop is carried out one or more times. A number of programming languages, including some versions of Basic, have a special statement to control a 'repeat until' loop.

Figure 7C1 illustrates the general idea of a 'repeat until' loop. Notice that the condition in the decision box must be written as one for continuing the repetition. It is the 'repeat until' condition turned around, as explained in section 4B. Figure 7C1 shows how the loop is always carried out at least once.

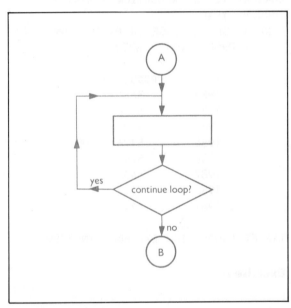

Figure 7C1   A 'repeat until' loop

Example 7C

A computer company produced 3291 microcomputers in 1981. If its production increases by 12% per year, in how many years will production exceed 8000 microcomputers per year?

Method

The program written to solve this program can, in fact, be used for a variety of similar situations. The program inputs the product name, year, production for that year, percentage increase in production and target production. The steps of the loop are then as follows:

    Repeat:
        Add 1 to year,
        Increase production by given percentage,
        Print year and production,
    Until production exceeds target production.

Variables

N\$	product name	**P**	production
Y	year	**I**	percentage increase
T	target production		

Formula

To increase production by given percentage:

$$P = P \times \left(1 + \frac{I}{100} \right)$$

Flow diagram

See figure 7C2. Note that the 'repeat until' condition is turned around, to become the condition for continuing the loop.

Program

```
100  REM EXAMPLE PROGRAM 7C
105  REM PRODUCTION FORECASTS
110  PRINT
115  PRINT "PRODUCTION FORECASTS"
120  PRINT "--------------------"
125  PRINT
130  PRINT "PRODUCT NAME";
135  INPUT N$
140  PRINT "CURRENT YEAR'S PRODUCTION";
145  INPUT P
150  PRINT "CURRENT YEAR";
155  INPUT Y
160  PRINT "PERCENTAGE INCREASE
                     IN PRODUCTION";
165  INPUT I
170  PRINT "TARGET PRODUCTION";
175  INPUT T
180  PRINT
185  PRINT TAB (5); "YEAR";
                 TAB (20); "PRODUCTION"
190  LET Y = Y + 1
195  LET P = P * (1 + I/100)
200  PRINT TAB (5); Y; TAB (20); P
205  IF P <= T THEN 190
```

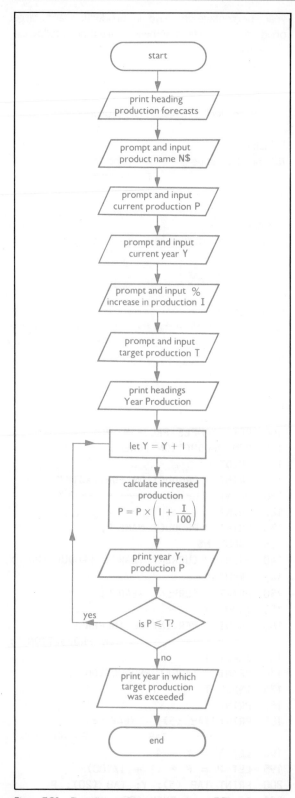

Figure 7C2 Flow diagram for example program 7C

```
210  PRINT
215  PRINT "TARGET PRODUCTION
                          EXCEEDED IN"; Y
220  END
```

Points to notice

- The condition for repetition (line 205) is at the end of the loop. It transfers control to line 190, the start of the loop.
- Even if the initial production exceeds the target production, the loop will be performed once.

Sample run

```
PRODUCTION FORECASTS
--------------------

PRODUCT NAME ? AMC
CURRENT YEARS PRODUCTION ? 3291
CURRENT YEAR ? 1981
PERCENTAGE INCREASE IN PRODUCTION ? 12
TARGET PRODUCTION ? 8000
```

YEAR	PRODUCTION
1982	3684
1983	4126
1984	4621
1985	5176
1986	5797
1987	6492
1988	7272
1989	8144

```
TARGET PRODUCTION EXCEEDED IN 1989
```

Exercise 7C

1 a) Briefly describe how a 'repeat until' loop works.
   b) How is a 'repeat until' loop constructed in Basic?
   c) Mention one difficulty with 'repeat until' loops in Basic.

Copy and complete the flow diagram and program for the task in question 2.

2 The height of a certain type of tree after a number of years is calculated by the formula:

$$H = \frac{M \times T}{1 + T}$$

H height (metres)   **M** maximum height (metres)
T time (years)   **G** required height (metres)

The maximum height is the height which the tree will approach after a very long time. Input the maximum height and then a required height, less than the maximum. Output the height of the tree each year until it reaches the required height.

Method

The processing steps of the program are as follows:

Start with time T = 0.

Repeat:

Add 1 to T,

Calculate height, using above formula,

Print time and height,

Until height reaches or exceeds required height.

Flow diagram

See figure 7C3. Note that the required height is validated.

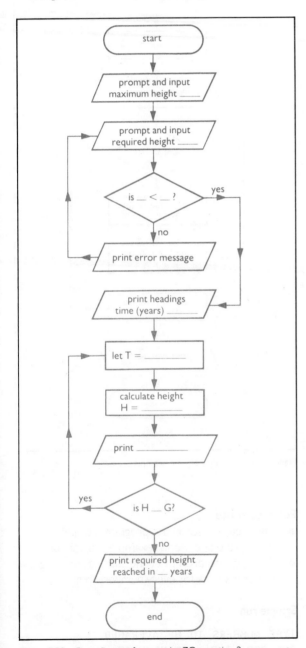

Figure 7C3   Flow diagram for exercise 7C, question 2

Program

```
100  REM EXERCISE 7C QUESTION 2
105  REM TREE HEIGHT CALCULATIONS
110  PRINT "MAXIMUM HEIGHT (M)";
115  INPUT ____
120  PRINT "REQUIRED HEIGHT (M);
125  _____
130  IF ___ < ___ THEN ____
135  PRINT "REQUIRED HEIGHT MUST BE"
140  PRINT "LESS THAN MAXIMUM"
145  PRINT "PLEASE RE-ENTER";
150  GO TO _____
155  LET T = 0
160  PRINT
165  PRINT TAB (__); "TIME
                       (YEARS)";     _____
170  PRINT
175  LET T = _____
180  LET H = _____
185  PRINT _____
190  IF H ___ G THEN _____
195  PRINT
200  PRINT "REQUIRED HEIGHT REACHED IN";
                       ____; "YEARS"

205  END
```

Draw flow diagrams and write programs for the tasks in questions 3 to 5. Validate input data where necessary, and pay attention to layout of output. Choose suitable test data to check the working of the programs.

3 A radioactive substance halves its activity every ten days. If its present activity is 1000 emissions per second, after how long (to the nearest ten days) will it drop below 1 emission per second?

4 A train travelling at 50 metres per second slows down by 2 metres per second every second. Print a table of time (at 1 second intervals), speed and distance (from where it started slowing down) until it has stopped.

   The distance travelled in a 1 second interval is approximately equal to the speed at the start of the interval.

5 A ball is thrown upwards at a certain speed. Print a table of heights at different times (at 0.2 second intervals) until the ball again reaches the ground. The height is calculated from the formula:

$$H = V \times T - 4.9 \times T^2$$

H height (metres)   **T** time (seconds)

V initial speed (metres per second)

7D   The use of end-of-data markers

Programs are frequently required to input and process long sets of data of unknown length. The commonest way of identifying the end of the data set is by means of an **end-of-data marker**, sometimes called a **terminator** or **rogue value**. The end-of-data value is never a 'realistic' value, so that it cannot be confused with a data item in the set. For numeric data, values of 0, −1 or a very large number are generally used. Sets of literal data are terminated by character strings such as XXXX or ★★★★.

The input and processing of data terminated by a rogue value is almost always done by means of a loop controlled by a condition. The condition for ending the loop is that the end-of-data marker has been reached. The condition is generally at or near the start of the loop.

Example 7D

Input a set of numbers and calculate their average. It is not known how many numbers are in the set, but the end of the set is marked with the number −1, which is not part of the set.

Method
The steps of the program are as follows:
Set a total and a counter to zero.
Repeat:
    Input a number.
    If the number is −1, then end the repetition.
    Add the number to the total.
    Add 1 to the counter.
Divide the total by the count to get the average.
Output the average.

Variables
T total   **N** number
K counter   **A** average

Flow diagram
See figure 7D1.

Program

```
100  REM EXAMPLE PROGRAM 7D
105  REM AVERAGE OF A SET OF
110  REM NUMBERS, USING END-
115  REM OF-DATA MARKER
120  PRINT "TYPE NUMBERS TO BE AVERAGED"
125  PRINT "ONE PER LINE, ENDING WITH -1"
130  PRINT
135  LET T = 0
140  LET K = 0
145  INPUT N
150  IF N = -1 THEN 170
155  LET T = T+N
160  LET K = K+1
165  GO TO 145
170  LET A = T/K
175  PRINT
180  PRINT "AVERAGE"; A
185  END
```

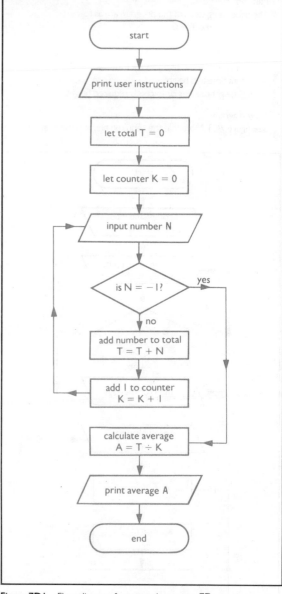

Figure 7D1   Flow diagram for example progrm 7D

Points to notice
- The method used in this program is similar in some ways to the one used in example program 6B.
- There is one prompt at the start of the program, rather than one for every number input.

Sample run

```
TYPE NUMBERS TO BE AVERAGED
ONE PER LINE, ENDING WITH -1
```

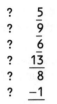

? 5
? 9
? 6
? 13
? 8
? −1

AVERAGE : 8.2

Exercise 7D

1 Write down the meaning of the term end-of-data marker.

Copy and complete the flow diagram and program for the task in question 2.

2 A charitable trust keeps computerised records of its donations. The record for one donation contains a date, donor's name and amount. Input the records for a number of donations, and calculate the total amount donated. The end of the input is marked as follows:

00/00/00, XXX, 0.00

Method
The steps of the program are:
   Set the total amount donated to zero.
   Repeat:
      Input data for a donation.
      If the date is 00/00/00, end the repetition.
      Add the amount to the total amount donated.
   Print the total amount donated.

Variables
D$	date	N$	donor's name
A	amount (£)	T	total amount (£)

Flow diagram
See figure 7D2.

Program

```
100  REM EXERCISE 7D QUESTION 2
105  REM DONATIONS TO CHARITY
110  PRINT " TYPE THE INFORMATION FOR "
115  PRINT " A NUMBER OF DONATIONS, "
120  PRINT " ONE DONATION PER LINE "
125  PRINT " END INPUT WITH "
130  PRINT " 00/00/00, XXX, 0.00 "
135  PRINT
140  LET _____
145  INPUT ___, ___, ___
150  IF _____ THEN _____
155  LET T = _____
160  GO TO _____
165  PRINT
170  PRINT _____
175  END
```

Draw flow diagrams and write programs for the tasks in questions 3 to 5. Validate input data where appropriate, and choose suitable test data to check the workings of the programs.

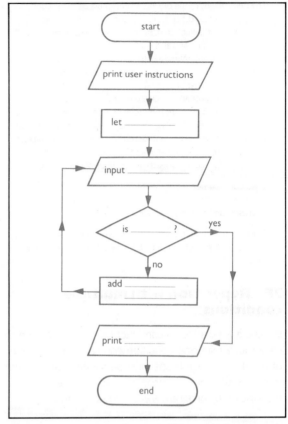

Figure 7D2 Flow diagram for exercise 7D, question 2

3 A certain kind of fencing requires 345 posts and 4.2 km of wire for every kilometre of fence. Input an order number and length of fence for each of a number of orders. Calculate the number of posts and length of wire required by each order, and the total number of posts and length of wire for the batch of orders. Use an end-of-data marker with order number zero.

Variables
N$	order number	N	number of posts
L	length of fence (km)	W	length of wire
T1	total number of posts	T2	total length of wire

Formulae
$N = 345 \times L$
$W = 4.2 \times L$

4 A ready mixed concrete firm makes up batches of concrete to order. Concrete is a mixture of sand, gravel, cement and water; the proportions of the dry ingredients may be varied to some extent according to the type of concrete required. An order processing program accepts the following information for each batch of concrete:

order number   date and time required
customer's name and address
proportions, expressed as percentages, of
sand (70% to 85%)   gravel (0% to 20%)   cement (15% to 25%)
quantity (kg)

The percentages of the dry ingredients must be in the above ranges, and must add up to 100%. For each order, the quantity of each ingredient is calculated, by multiplying the percentage by the quantity of cement, and all the information is displayed or printed in a suitable layout. When a batch of orders, ending with an order number of zero, has been processed, the total amount of each material is displayed or printed.

5   Electricity accounts are calculated from a present and a past meter reading. These are subtracted to find the number of units used. The number of units is multiplied by the cost per unit and added to a standing charge to determine the amount payable.

   Input the date, fixed charge and cost per unit, and then the following information for each of a number of customers:

   account number
   name and address
   present and past meter readings.

Calculate the amount payable, as explained above, and print an electricity bill, suitably set out. Use a suitable end-of-data marker to terminate input.

7E   Repetition with multiple conditions

In Basic it is possible to construct program loops which have more than one condition controlling the number of repetitions. Such loops must be treated with caution to ensure that they are programmed correctly, and that the logic of the program is easy to understand.

Example 7E

This program provides a simple number guessing game for young children. The computer 'thinks of a number' between 1 and 100, and invites the user to guess what it is. Repeated guesses may be tried, until one is correct, or the user gives up by typing 0. If a guess is too high, the computer displays the message TOO HIGH, and similarly the message TOO LOW is displayed if the guess is too low.

Method

The two conditions for ending the loop are that a guess is correct, or that a guess is zero. The steps of the program are:

   Display instructions to user.
   'Think of a number' between 1 and 100.
   Repeat:
      Input a guess.
      If the guess is correct, then Exit 1.
      If the guess is zero, then Exit 2.
      If the guess is too high,
         then display TOO HIGH,
         else display TOO LOW.

Exit 1 : Display message WELL DONE.
Exit 2 : Display message TOO BAD and the correct number.

The process of 'thinking of a number' is discussed in section 9C. All the whole numbers between 1 and 100 have an equal chance of being selected.

Variables
N   number 'thought of'   **G**   guess

Flow diagram
See figure 7E1.

Program

```
100   REM EXAMPLE PROGRAM 7E
105   REM NUMBER GUESSING GAME
110   PRINT "I HAVE THOUGHT OF A"
115   PRINT "NUMBER BETWEEN 1 AND 100"
120   PRINT "TRY TO GUESS WHAT IT IS"
125   PRINT
130   RANDOMIZE
135   LET N = INT (RND (1) * 100) + 1
140   INPUT G
145   IF G = N THEN 180
150   IF G = 0 THEN 190
155   IF G > N THEN 170
160   PRINT "TOO LOW. GUESS AGAIN"
165   GO TO 140
170   PRINT "TOO HIGH. GUESS AGAIN"
175   GO TO 140
180   PRINT "WELL DONE. THAT IS RIGHT"
185   GO TO 195
190   PRINT "TOO BAD. THE NUMBER IS"; N
195   END
```

Points to notice
- The process of 'thinking of a number' takes place in lines 130 and 135. See section 9C for an explanation of these statements.
- The conditions for ending the loop are in lines 145 and 150.

Sample run

```
I HAVE THOUGHT OF A
NUMBER BETWEEN 1 AND 100
TRY TO GUESS WHAT IT IS

?  70
TOO HIGH. GUESS AGAIN
```

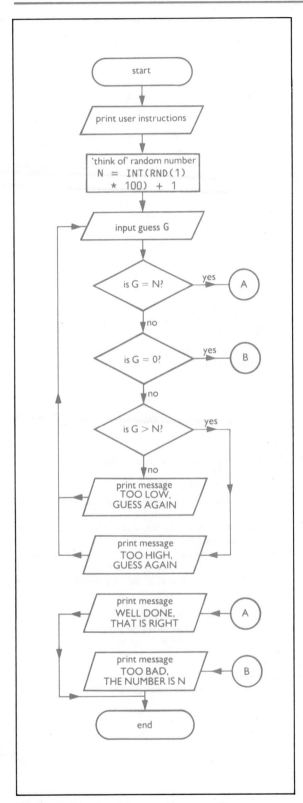

Figure 7E1 Flow diagram for example program 7E

```
?   50
TOO HIGH. GUESS AGAIN
?   30
TOO LOW. GUESS AGAIN
?   40
TOO LOW. GUESS AGAIN
?   45
TOO HIGH. GUESS AGAIN
?   42
WELL DONE. THAT IS RIGHT.
```

Exercise 7E

1 Modify the general knowledge quiz (example program 6H) so that the user may have repeated attempts to answer a question, until the answer is correct or the message GIVE UP is typed. No points are scored after the third attempt.

Draw flow diagrams and write programs for the tasks in questions 2 to 4. Validate input data where necessary, and choose suitable test data to check the working of the programs.

2 Use the method of 'thinking of a number' between 1 and 100 to produce a simple multiplication tester. Two numbers are 'thought of' and displayed, and the user is asked to type their product. Repeated attempts are allowed, until the answer is correct, or 0 is typed to indicate that the user has given up. If the user gives up, the correct answer is displayed. After each sum, the user is given the opportunity to try another sum. A suitable method of scoring may be used.

3 Input and print a number of destination addresses and weights (kg) of parcels to be delivered in a van. The input halts either when a suitable end-of-data marker is typed, or when the capacity of the van (1000 kg) is reached.

4 Input the name of an article, its current price, and the expected percentage increase in the price per year. Display the price each year until it has doubled or the year 2000 is reached.

Variables

P	price (£)	I	% increase
Y	year	C	current price
N$	name of article		

Formula

$$P = P \times \left(1 + \frac{I}{100}\right)$$

7F   End-of-chapter summary

This chapter has introduced the idea of controlling a loop by a condition, or combination of conditions. The main points of the chapter are as follows:

● In general, the condition controlling the loop may be anywhere in the loop. However, it is customary to place the condition either at the start or at the end of the loop.

- A 'repeat while' loop has the condition at the start of the loop. The loop is repeated zero or more times.
- A 'repeat until' loop has the condition at the end of the loop. The loop is repeated one or more times.
- Large sets of data, of unknown length, are frequently ended by an end-of-data marker. Input and processing of such data is generally done by a loop controlled by a condition related to the end-of-data marker.
- It is possible to control a loop by a combination of conditions.

Exercise 7F

Questions in this exercise cover topics introduced in this or previous chapters.

1   The section of a program shown below attempts to calculate the number of years a quantity takes to double if it increases at 5% per year. The input section is omitted.

Variables

Q1   original quantity   Q   current quantity
T   time (years)

Formula

Increasing Q by 5% is achieved by the formula:

$$Q = Q \times 1.05$$

Program

```
100  REM EXERCISE 7F QUESTION 1
105  REM INPUT Q1, ETC
110  REM
150  LET Q = Q1
155  LET T = 0
160  LET Q = Q * 1.05
165  LET T = T + 1
170  IF Q <> 2 * Q1 THEN 160
175  PRINT T
```

a) What will happen if the program segment is run as it is?
b) Correct the error in the program segment.

2   Write a user guide for example program 7E, assuming that the users are young children.

Draw flow diagrams and write programs for the tasks in questions 3 to 5. Validate input data where necessary, and choose suitable test data to check the workings of your program.

3   A common method of checking numeric input data is the use of **check totals**, also known as **hash totals**. A check total is the sum of a set of input data, which is added up manually and input with the data. The computer also adds up the data figures, and compares the total with the check total input. If the two do not match, then a data item has been typed incorrectly (or, of course, the check total has been calculated or typed incorrectly).

Use a check total to validate the input data in the following task:

A wage processing system requires the input, for each employee, of a name, works number, ordinary and overtime pay rates and five sets of clocking-on and clocking-off times (in hour's and decimals of an hour, e.g. 17.30 hours is input as 17.5), and a check total, being the sum of all the numeric data. If the check total indicates an error, then the entire set of input data must be re-entered.

The total hours worked for the week are calculated from the clocking-on and clocking-off times, and the wages calculated on the basis of ordinary pay rate for the first 35 hours, and overtime rate for the rest. A suitable end-of-data marker is used to terminate input. Output comprises the works number, name, total hours worked and wage, in a suitably printed payslip.

4   Roman numerals consist of a set of capital letters representing the following quantities:

I   units
V   fives
X   tens
L   fifties
C   hundreds
D   five hundreds
M   thousands

A slight variation on the standard set of Roman numerals, which is nevertheless quite acceptable, is shown in the first ten numerals below:

I   II   III   IIII   V   VI   VII   VIII   VIIII   X

The basis of one method of converting a decimal number D to Roman numerals is as follows:
For the thousands:
   While D is greater than or equal to 1000, repeat
      Output 'M',
      Reduce D by 1000.
The other letters of the Roman numeral are dealt with in a similar way.
   Input a decimal number in the range 0 to 5000 and output the equivalent Roman numeral.

☐5   The depletion of natural resources such as oil is a very serious long-term problem. Write a program to estimate the lifetime of a particular resource such as an oilfield, using the following input information:

The current size of the reserve.
The current amount extracted per year.
The estimated percentage change, per year, of the amount extracted.

Calculate the amount extracted each year and the remaining reserve until the resource is exhausted. Print the results in a suitable table.

8
Arrays

Computers are very frequently required to store information, not as individual data items, but as sets of data. One of the simplest and most widely used methods of storing a set of data in a computer memory is by means of an **array**. This chapter explains what an array is, and introduces some ideas related to arrays. The examples and exercises show a few of the many ways in which arrays can be used.

8A Dimensions

An array might be thought of as a set of related data items, stored one behind the other in the memory of a computer. A single variable name is used to refer to the whole array. Individual data items are referred to by a number which indicates their position in the array.

If a variable is to be used to represent an array, this fact must be declared in a **dimension** statement at the start of the program or segment of program in which the variable is used. A dimension statement starts with the word **DIM**, and includes the number of elements in each array. For example:

```
110  DIM A(12), B$(7)
```

declares a numeric array **A** of twelve items, and a literal array **B$** of seven items. Note that in most versions of Basic an array name must be a single letter; the name **A1(12)** cannot be used.

Individual data items in an array are identified by the number in the brackets after the array name. For example **A(5)** is the fifth item in array **A**, and **B$(3)** is the third item in array **B$**.

Example 8A

Input the names and heights of four mountains. Print this information in a table.

Method
Since the printing takes place after the input is complete, all the data must be stored in the computer memory. Two arrays are used, one for the names of the mountains, and the other for their altitudes. The steps of the program are:
Declare the two arrays.
Input the names of the mountains and their altitudes.
Print headings.
Print the names and altitudes.

Variables
N$(4) array of names   **H(4)** array of altitudes

Flow diagram
See figure 8A1. Notice that it is not usual to mention the dimension statement in a flow diagram.

Program

```
100  REM EXAMPLE PROGRAM 8A
105  REM HEIGHTS OF MOUNTAINS
```

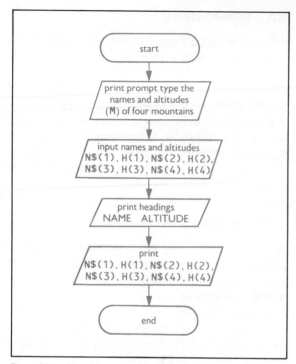

Figure 8A1   Flow diagram for example program 8A

```
110  DIM N$(4), H$(4)
115  PRINT  "TYPE THE NAMES AND "
120  PRINT  "ALTITUDES (M) OF FOUR "
125  PRINT  "MOUNTAINS "
130  PRINT
135  INPUT  N$(1), H(1)
140  INPUT  N$(2), H(2)
145  INPUT  N$(3), H(3)
150  INPUT  N$(4), H(4)
155  PRINT
160  PRINT  TAB (5); "NAME"; TAB (20);
                      "ALTITUDE (M) "
165  PRINT
170  PRINT  TAB(5); N$(1); TAB(20); H(1)
175  PRINT  TAB(5); N$(2), TAB(20), H(2)
180  PRINT  TAB(5); N$(3), TAB(20); H(3)
185  PRINT  TAB(5); N$(4); TAB(20); H(4)
190  PRINT
195  END
```

Points to notice

- Each element of an array is referred to by the name of the array and the number of the element within the array.
- The dimension statement (line 110) is near the start of the program.

Sample run

```
TYPE THE NAMES AND
ALTITUDES (M) OF FOUR
MOUNTAINS
?  EVEREST, 9063
?  BLANC, 4924
?  MITCHELL, 2086
?  ACONCAGUA, 7129
```

NAME	ALTITUDES (M)
EVEREST	9063
BLANC	4924
MITCHELL	2086
ACONCAGUA	7129

Exercise 8A

1 a) What is an array?
   b) How is an array declared in a Basic program?
2 Which of the following array names are incorrect?

   J$(5), A3(9), A(5)$, $J(2),
   J9($), T(5000), A(12)

3 Write a dimension statement to declare a numeric array of 15 items and two literal arrays, each of 17 items.
4 Write a program to input a person's name and address, and print it on a suitable label. Use an array for the four lines of the address.

8B Index variables

In the previous section you learned that an individual item in an array is referred to by a number which indicates its position in the array. For example, **A(5)** is the fifth item of array **A**. A variable may also be used to indicate an item in an array. For example, **A(N)** is the Nth item of array **A**. If **N = 5**, then it is **A(5)**. A variable which identifies an item in an array is sometimes called an **index** variable.

If a loop counter is used as an index variable, then it 'scans through' the array, one item at a time. This technique is illustrated in the example which follows:

Example 8B

At a car factory, the production figures for the four quarters of the current year are input, together with the corresponding figures for the previous year. A table is printed of these figures, together with the differences between the current year's figures and the corresponding figures for the previous year.

Method

An array **A(4)** is used to store the current year's figures. Array **B(4)** stores the previous year's figures and array **D(4)** contains the differences.

Three loops are used: the first inputs the current year's figures, the second inputs the previous year's figures and the third calculates the differences and prints all the data. In each case the loop counter is also the index variable, 'scanning through' the arrays item by item.

Variables

Y	current year
A(4)	production figures for the four quarters of the current year
B(4)	production figures for the four quarters of the previous year
D(4)	differences between corresponding production figures
K, L, M	loop counters

Formula
$C(M) = A(M) - B(M)$

Flow diagram
See figure 8B1.

Program

```
100  REM EXAMPLE PROGRAM 8B
105  REM QUARTERLY CAR PRODUCTION
110  REM FIGURES
115  DIM A(4), B(4), D(4)
120  REM
200  REM INPUT CURRENT YEARS FIGURES
205  PRINT " CURRENT YEAR ";
210  INPUT Y
215  PRINT " ENTER QUARTERLY PRODUCTION
                              FIGURES "
220  FOR K = 1 TO 4
225  INPUT A(K)
230  NEXT K
235  REM
300  REM INPUT PREVIOUS YEARS FIGURES
305  PRINT " ENTER QUARTERLY PRODUCTION
                              FIGURES " ;
310  PRINT " FOR " ; Y-1
315  FOR L = 1 TO 4
320  INPUT B(L)
325  NEXT L
330  REM
400  REM CALCULATE DIFFERENCES AND OUTPUT
                              RESULTS
405  PRINT
```

```
410  PRINT " PRODUCTION FIGURES "
415  PRINT " QUARTER " ; TAB (10); Y;
420  PRINT TAB (20); Y-1; TAB (30);
                              " DIFFERENCE "
425  PRINT
430  FOR M = 1 TO 4
435  LET D(M) = A(M) - B(M)
440  PRINT M; TAB (10); A(M);
445  PRINT TAB (20); B(M); TAB (30); D(M)
450  NEXT M
455  END
```

Points to notice

- In each loop, the loop counter is used as an index variable for one or more of the arrays.
- Array elements are accessed one at a time in the loops. For example, in the first loop, when K = 1, **A(1)** is input, when K = 2, **A(2)** is input, etc.
- Each segment of the program starts on a line number which is a multiple of 100, with a **REM** statement as a 'header'. This is a recommended technique for longer programs.
- Lines 310 and 420 show how calculations may be carried out in **PRINT** statements. In these statements, the value of $Y-1$ is calculated and printed.

Sample run

```
CURRENT YEAR ? 1982
ENTER QUARTERLY PRODUCTION FIGURES
3269
3847
5361
3016
ENTER QUARTERLY PRODUCTION FIGURES FOR 1981
3365
3752
4919
3215
```

PRODUCTION FIGURES			
QUARTER	1982	1981	DIFFERENCE
1	3269	3365	−96
2	3847	3752	95
3	5361	4919	442
4	3016	3215	−199

Exercise 8B

1 a) What is an index variable?
   b) Explain how a loop counter may be used to 'scan through' the individual items in an array.
2 Write down the value of the items in the arrays after each of the following program segments:

a) `100  FOR K = 1 TO 5`

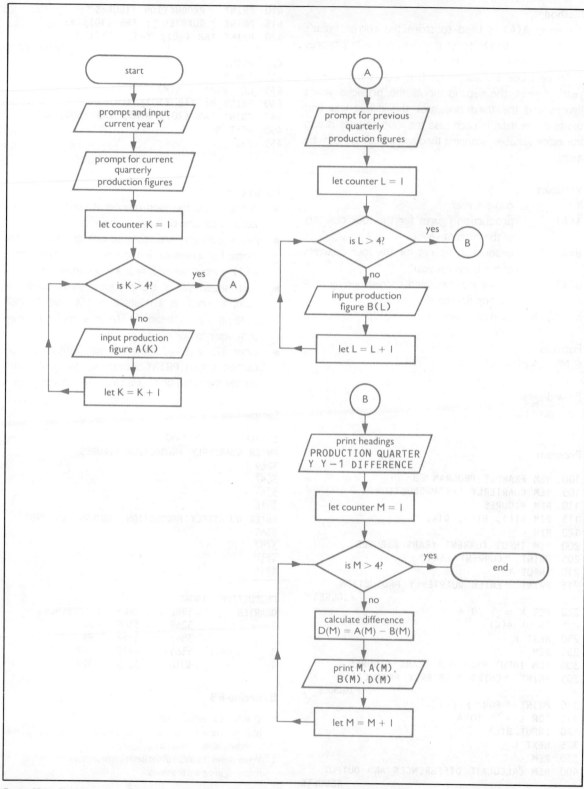

Figure 8B1   Flow diagram for example program 8B

```
105  LET M(K) = 3*K
110  NEXT K
```

b)
```
100  FOR J = 1 TO 3
110  READ B$(J)
115  NEXT J
120  DATA  " INPUT "
125  DATA  " PROCESSING "
130  DATA  " OUTPUT "
```

c)
```
100  FOR L = 5 TO 1 STEP −1
105  LET A(L) = L+1
110  NEXT L
```

Draw flow diagrams and write programs for the tasks in questions 3 to 7. Validate input data where necessary, and choose suitable test data to check the working of the programs.

3 Input the names and prices of four types of car. Print this information, suitably set out in a table.

4 An electrical appliance shop has fifteen appliances in stock. Input the name, price and number in stock of each appliance. Calculate the value of the stock of each appliance, and the total stock value. Print all the information in a suitable table.

Variables

N$(15)	array of names	P(15)	array of prices
S(15)	array of stock levels	V(15)	array of stock values

Formula

V(K) = S(K) × P(K)

where K is an index variable.

5 Three branches of a newsagent each sell six newspapers. Input the names of the newspapers and, for each branch, its weekly sales of each newspaper. Calculate the total sales of each newspaper. Output all the information in a table, with a column for the name of the newspapers, the sales for each branch and for the total sales. Each row of the table shows the name of a newspaper, its three sales figures and the total sales.

Variables

P$(6)	array of names of newspapers
A(6)	sales of newspapers for branch A
B(6)	sales of newspapers for branch B
C(6)	sales of newspapers for branch C
T(6)	total sales of the six newspapers

Formula

T(N) = A(N) + B(N) + C(N)

where N is an index variable.

6 A survey is carried out to find out the average family size of the pupils in a class. An array F(6) stores the information, where F(1) is the number of pupils with families of 1 child, F(2) is the number with families of 2 children, etc. The numbers are input, and output in a suitable table.

The average family size is calculated as follows:
The total number of families is:
T1 = F(1) = F(2) + ... + F(6)
The total number of children in all the families is:
T2 = 1 × F(1) + 2 × F(2) + 3 × F(3) + ... + 6 × F(6)

The average family size is: $A = \dfrac{T2}{T1}$

7 Input a set of numbers and calculate their average. Then calculate the percentage by which each number differs from the average.

Suggested method
Declare a sutiably large array to store the numbers. First input the number of numbers in the set, and check that it is not greater than the size of the array. Use a loop of variable length to input the numbers and calculate their total. Then calculate the average. Use another loop of the same length to calculate the percentage differences, and output them, together with the numbers. Finally output the average.

Variables

X(50)	array of numbers
P(50)	array of percentage differences
N	number of numbers input
T	total of the numbers
A	average
J,K	loop counters

Formulae

$A = \dfrac{T}{N}$

$P(K) = \dfrac{(X(K)-A) \times 100}{A}$

8C Tables of information

Arrays can be used to store tables of reference information. For example, if a program is required to display the name of a month given the number of the month, then a table of the names of the months is stored in an array:

M$(1) = January
M$(2) = February
⋮
M$(12) = December

Notice that the index of each month is the number of the month in the year.

This section shows how tables of data can be stored in arrays, and demonstrates some uses of such tables. The next section investigates an associated topic, that of searching a table for a particular element.

Example 8C

A shop uses **point-of-sale terminals** instead of cash registers, to record sales. These are specially designed computer terminals, connected to a central computer in the shop. A simplified version of the action of a terminal to record a cash sale is as follows:

The stock number and quantity of each item sold are entered. The price is found from a table of prices.

The stock number, price, quantity and cost (cost = price × quantity) are printed for each item, together with the total cost. The amount of money paid is then entered, and the change calculated. Both of these quantities are printed.

Method
The prices of the goods are stored in an array, in order of stock number. In other words, the stock number is also the array index. The steps of the program are as follows:

Read prices into array,
Input date
Repeat indefinitely:
    Set sale total to zero,
    Print sale slip heading and date,
    Input stock number,
    While stock number is not equal to zero, repeat:
        Input quantity,
        Look up price from table of prices,
        Calculate cost (cost = price × quantity),
        Add cost to sale total,
        Print stock number, price, quantity and cost,
        Input next stock number.
    Print sale total.
    Input amount paid.
    Calculate and print change.

Notice that a stock number of zero is used to end the input for one sale.

Variables

P(20)	array of prices (£)	D$	date
T	sale total (£)	N	stock number
Q	quantity	C	cost (£)
A	amount paid (£)	G	change (£)
K	loop counter		

Formula
$C = Q \times P(N)$

Flow diagram
See figure 8C1.

Program

```
100 REM EXAMPLE PROGRAM 8C
105 REM POINT-OF-SALE TERMINAL
110 DIM P(20)
115 REM
200 REM READ TABLE OF PRICES
205 FOR K = 1 TO 20
210 READ P(K)
```

```
215 NEXT K
220 DATA 12.65, 29.95, 34.95, 2.50
225 DATA 87.95, 30.85, 69.45, 34.80
230 DATA 15.45, 19.95, 19.95, 99.95
235 DATA 9.95, 12.45, 18.65, 10.35
240 DATA 56.45, 28.35, 3.75, 2.35
245 REM
250 REM INPUT DATE
255 PRINT "DATE";
260 INPUT D$
265 REM
300 REM SALES SLIP : INITIALISE AND HEADING
305 LET T = 0
310 PRINT "UNIVERSAL SUPPLIES LIMITED"
315 PRINT D$
320 PRINT "STCK NO"; TAB (8); "PRICE";
325 PRINT TAB(16); "QTY"; TAB(24); "COST"
330 INPUT N
335 REM
400 REM REPEAT FOR EACH ITEM
405 IF N = 0 THEN 500
410 INPUT Q
415 LET C = Q*P(N)
420 LET T = T + C
425 PRINT N; TAB (8); P(N);
430 PRINT TAB (16); Q; TAB (24); C
435 INPUT N
440 GO TO 400
445 REM
500 REM SALE TOTAL AND CHANGE
505 PRINT TAB (16); "TOTAL"; TAB (24); T
510 INPUT A
515 LET G = A-T
520 PRINT TAB (16); "CASH"; TAB (24); A
525 PRINT TAB (16); "CHANGE"; TAB (24); G
530 REM
600 REM NEXT SALE
605 GO TO 300
610 END
```

Points to notice
- The program is written as a set of short segments, each starting at a line number which is a multiple of 100.
- The table of prices is read from **DATA** statements. In these statements, the prices are in order of stock number.
- In lines 415 and 425, the stock number (variable N) locates the price in the array. For example, if the stock number is 3, the data item P(3) is accessed.
- The above is a 'bare bones' program for a point-of-sale terminal. It can be extended in a number of ways, as suggested in question 7 of exercise 8C.

Sample run
For added realism, keyboard input and printed output

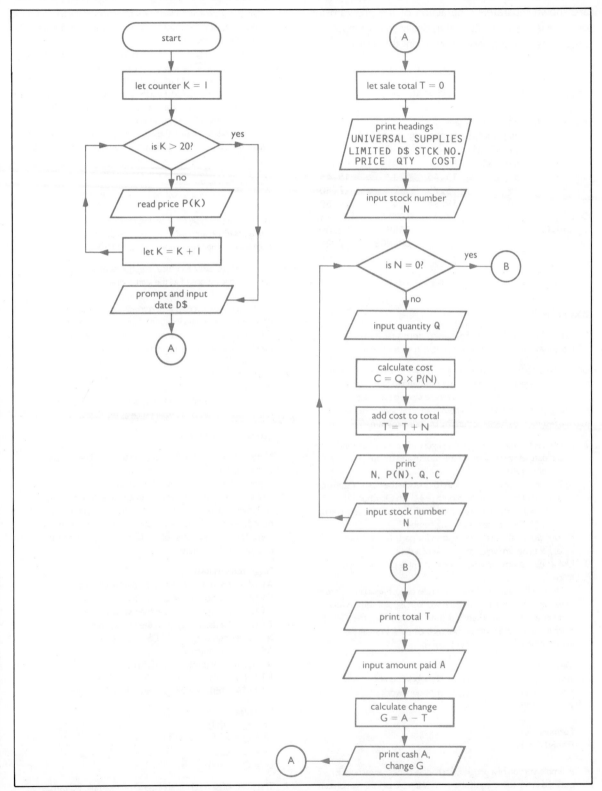

Figure 8C1 Flow diagram for example program 8C

are shown separately. The action of the program for one sale is shown. Note that in order to align input and output, two inputs are shown on the same line in certain places.

Keyboard input   Printed output

Date? 11/10/81
```
                UNIVERSAL SUPPLIES LIMITED
                11/10/81
                STK NO    PRICE     QTY     COST
? 5 ? 1         5         15.45     1       15.45
? 19 ? 2        19         3.75     2        7.50
? 10 ? 4        10        19.95     4       79.80
? 0                                 TOTAL  102.75
? 110.00                            CASH   110.00
                                    CHANGE   7.25
```

Exercise 8C

1 Explain how an array may be used to store a table of data. What is the significance of the index variable in such an array?

Draw flow diagrams and write programs for the tasks in questions 2 to 6. For the longer programs, it is recommended that segments be used, as in example program 8C. Validate input data where necessary, particularly if the data item is an array index. Choose suitable test data to check the running of your program.

2 a) Input a day, month and year in figures (e.g. 11,10,81) and print the date using the name of the month and the full year (e.g. 11 October 1981).
   b) Extend the program in part a) to provide the correct suffix on the end of the day of the month (e.g. 11th October 1981). A suggested method is to use a table of 31 elements, each being the suffix for the corresponding number.
   c) Incorporate the program written for parts (a) or (b) into a larger program which makes use of a date.

3 Use a table of worker's pay rates in a simple payroll program as follows:
   Store in the table the hourly pay rate of each worker, in order of works number. Then, for each worker, input a name, works number and hours worked. Calculate the pay, using the pay rate from the table, and multiplying it by the hours. Print all the information in a suitably set out payslip.

Variables

R(20)	table of pay rates	N	works number
N$	name	H	hours worked
P	pay		

Formula
$P = R(N) \times H$

4 A simple version of a program to handle bank transactions is outlined in the following. It shows how a table of information can be updated by a program.

The program is intended to keep records of the bank's trading for one day. At the start of the day, the balances of the accounts at the bank are read into a table, in order of account number. The date is also input. For each transaction, an account number, transaction type (D for deposit, W for withdrawal) and amount are input. The account number, transaction type and amount are validated and re-entered if necessary. Deposits are added to the balance for the particular account, withdrawals are subtracted. The date, input data and new balance are printed.

At the end of the day, the account number -1 is input. This causes the current balances in all the accounts to be printed, with their corresponding account numbers.

Note on validation

The account number must be between 1 and the highest account number used.

The transaction type must be the character D or W.

The transaction amount must be a positive number not exceeding some transaction limit (say £10 000).

5 A program to assist an office telephonist uses a table of the names and locations of all the staff, stored in two arrays. The data is stored in order of extension number.

The program accepts an extension number as input, and displays the name and location of the person at that extension. (This program can be extended to display an extension number given a name, as discussed in the next section. See question 5 of exercise 8D.)

☐ 6 A paint factory produces twelve colours by mixing four dyes in different ratios. An order processing program used by the factory has a table of the ratios of the dyes for each colour. The data for one colour is a set of numbers such as the following:

  0.37, 0.18, 0.09, 0.36

Note that the four numbers add up to 1.00. The table is contained in four arrays, one for each dye.

For each order, an order number, customer's name and address, colour number and quantity are entered. The quantity of each dye required to make up the order is displayed. A sequence of orders is processed, terminating with an order number of zero. The total quantities of the four dyes required by the batch of orders is then output.

Suggested variables

A(12)	fraction of dye 1 in the twelve colours
B(12)	fraction of dye 2 in the twelve colours
C(12)	fraction of dye 3 in the twelve colours
D(12)	fraction of dye 4 in the twelve colours
N	order number C$ customer name
A$	customer address
Q	quantity of paint ordered (litres)
L1 to L4	quantities (litres) of the four dyes
T1 to T4	total quantities (litres) of the four dyes

Formulae
$L1 = Q \times A(U)$
$L2 = Q \times B(U)$
$L3 = Q \times C(U)$
$L4 = Q \times D(U)$

7 The point-of-sale terminal program in example 8C can be extended in a number of ways. Some suggestions are as follows:

Validate the stock number. It must be in the range 1 to 20.

Include a stock level for each item. The initial stock levels are read into a table at the start of the program. The number sold in each transaction is subtracted from the stock level. At the end of the program, indicated by a stock number of −99, the current stock levels are printed.

Incorporate the date manipulation program (question 2) into the point-of-sale program.

8D Searching a table

The previous section introduced the idea of using an array to store a table of information. This section extends the idea, showing a way of 'looking up' an item in a table. The method introduced in this section is very simple, but very widely used. Its only limitation is that it is rather slow if the table is fairly large.

Example 8D

The objective of the program shown below is to translate words from English to French. An English word is typed and, provided that the word is in the 'dictionary' of the program, the corresponding French word is displayed.

Method

A table of the English and French words is stored in two arrays, in such a way that the index values of corresponding words are the same. For example:

if E$(5) = BIG, then F$(5) = GRAND,
its French equivalent.

To translate an English word, it is 'looked up' in the array of English words, by comparing it with each word in the array, until a match is found. The French word with the same index value as the matching English word is the one required. It is displayed.

If the whole array is searched without a matching word being found, then a message is displayed, apologising for the fact that the word is not in the program's dictionary.

The main steps of the program are as follows:

Display user instructions.
Load table of English and French words.
Input an English word.
For each English word in the table, repeat:
Compare word input with word in the table.
If they match, note the index of the word in the table and end the repetition.

If a matching word has been found
then display the corresponding French word,
else display a message that the English word cannot be translated.

Variables

E$(25)	array of English words
F$(25)	array of French words
J, K	loop counters
E1$	English word to be translated
C	check digit. C = 0 if no match is found, otherwise C = index of matching English word.

Flow diagram

See figure 8D1.

Program

```
100 REM EXAMPLE PROGRAM 8D
105 REM ENGLISH TO FRENCH
110 REM TRANSLATION PROGRAM
115 DIM E$(25), F$(25)
120 REM
200 REM DISPLAY USER INSTRUCTIONS
205 PRINT "THIS PROGRAM TRANSLATES"
210 PRINT "AN ENGLISH WORD TO FRENCH"
215 PRINT "TYPE THE ENGLISH WORD,"
220 PRINT "AND THE FRENCH WORD WILL"
225 PRINT "BE DISPLAYED"
230 PRINT
235 REM
300 REM LOAD TABLE OF ENGLISH
305 REM AND FRENCH WORDS
310 FOR J = 1 TO 25
315 READ E$(J), F$(J)
320 NEXT J
325 REM
400 REM INPUT ENGLISH WORD
405 PRINT "ENGLISH WORD";
410 INPUT E1$
415 PRINT
500 REM LOOK UP WORD IN TABLE
505 LET C = 0
510 FOR K = 1 TO 25
515 IF E1$ <> E$(K) THEN 535
520 REM MATCHING WORD FOUND
525 LET C = K
530 LET K = 25
535 NEXT K
540 REM
```

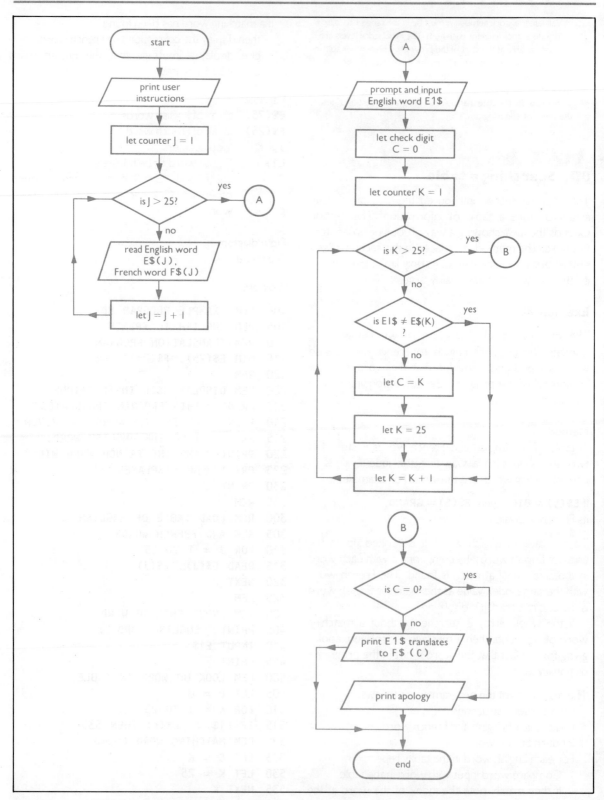

Figure 8D1 Flow diagram for example program 8D

```
600  REM DISPLAY FRENCH WORD OR
605  REM FAILURE MESSAGE
610  IF C = 0 THEN 625
615  PRINT E1$; "TRANSLATE TO"; F$(C)
620  GO TO 640
625  PRINT "SORRY, BUT"; E$; "IS NOT "
630  PRINT "IN THE DICTIONARY"
635  PRINT
640  REM
700  REM DICTIONARY OF ENGLISH
705  REM AND FRENCH WORDS
710  DATA "AFTER", "APRES"
715  DATA "AGAIN", "ENCORE"
720  DATA "BEFORE", "AVANT"
725  DATA "BETWEEN", "ENTRE"
730  DATA "BIG", "GRAND"
735  DATA "COLD", "FROID"
740  DATA "DRINK", "BOIRE"
745  DATA "EAT", "MANGER"
750  DATA "EARTH", "TERRE"
755  DATA "ENOUGH", "ASSEZ"
760  DATA "EVERYTHING", "TOUT"
765  DATA "FAST", "VITE"
770  DATA "GOOD", "BON"
775  DATA "HERE", "ICI"
780  DATA "HIGH", "HAUT"
785  DATA "HOW", "COMMENT"
790  DATA "IN", "DANS"
795  DATA "LESS", "MOINS"
800  DATA "LITTLE", "PETIT"
805  DATA "MORE", "PLUS"
810  DATA "NO", "NON"
815  DATA "OPEN", "OUVERT"
820  DATA "UNDER", "SOUS"
825  DATA "VERY", "TRES"
830  DATA "YES", "OUI"
835  REM
900  END
```

Points to notice

- The method of branching out of a loop, introduced in section 6H, is used here.
- The check variable C is set to zero at the start. If no match is found during the search of the table, C remains zero.
- The method of searching a table used in this program is called a **sequential search**.
- This program can be extended in a number of ways. Some of these are suggested in question 6 of exercise 8D.

Sample run

```
THIS PROGRAM TRANSLATES
AN ENGLISH WORD TO FRENCH.
TYPE THE ENGLISH WORD,
AND THE FRENCH WORD WILL
BE DISPLAYED.

ENGLISH WORD ? UNDER

UNDER TRANSLATES TO SOUS
```

Exercise 8D

1 Briefly describe the method of searching a table introduced in this section.

Draw flow diagrams and write programs for the tasks in questions 2 to 6. Validate input data where necessary, and pay attention to the layout of output. Choose suitable test data to check the workings of the programs.

2 Store a table of people's names and telephone numbers. Type a person's name, and display their telephone number.
3 Store a table of your personal school timetable. Together with each subject, store the name of the teacher, and the days, times and rooms of the lessons. For example:

GERMAN MR SMITH MON 3RD C 14 WED 4TH C 12

Type the name of a subject, and display the timetable for the subject.
4 Store the common names and chemical formulae of a number of substances. For example

SALT   NACL

Type the common name of a substance, and display its chemical name. Allow the program to be used repeatedly, looking up a series of names.
5 Extend the office telephonist's program (question 5 of exercise 8C) to allow a name to be typed and an extension to be displayed.
6 The English to French translation program can be modified or extended in a number of ways. Some suggestions are:
   Allow the program to be used repeatedly, translating a series of words.
   Extend the program to translate from French to English as well as from English to French.
   Modify the program to translate to or from a different foreign language, or to or from a number of languages.
   Enlarge the 'dictionary' of words used by the program.

8E Two-dimensional arrays

The arrays introduced up to now all have a single index, and can be imagined as a column of numbers or words. These arrays are known as **one-dimensional arrays**. In most versions of Basic it is possible to have arrays with two index numbers. These arrays can be imagined as a rectangular pattern of rows and columns. Such arrays are called **two-dimensional arrays**.

For example, if an array is dimensioned as A$(3, 4), then the items in the array can be thought to be in rows and columns as follows:

```
A$(1, 1)  A$(1, 2)  A$(1, 3)  A$(1, 4)
A$(2, 1)  A$(2, 2)  A$(2, 3)  A$(2, 4)
A$(3, 1)  A$(3, 2)  A$(3, 3)  A$(3, 4)
```

Note that the first index indicates the row and the second index the column. In the above example, A$(2, 3) is in the second row, third column.

Example 8E

Input the four quarterly sales figures for the three branches of a company. Display these figures in a table, with quarterly totals for the three branches, annual totals for each branch and an overall total figure. Set out the table as follows:

Sales figures for . . .

	1st	2nd	3rd	4th	(£000)
	Quarter	Quarter	Quarter	Quarter	Total
Branch 1					
Branch 2					
Branch 3					
Total					

Method

A two dimensional array is used to store the sales figures. Each row of the array is for a branch, and each column is for a quarter. Input, processing and output of the figures in the array is done by means of nested loops, using the loop counters as array index numbers. In this way the array is 'scanned' row by row and column by column. The method of adding up totals in a loop, first introduced in section 6C, is used several times.

The overall steps of the program are as follows:
  Input year and display user instructions.
  Repeat, for each branch:
    Repeat, for each quarter:
      Input quarterly sales figure.
  Display headings.
  Repeat for each branch:
    Let branch total sales = 0.
    Display branch number.

    Repeat for each quarter:
      Add quarterly sales figure to total.
      Display quarterly sales figure.
    Display branch total sales.
  Let overall total sales = 0.
  Repeat, for each quarter:
    Let quarterly total sales = 0.
    Repeat, for each branch:
      Add quarterly sales figure to total.
    Add quarterly total sales to overall total sales.
    Display quarterly total sales.
  Display overall total sales.

Variables

S(3, 4)	quarterly sales figures for the three branches
T1	branch total sales
T2	quarterly total sales
T3	overall total sales
I, J, K, L, M, N, P	loop counters
Y	year

Flow diagram
See figure 8E1.

Program

```
100  REM EXAMPLE PROGRAM 8E
105  REM QUARTERLY BRANCH SALES ANALYSIS
110  DIM S(3, 4)
115  REM
200  REM INPUT YEAR AND DISPLAY USER
205  REM INSTRUCTIONS
210  PRINT  "YEAR";
215  INPUT Y
220  PRINT  "TYPE QUARTERLY SALES FIGURES"
225  PRINT  "(£000) FOR EACH BRANCH"
230  PRINT  "TYPE ONE FIGURE PER LINE"
235  REM INPUT SALES FIGURES
240  FOR I = 1 TO 3
245  PRINT  "BRANCH"; I
250  FOR J = 1 TO 4
255  INPUT S(I, J)
260  NEXT J
265  NEXT I
270  REM
300  REM DISPLAY HEADINGS
305  PRINT
310  PRINT
315  PRINT  "SALES FIGURES FOR"; Y;
320  PRINT TAB (33);  "(£000)"
```

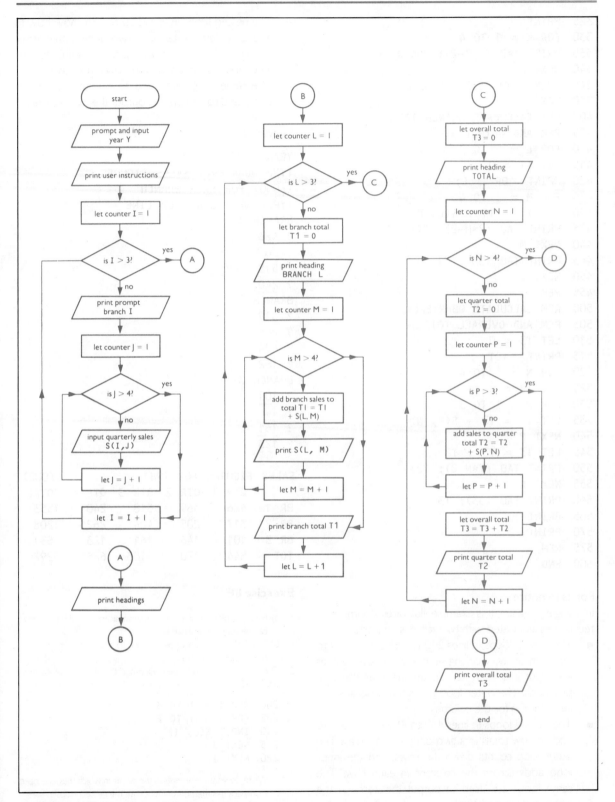

Figure 8E1 Flow diagram for example program 8E

```
325  PRINT
330  FOR K = 1 TO 4
335  PRINT TAB (7*K-2); "QTR"; K;
340  NEXT K
345  PRINT TAB (33); "TOTAL"
350  REM
400  REM CALCULATE BRANCH TOTALS
405  REM AND OUTPUT
410  FOR L = 1 TO 3
415  LET T1 = 0
420  PRINT "BR"; L;
425  FOR M = 1 TO 4
430  LET T1 = T1 + S(L, M)
435  PRINT TAB (7*M-2); S(L, M);
440  NEXT M
445  PRINT TAB (33); T1
450  NEXT L
455  REM
500  REM CALCULATE QUARTERLY
505  REM AND OVERALL TOTALS
510  LET T3 = 0
515  PRINT "TOT";
520  FOR N = 1 TO 4
525  LET T2 = 0
530  FOR P = 1 TO 3
535  LET T2 = T2 + S(P, N)
540  NEXT P
545  LET T3 = T3 + T2
550  PRINT TAB (7*N-2); T2;
555  NEXT N
560  PRINT TAB (33); T3
565  PRINT
570  PRINT
575  REM
600  END
```

Points to notice

In a single program, this example illustrates a number of techniques associated with two-dimensional arrays:

- The nested loops in lines 240 to 265 show how to 'scan' an array, working across each row. Values are input into each item in the array as the scan proceeds. The outer loop is for the rows and the inner loop is for the columns.
- The nested loops in lines 410 to 450 show how to add up row totals in a two-dimensional array. The outer loop counts down the rows, and the inner loop adds across the columns in each row. The same loops are used to output the items in the array, and the row totals.

- The nested loops in lines 520 to 555 show how to add up column totals in a two-dimensional array. The outer loop counts across the columns, and the inner loop adds down the rows in each column. The same loops are used to output the column totals, and to add up and output the overall total.

Sample run

```
YEAR ? 1981
TYPE QUARTERLY SALES FIGURES
(£000) FOR EACH BRANCH
TYPE ONE FIGURE PER LINE
BRANCH 1
? 426
? 369
? 518
? 240
BRANCH 2
? 319
? 205
? 424
? 162
BRANCH 3
? 101
? 146
? 161
? 123
```

SALES FIGURES FOR 1981				(£000)
	QTR 1	QTR 2	QTR 3	QTR 4	TOTAL
BR 1	426	369	518	240	1553
BR 2	317	205	424	262	1208
BR 3	101	146	161	123	531
TOT	844	720	1103	625	3292

Exercise 8E

1 a) Briefly explain what a two-dimensional array is, and how one can be represented in Basic.
   b) Explain how nested loops are used to 'scan' the items in a two-dimensional array.

2 The nested loops shown below input all the elements of the array X(2, 3)

```
200  FOR I = 1 TO 3
205  FOR J = 1 TO 2
210  INPUT X(J, I)
215  NEXT J
220  NEXT I
```

a) Write down the elements in the order in which they are input.
b) Compare this method of input with the nested loops in lines 240 to 265 of example program 8E.

Draw flow diagrams and write programs for the tasks in questions 3 to 6. Validate input data where necessary, and pay particular attention to the layout of output. Choose suitable test data to check the working of the programs.

3   One of the commonest applications of arrays is to store and process matrices. Some matrix operations are extremely complicated; others, such as addition, are relatively simple.

When two matrices are added, each element of the sum matrix is obtained by adding corresponding elements in the original matrices. If the matrices are **A**, **B** and **C**, then, in Basic notation:

```
C(I, J) = A(I, J) + B(I, J)
```

where **I** is the row index and **J** the column index.

Write a program to input two matrices of a suitable size, and calculate and output the sum of the matrices.

4   A simple accounting program accepts as input a company's income and expenditure figures for each month of a year. For each month, the operating profit (income − expenditure) is calculated. The figures are displayed in a table as follows:

Month	Income	Expenditure	Profit
1	561 273	481 906	79 367
2	306 415	291 913	14 502
...	...	...	...

Suggested variables

F(12, 3) stores the three columns of figures for the twelve months.

5   Use one or more arrays to store the rows and columns of a large character or other symbol to be displayed. Use 5 rows of 3 columns or 7 rows of 5 columns for one large character. Display various combinations of the stored character(s).

6   Extend the matrix addition program (question 3) to deal with the subtraction of matrices, and with the multiplication of a matrix by a number.

7   Several of the programs described in exercise 8D can be modified to use two-dimensional arrays. Particularly suitable are questions 3 and 6.

8F   End-of-chapter summary

This chapter has introduced the idea of an array, and demonstrated a number of programming techniques using arrays. The main points in the chapter are as follows:

- An array may be thought of as a set of related data items, stored one behind the other in the memory of a computer.
- A single variable name refers to a whole array; individual data items are referred to by a number called an index which indicates their position in the array.
- A dimension statement declares that a variable is to represent an array, and indicates the size of the array.
- A very common method of 'scanning' an array is by

means of a loop, with the loop counter used as the index variable.

- One or more arrays can be used to store a table of reference information.
- A common method for 'looking up' a data item in a table is the sequential search, in which each item in turn is examined until the required item is found.
- A two-dimensional array can be imagined as a rectangular pattern of rows and columns. Two index numbers are used, the first identifying the row and the second identifying the column.

Exercise 8F

The questions in this exercise cover topics introduced in this and previous chapters.

1   On average, how many comparisons are made in a sequential search of a table, before the required data item is found?
2   Identify the incorrect variable names in the following:

```
A$(50), P(I, J, K), $J(4), J(3)$, M(−1), K(L$)
```

Draw flow diagrams and write programs for the tasks in questions 3 to 4. Validate input data where necessary, and pay particular attention to the layout of output. Choose suitable test data to check the working of the programs.

3   Choose a number (say 6) of popular makes of motor car, and conduct a survey to find out which car people would prefer to have. Record the results as a set of numbers (e.g. 3, 1, 2, 5 etc.) where each number is a vote for a particular make of car.

Input the sequence of numbers, validating each one, and counting the total number of votes for each type of car. Also count the overall total number of votes, and express the total for each car as a percentage of the overall total. Display the results in a suitable layout.

Suggested method

Use an array for the total votes for the cars. Set all the totals to zero at the start of the program. Then as each number is input, the corresponding total is increased by 1. For example, if 3 is input then T(3) is increased by 1, or, in general, if J is the variable input, then T(J) is increased by 1.

Similarly, use an array for the percentages of the total votes. Each percentage is calculated from the formula

$$P(J) = (T(J) \times 100)/G$$

where G is the overall total.

4   **Top of the pops**

Make a list of the current hit single titles. Input these titles into an array **R$(10)** where **R$(1)** is the title of record 1, etc.

Get a number of people to vote for their favourite title. Input these votes as a sequence of numbers; 3 as a vote for record 3, etc. Set a count for each record to zero, and use it to count the votes for each record. See question 3 for details of the method.

After the votes have been input, terminating with a suitable end-of-data marker, use the method introduced in section 6F to find the record with the highest total marks.

Print: TOP OF THE POPS IS . . .

Functions

One of the most powerful features of Basic language is the number of functions it includes. These fall roughly into two groups, namely character handling functions and mathematical functions. In addition, it is possible for a programmer to define a function for use during a program.

This chapter briefly considers the nature of a function, and then introduces the various types of functions available in Basic language.

9A   Functions and arguments

Before discussing functions in Basic language, it is important to be clear about what a function is, and to introduce some ideas associated with functions.

A function may be thought of as a transformation from one quantity to another. For example, a very common function is the one which produces the square of a number. Given the number 3, this function transforms it to the number 9. Similarly, it transforms 4 to 16 and 10 to 100.

The quantity which is 'given to' a function is called the **argument**. In the above example, the numbers 3, 4 and 10 are arguments. Arguments do not have to be numbers.

The quantity 'produced by' a function, given a certain argument, is called the **value** of the function. In the above example, the numbers 9, 16 and 100 are values of the function, each corresponding to a particular argument.

To summarise, a function transforms one quantity (the argument) to another quantity (the value). Neither the argument nor the value are necessarily numbers.

9B   Character handling functions

Some of the most important and widely used functions in Basic language are those which manipulate characters or strings of characters. Many of these functions are not available in other programming languages. Unfortunately, different versions of Basic use different character handling functions. The ones included here are the most widely used, and are available on the majority of computers which support Basic language. Each function is briefly discussed, and then an example program is introduced which uses some of them. Questions in the exercise which follows make use of all the functions introduced.

LEN (X$)
The **LEN** function accepts a string of characters and produces the number of characters in the string. For example:

```
LEN ( " SHAKESPEARE " )  =  11
LEN (A$)  =  4  if A$  =  " FRED "
```

MID$ (X$, A, B)
The **MID$** function extracts a substring from a given string of characters. It has three arguments, namely the

string, the position of the start of the substring and the number of characters in the substring. For example:

> if J$ = " AMY 349T "
> then MID$ (J$, 1, 3) = " AMY "
> MID$ (J$, 5, 3) = "349 "
> MID$ (J$, 8, 1) = " T "

Notice that the space is counted as a character.

The + operator

The opposite process to extracting a substring from a string, is joining two strings to form a larger string. This is achieved by the + operator which, when used with strings, attaches them one behind the other. For example:

> if A$ = " AMY " B$ = " " (space)
> C$ = " 349 " D$ = " T "
> then the statement
> LET J$ = A$ + B$ + C$ + D$
> assigns to variable J$ the value " AMY 349T "

VAL (X$)

If a literal variable comprises a string of digits, then the VAL function produces a numeric variable of the same value. For example:

> if C$ = " 349 " then VAL (C$) = 349

Note that if the character string does not contain a number, then an error will arise.

STR$ (X)

Transforming in the opposite direction to VAL, the STR$ function produces a literal variable containing the same characters as a given numeric variable. For example:

> STR$ (349) = " 349 "
> and, if Y = −72.9 "
> then STR$ (Y) = " −72.9 "

Example 9B

A date is input in the form 29/12/81 and is stored as a single variable. Output of the date is required in the form 29 December 1981. Write the portion of the program which transforms the date from the one form to the other.

Method

A table of months is read into an array, in order, so that the index of each month is the number of the month in the year.

A date is input as a single variable, and the MID$ function used to separate the day, month and year. The VAL function is used to obtain the numeric value of the month, which is checked to see that it is in the range 1 to 12. The date in the required output form is then "assembled" using the + operator, and output.

Variables

N$(12)	array of months
D1$	date in input form
D$	day
M$	month
Y$	year
M	numeric value of month
D2$	date in output form

Flow diagram
See figure 9B1.

Program

```
100  REM EXAMPLE PROGRAM 9B
105  REM DATE DISPLAY SEGMENT
110  DIM N$ (12)
200  REM READ TABLE OF MONTHS
205  FOR K = 1 TO 12
210  READ N$ (K)
215  NEXT K
220  DATA " JANUARY " , " FEBRUARY "
225  DATE " MARCH " , " APRIL "
230  DATA " MAY " , " JUNE "
235  DATA " JULY " , " AUGUST "
240  DATA " SEPTEMBER " , " OCTOBER "
245  DATA " NOVEMBER " , " DECEMBER "
250  REM
300  REM INPUT AND CONVERT DATE
305  PRINT " DATE " ;
310  INPUT D1$
315  LET D$ = MID$ (D1$, 1, 2)
320  LET M$ = MID$ (D1$, 4, 2)
325  LET YS = MID$ (D1$, 7, 2)
330  LET M = VAL (M$)
335  IF M >= 1 AND M <= 12 THEN 350
340  PRINT " INVALID INPUT. PLEASE
                            . RE-ENTER "
345  GO TO 305
350  LET D2$ = D$ + "   " + N$ (M)
                    + "   " + " 19 " + Y$
```

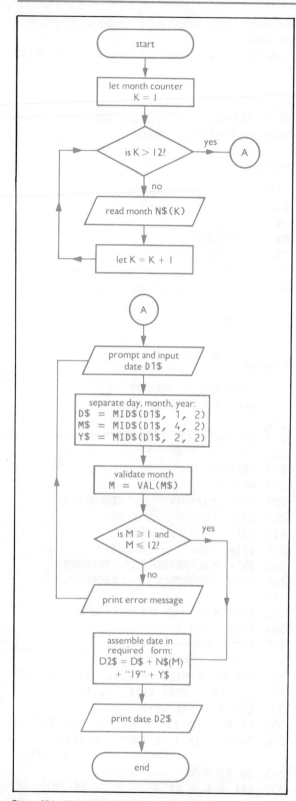

Figure 9B1 Fow diagram for example program 9B

```
355  PRINT
360  PRINT TAB (10); D2$
365  PRINT
370  END
```

Points to notice

- The variable **M** is used to locate the months in the table.
- This program is intended to form part of a longer program. As such, the section which reads the table of months (lines 200 to 250) should be placed near the front of the program, since it is only required once. The remaining portion can then be inserted whenever it is needed, or become a subprogram (see chapter 10).

Sample run

DATE ? <u>27/06/81</u>
        27 JUNE 1981

Exercise 9B

1 Briefly define the terms function, argument and value (of a function).

2 If **A$ = " UB40 "** and
   B$ = " JOAN ARMATRADING " , write down the values of the following functions.

   a) **LEN (A$)**
   b) **LEN (B$)**
   c) **MID$ (A, 1, 2)**
   d) **VAL (MID$ (A$, 3, 2))**
   e) **MID$ (B$, 1, 4)**
   f) **LEN (A$ + " AND " + B$)**

Draw flow diagrams and write programs for the tasks in questions 3 to 6. Validate input data where necessary, and pay attention to the layout of output. Choose suitable test data to check the working of your programs.

3 Input a car registration mark and output the year of manufacture of the car.

   Suggested Method
   Store a table of final registration letters and years of manufacture. Note that certain registration letters such as I and O have not been used. Search this table, using the method introduced in section 8D, to find the year of manufacture corresponding to the final registration letter input.

4 Add up the total of a number of sums of money which are input in the form £43.45. Either use an end-of-data marker to terminate input, or start by entering the number of amounts to follow.

5 Input a string of text, as a single variable, and output the same string with all the spaces removed.

6 Input a number (preferably restricted to the range 0 to 100) and output the number in words. For example, if the input is 23, the output is TWENTY THREE. (See exercise 9H for an enhanced version of this program).

9C   Random numbers

Basic language includes a function which chooses a number at random. This function has a very wide variety of uses, including the simulation of chance events, games and producing tables of random numbers. Regrettably, the function works slightly differently on different types of computer. The most common version is described below.

RND (X)

The random number generating function **RND** produces a value between 0 and 1 in the form of a fraction, to six decimal places. All values in the range 0 to 1 have an equal chance of being selected.

The argument, which may be a positive of negative number of any size, affects the random number chosen in the following way:

If the argument is negative, then the random number chosen depends on the argument. For example, **RND (−1)** always produces the same number on the same computer.

If the argument is positive, the random number chosen depends on the previous random value. For example, **RND (1)** produces a sequence of random numbers.

If the argument is zero, the previous random number is repeated.

The most common use of the **RND** function is as follows:

A negative argument is used to select an initial random number.

A positive argument is then used repeatedly to produce a sequence of random numbers. This sequence does, however, depend on the initial (negative) argument; the same initial argument produces the same sequence of random numbers.

If a completely random sequence of numbers is required, the instruction **RANDOMIZE** at the start of the program will choose an initial random number at random.

It is convenient to introduce the whole number function **INT** at this point, as it is often used in conjunction with the **RND** function. Further uses of the **INT** function are discussed in the next section.

INT (X)

The integer function **INT** produces the whole number part of its argument. For example:

$$INT\ (\ 5.9) = 5$$
$$INT\ (10) \quad = 10$$
$$INT\ (−2.1) \quad = −3$$

Note the effect of the **INT** function on negative numbers.

Example 9C

Print a table of 100 integers in the range 1 to 10, chosen at random.

Method

The most convenient layout of the table is 10 rows of 10 columns. The steps of the program are as follows:

    Input a number to initialise the random number generator.
    Print a suitable heading.
    Repeat, for each row:
        Repeat, for each column:
            Generate a random integer in the range 1 to 10,
            Print the random integer,
        End column repetition,
        Start new print line
    End row repetition.

The only step which needs further explanation is the one which produces a random integer in the range 1 to 10. This is programmed as follows:

    THE **RND** function produces a fraction in the range 0 to 1.
    Multiplying by 10 produces a number in the range 0 to 10 which may be a fraction.
    Taking the whole number part produces an integer in the range 0 to 9.
    Adding 1 produces an integer in the range 1 to 10.
The statement which achieves this is:

```
LET X = INT (10 * RND (1)) + 1
```

Variables
X   random integer in range 1 to 10
R   row counter

C column counter
I initial random number
J number to set random number generator

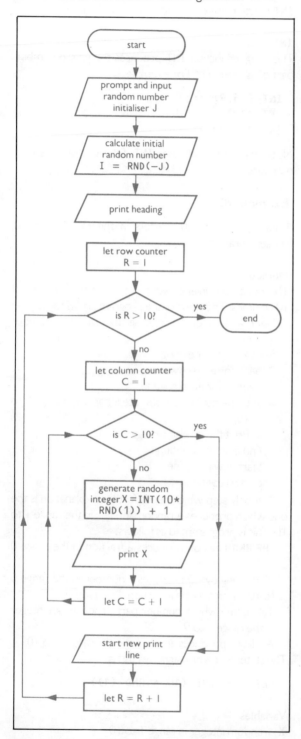

Figure 9C1 Flow diagram foe example program 9C

Flow diagram
See figure 9C1.

Program

```
100  REM EXAMPLE PROGRAM 9C
105  REM TABLE OF RANDOM INTEGERS
110  PRINT "TYPE A POSITIVE NUMBER"
115  PRINT "TO START THE RANDOM"
120  PRINT "NUMBER GENERATOR";
125  INPUT J
130  LET I = RND (-J)
135  PRINT
140  PRINT "TABLE OF RANDOM INTEGERS"
145  PRINT "IN RANGE 1 TO 10"
150  PRINT
155  FOR R = 1 TO 10
160  FOR C = 1 TO 10
165  LET X = INT (10 * RND (1)) + 1
170  PRINT TAB (5 + 3*C); X;
175  NEXT C
180  PRINT
185  NEXT R
190  PRINT
195  END
```

Points to notice

- The initial random number I is not output. Its purpose is to set the random number generator.
- The **TAB** function in line 170 is used to create the columns of the table.

Sample run

```
TYPE A POSITIVE NUMBER
TO START THE RANDOM
NUMBER GENERATOR ? 22

TABLE OF RANDOM INTEGERS
IN RANGE 1 TO 10
9   9   7   7   5   7   7   2   9   4
3   5   2  10   9   2   1   8  10   4
5  10   8   3   1  10  10   5   9   5
7  10   9   7   9  10   3  10   7   1
8   3   5   2   4   8   6  10   1   3
7   9   7   7   5   2   7   7   2   1
6   3  10   4   9   1   8   7   8   6
6   5   5   6   8   6   4   9   7   8
6   6   4   6  10  10   8   8   8   8
5   5  10   2   3   6   6   3   9   1
```

Exercise 9C

1 Write down the values of
 a) INT (9.95) b) INT (−6)
 c) INT (0) d) INT (35)
 e) INT (−3.01)

Copy and complete the flow diagram and program for the task in question 2.

2 Simulate 100 spins of a coin.

Method
A spin of a coin has 0.5 probability of coming up heads, and the same for tails. The simplest way to simulate it is to choose a random number in the range 0 to 1. If the random number is more than 0.5, then the result is heads, otherwise it is tails.
 Output from the program is in the form of a table of ten rows and ten columns, with the letter H or T as appropriate.

Variables
X random number in range 0 to 1
R row number
C column number
A$ result of spin, either H or T.

Flow diagram
See figure 9C2.

Program

```
100  REM EXERCISE 9C QUESTION 2
105  REM 100 SPINS OF A COIN
110  RANDOMIZE
115  PRINT "_____"
120  PRINT
125  FOR R = 1 TO 10
130  FOR _____
135  LET X = RND (__)
140  IF X > 0.5 THEN ____
145  LET A$ = "T"
150  GO TO ____
155  LET _____
160  PRINT TAB (5 + 3*C); A$;
165  NEXT ____
170  _____
175  NEXT ____
180  PRINT
185  END
```

Draw flow diagrams and write programs for the tasks in questions 3 to 5. Validate input data if necessary, and pay careful attention to the layout of output. Use suitable test data to check the working of the programs.

3 The probability that an electrical component is defective is 0.05. Simulate a batch of 200 such components as follows:
 For each component, generate a random number in the range 0 to 1. If the number is less then 0.05 then the component is defective, otherwise it is not. Count the number of defective components in each batch.

4 The probabilities of various types of weather at a particular place are as follows:

 sunny : 0.3 overcast : 0.6 rain : 0.1

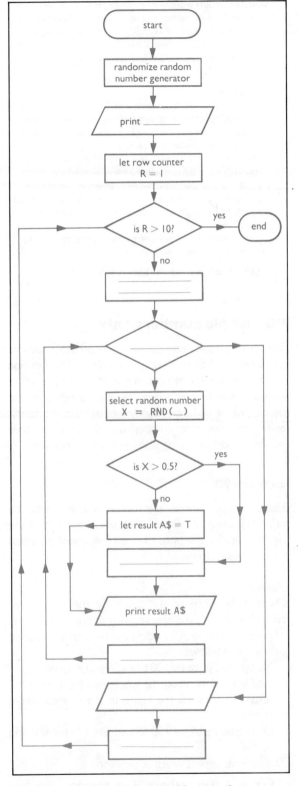

Figure 9C2 Flow diagram for exercise 9C, question 2

Simulate a month's weather by generating a random number in the range 0 to 1 for each day. If the number is less then 0.3, the weather is sunny, if it is between 0.3 and 0.9 the weather is overcast, and if it is more than 0.9 there is rain. Print a table of the weather for each day, and add up the number of days having each type of weather.

Modification

Keep a record of your local weather for a month, and work out the probabilities of the weather types from the results. Use these probabilities to simulate the month's weather, and compare the results with the actual weather record.

5 Each move in a game for two players is as follows: each player throws a dice, and the one with the higher number scores one point (there is no score if the numbers are equal). Simulate ten moves of this game, adding up the total score for each player. At the start, input each player's lucky number to set the random number generator.

The statement to simulate one throw of a dice, producing a random integer in the range 1 to 6 is:

```
LET X = INT (6 * RND (1)) + 1
```

9D   Whole numbers only

The **INT** function, introduced in the previous section, produces the integer part of a number. This function has a wide variety of uses, some of which are introduced in this section. These include rounding to the nearest whole number, rounding to the nearest penny, testing whether one number is a factor of another number, and thus finding all the factors of a number.

Example 9D

Electronic components are sold in batches. Input the price of a batch, and the number of components in the batch. Calculate the price of one component, rounded to the nearest penny.

Method

Dividing the price of the batch by the number of components gives the precise price of one component. The steps involved in rounding this price to the nearest penny are as follows:

Multiply the price by 100 to express it in pence.

Add 0.5 and then take the whole number part of the result. This rounds the figure to the nearest whole number.

Divide the result by 100 to express it in pounds and pence.

The Basic statement which achieves this is:

```
LET R = INT (100*P + 0.5)/100
```

where   P   is the precise price,
        R   is the rounded price.

Other variables
B   batch price
N   number of components in the batch

Flow diagram
See figure 9D1.

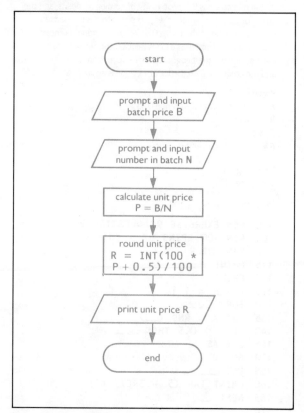

Figure 9D1   Flow diagram for example program 9D

Program

```
100   REM EXAMPLE PROGRAM 9D
105   REM CALCULATE UNIT PRICE OF
110   REM ELECTRONIC COMPONENTS,
115   REM ROUNDED TO NEAREST PENNY
120   PRINT "BATCH PRICE";
125   INPUT B
130   PRINT "NUMBER IN BATCH";
135   INPUT N
140   LET P = B/N
145   LET R = INT (100*P + 0.5)/100
150   PRINT "PRICE PER COMPONENT : £"; R
155   END
```

Sample run

```
BATCH PRICE ? 126.50
NUMBER IN BATCH ? 17
PRICE PER COMPONENT : £7.44
```

Exercise 9D

1   Write down the value of INT (X + 0.5) in each of the
    following cases:
    a) X = 1   b) X = 1.9
    c) X = 1.5   d) X = 2.0
    e) X = 1.4999
    What is the effect of the function INT (X + 0.5)?

2   Dry run the following program segment in each of the cases
    below:

```
200  REM EXERCISE 9D QUESTION 2
205  INPUT J
210  IF J >= 1 AND J <= 3 AND J =
                         INT(J) THEN 225
215  PRINT  " INVALID "
220  GO TO 230
225  PRINT  " VALID "
230  REM CONTINUE
```

    a) J = 1   b) J = 1.5
    c) J = 20   d) J = 2.9
    e) J = 2   f) J = −10
    g) J = 3
    From your results, state which values of J are accepted by the
    condition in line 210.

Draw flow diagrams and write programs for the tasks in questions 3
to 8. Validate input data where necessary, and pay attention to the
layout of output. Choose suitable test data to check the running of
the programs.

3   Input a set of ten whole numbers, and test whether each is even
    or odd (an even number gives a whole number when divided by
    2).

4   Insulating material is sold in rolls measuring 5 m by 0.5 m. Input
    the length and breadth of a number of surfaces to be insulated,
    and calculate the area of each. Calculate the total area, add 5%
    for wastage and then calculate the number of rolls required.

5   Input a sum of money, and work out how it can be made up in
    the least number of notes and coins.

    Suggested method
    If the sum of money (variable M) is input with a decimal point
    separating pounds and pence, then

    number of £5 notes = INT (M/5)

    Subtract the sum of money this represents from the original sum,
    and then find the number of £1 notes, etc.

6   A number is a factor of another number if it divides into it exactly.
    Input a (whole) number, and output a list of its factors. (Try all the
    numbers from 2 to half the input number and see if they divide
    exactly.)

7   A number is prime if it has no factors other than 1 and itself. Input
    a set of numbers and test whether each is prime. (Adapt the
    program from question 6 to test whether a number is prime.)

8   Output all the prime numbers between 1 and a suitable limit.
    (The classical method is to test each number in turn, rejecting all
    those which are not prime. Adapt the program from question 7
    to carry out the test.)

9E   Mathematical functions

In addition to the **RND** and **INT** functions introduced in
the previous two sections, a number of mathematical
functions are available in Basic language. The commonest of these are discussed in this section.

ABS(X)

The **ABS** function produces the absolute value of its
argument. This is the size of the number, whether or
not it is positive. For example:

ABS (−9) = 9 and ABS (8) = 8

A simple test whether a number X is positive is:

is **ABS** (X) = X?

SGN(X)

The sign function **SGN** tests the sign of a number:

SGN(X) = + 1 if X is positive
SGN(X) =   0 if X is zero
SGN(X) = − 1 if X is negative

SQR(X)

The function **SQR** produces the square root of its
argument, which must be positive. For example:

SQR (16) = 4 and SQR (7.51) = 2.74

SIN(X), COS(X) and TAN(X)

The trigonometrical functions **SIN**, **COS** and **TAN** produce the sign, cosine and tangent respectively of their
arguments. The arguments, which are angles, are not
measured in degrees but in **radians**. Conversion between radians and degrees is based on the fact that
        π radians = 180 degrees
or   3.14159 radians = 180 degrees

ATN(X)

The arc tan function **ATN** produces the angle (in
radians) having a tangent equal to the argument. For
example:

ATN (1) = 0.786 (= π/4) radians,

or 45°, since the tangent of 45° is 1.

Example 9E

Input the angle at which an aeroplane takes off, and its take-off velocity. Calculate its increase in altitude after 10 seconds.

Method

Figure 9E1 illustrates the aeroplane taking off. The required increase in altitude is one side of a right-angled triangle of which the length of the hypotenuse can be calculated, and the size of the opposite angle is known.

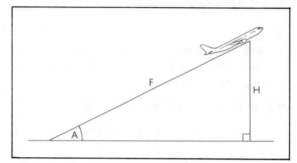

Figure 9E1   Example program 9E: Aeroplane taking off

From the theory of trigonometry:

$$\sin A = \frac{\text{length H}}{\text{length F}}$$

i.e.,   length H = length F × sin A
         length F = velocity of plane × 10 seconds

To change the angle to radians for the calculation:

$$180° = 3.14159 \text{ radians}$$
$$1° = 3.14159 \div 180 \text{ radians}$$
$$A° = 3.14159 \div 180 × A \text{ radians}$$

Variables

V   velocity of plane (metres per second)
F   distance flown in 10 seconds (metres)
A   angle of take-off (degrees)
R   angle of take-off (radians)
H   increase in altitude (metres)

Flow diagram

See figure 9E2.

Program

```
100  REM EXAMPLE PROGRAM 9E
105  REM AIRCRAFT ALTITUDE
110  REM AFTER 10 SECONDS
115  PRINT "ANGLE OF TAKE-OFF (DEGREES)";
120  INPUT A
```

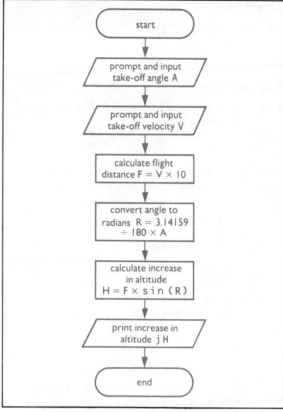

Figure 9E2   Flow diagram for example program 9E

```
125  PRINT "TAKE-OFF VELOCITY (M/SEC)";
130  INPUT V
135  LET F = V*10
140  LET R = 3.14159/180*A
145  LET H = F*SIN(R)
150  PRINT "INCREASE IN ALTITUDE";
155  PRINT "AFTER 10 SECONDS:"; H; "M"
160  PRINT
165  END
```

Points to notice

● The angle is converted to radians before use in the **SIN** function.

Sample run

```
ANGLE OF TAKEOFF (DEGREES) ? 11
TAKEOFF VELOCITY (M/SEC) ? 100
INCREASE IN ALTITUDE AFTER 10 SECONDS: 190.81 M
```

Exercise 9E

I   Which of the following functions have invalid arguments:
    a) **SQR (10)**   b) **SQR (−10)**
    c) **ABS (−10)**   d) **SGN (0)**
    e) **TAN (X/2)**   where **X** = 3.14159

Copy and complete the flow diagram and program for the task in question 2.

2 The sugar content of a certain soft drink is supposed to be 7%. If the percentage for a sample from a batch is within 0.2% of 7%, then the batch is accepted, otherwise it is rejected.

Input a batch number, weight of sugar (grams) in the sample, total sample weight (grams) and calculate the percentage sugar content. Print the message REJECT if this differs from 7% by more than 0.2%. Otherwise print the message ACCEPT.

Method

The percentage of sugar is:

$$P = \frac{S}{W} \times 100$$

where:

P	percentage sugar	**S**	weight of sugar
W	sample weight	**B**	batch number

The difference between this and 7% is:

$D = 7 - P$

D   difference

The sample is rejected if the size of the difference, not counting sign, is more than 0.2%, in other words:

if **ABS(D)** > 0.2

Flow diagram

See figure 9E3.

Program

```
100  REM EXERCISE 9E QUESTION 2
105  REM SOFT DRINK ACCEPTANCE TEST
110  REM
115  PRINT  " BATCH NUMBER " ;
120  INPUT B
125  PRINT  " SAMPLE SUGAR WEIGHT(GM) " ;
130  INPUT ___
135  PRINT  " SAMPLE WEIGHT (GM) " ;
140  INPUT ___
145  LET  P = _____
150  IF ABS(P) > 0.2 THEN _____
155  PRINT  " ACCEPT "
160  _____
165  PRINT  " ____ "
170  END
```

Draw flow diagrams and write programs for the tasks in questions 3 to 8. Validate input data where necessary, and pay attention to the layout of output. Choose suitable test data to check the working of the programs.

3 Print a table of the sines, cosines and tangents of angles from 0° to 90° in steps of 1°.

4 Figure 9E4 shows a point P plotted with co-ordinates (x, y).
   a) Input the co-ordinates of the point, and calculate its distance D from the origin and the angle A between D and the x-axis.
   b) Input the distance D and angle A, and calculate the co-ordinates of the point.
   c) Use the method of co-ordinates to display various shapes and patterns on the screen. Circles, ellipses and spirals can be created by this method.

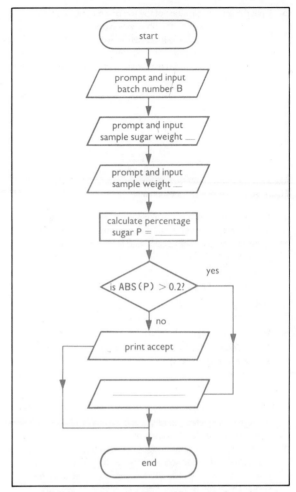

Figure 9E3   Flow diagram for exercise 9E, question 2

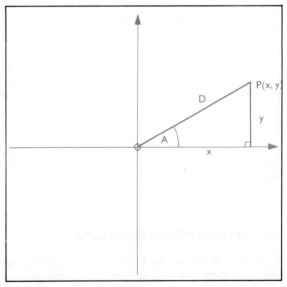

Figure 9E4   Exercise 9E, question 4

5 Input the angle of elevation of the top of a mountain, and the horizontal distance from the observation point to the mountain. Calculate the height of the mountain above the observation point.

6 Calculate the total length of all the beams in the structure shown in figure 9E5. All the angles marked are 53.6°, and the total length of the structure is 20 m.

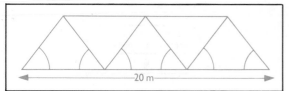

Figure 9E5 Exercise 9E, question 6

7 A shell is fired from a gun with velocity V m/sec at an angle A to the horizontal. The horizontal distance it travels before returning to the ground (its range) is calculated from the formula

$$R = \frac{V^2}{G} \sin 2A$$

The maximum height reached is:

$$H = \frac{V^2}{2G} (\sin A)^2$$

V speed on firing (m/sec)
G acceleration due to gravity (9.8 m/sec²)
A angle if firing (radians)
R range (m)
H maximum height (m)

Input a value of the velocity **V** (usually between 500 and 1000 m/sec) and print a table of ranges and maximum heights for angles of firing from 10° to 80° in steps of 5°.

8 Figure 9E6 shows a swing bridge in its open position. Calculate the angle that the road sections make with the horizontal in this position, and the speed (in degrees per second) at which the sections must rotate for the bridge to open in 45 seconds.

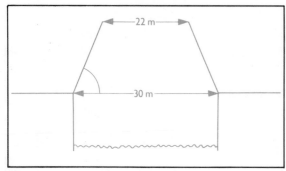

Figure 9E6 Exercise 9E, question 8

9F User-defined functions

In addition to the standard functions in Basic language discussed in the previous sections of this chapter, it is possible to define a function at the start of a program,

which can then be used as often as necessary during the program.

The defining statement contains:
the word **DEF**
the name of the function, consisting of the letters **FN** followed by a letter identifying the function,
a variable (in brackets), the argument,
a formula for calculating the value of the function from its argument,

For example, the statement

```
110  DEF FNS (X) = X * X
```

defines a function **FNS** which produces the square of its argument.

Later in the program, the statements

```
150  LET A = 3.2
155  LET B = FNS (A)
```

assign to variable **B** the value 10.24, the square of 3.2.

A defined function may use a standard Basic function in its formula, for example:

```
120  DEF FNR (X) = INT (X + 0.5)
```

defines a function **FNR** which rounds a number of the nearest integer.

Example 9F

At a clothes shop, the selling price of each article is calculated as follows:

For each consignment, an identification code, number of articles, total cost and percentage increase from cost price to selling price (the 'mark up') are input.

The cost price for one article is:

$$C = \frac{T}{N}$$

C cost price per article (£)
T total consignment cost (£)
N number of articles in consignment

The selling price for each article is:

$$S = \left(1 + \frac{P}{100}\right) \times C$$

S selling price (£)
P percentage 'mark up'

The price plus VAT is:

$$T = \left(1 + \frac{V}{100}\right) \times S$$

T price plus VAT
V VAT rate (currently 15%)

The cost price, selling price and price plus VAT are output, rounded to the nearest penny. A defined function is used for the rounding, based on the formula introduced in example 9D.

The calculation is carried out for a number of consignments, ending when a consignment identity code **XXX** is entered.

Flow diagram
See figure 9F1.

Program

```
100  REM EXAMPLE PROGRAM 9F
105  REM CLOTHES SHOP PRICE
110  REM CALCULATIONS
115  REM
200  REM DEFINE ROUNDING FUNCTION
205  DEF FNR(X) = INT (100*X + 0.5)/100
210  REM PRINT HEADING
215  PRINT
220  PRINT "PRICE CALCULATIONS"
225  PRINT
230  LET V = 15
300  REM CALCULATION LOOP
305  PRINT "CONSIGNMENT CODE";
315  INPUT C$
320  IF C$ = "XXX" THEN 400
325  PRINT "NUMBER OF ARTICLES";
330  INPUT N
335  PRINT "CONSIGNMENT COST (£)";
340  INPUT C
345  PRINT "CONSIGNMENT MARK UP (%)";
350  INPUT P
355  LET C = T/N
340  LET S = (1 + P/100)*C
345  LET T = (1 + V/100)*S
350  PRINT "COST PRICE : £"; FNR(C)
355  PRINT "SELLING PRICE : £"; FNR(S)
360  PRINT "PRICE + VAT : £"; FNR(T)
365  PRINT
370  GO TO 300
400  PRINT "END OF PROGRAM"
405  END
```

Points to notice
- The rounding function **FNR** is defined in line 205.
- The rounding function is used in the **PRINT** statements in lines 350 to 360. Functions may be used in **PRINT** statements as well as in **LET** statements.

- This program is another example of the use of an end-of-data marker.

Sample run

```
PRICE CALCULATIONS

CONSIGNMENT CODE ? J397
NUMBER OF ARTICLES ? 20
CONSIGNMENT COST (£) ? 437.50
CONSIGNMENT MARK UP (%) ? 40
COST PRICE : £21.88
SELLING PRICE : £30.63
PRICE + VAT : £35.22


CONSIGNMENT CODE ? XXX
END OF PROGRAM
```

Exercise 9F

1 Describe in words, or algebraic formulae, the effects of the following functions:
   a) DEF FNP(Y) = 100−Y
   b) DEF FNQ(X) = 3*X*X − 2*X + 17
   c) DEF FNR(A) = INT (10* RND(A) + 1)
   d) DEF FNS(M) = SQR (1−M*M)
   e) DEF FNT(K) = (K + 1)/(K − 1)
   f) DEF FNH(X,Y) = SQR (X*X + Y*Y)

   Note that in some versions of Basic a defined function may have more than one argument.

2 Two of the functions defined in question 1 will give errors if their arguments have certain values. Which functions are they, and what values are not permitted?

3 In the functions defined in question 1:
   a) If K=47, what is FNP(K)?
   b) If Y=2, what is FNQ(Y)?
   c) If M=3, what values can FNR(M) have?
   d) If L=0.6, what is FNS(L)?
   e) If A=0.5, what is FNT(A)?
   f) If A=7, B=24, what is FNH(A,B)?

4 Define functions to calculate the sine, cosine and tangent of an angle when the angle is in degrees. Use these functions in programs from the trigonometry exercise.

Draw flow diagrams and write programs for the tasks in questions 5 to 8. In each case, define a suitable function at the start of the program. Choose suitable test data to check the working of the programs.

5 Define a function to convert temperatures from degrees Centigrade to degrees Fahrenheit (optionally rounded to the nearest 0.1 degree). Print a conversion table over the range 1 °C to 100 °C.

Conversion formula
$F = \frac{9}{5} \times C + 32$
F degrees Fahrenheit
C degrees Centigrade

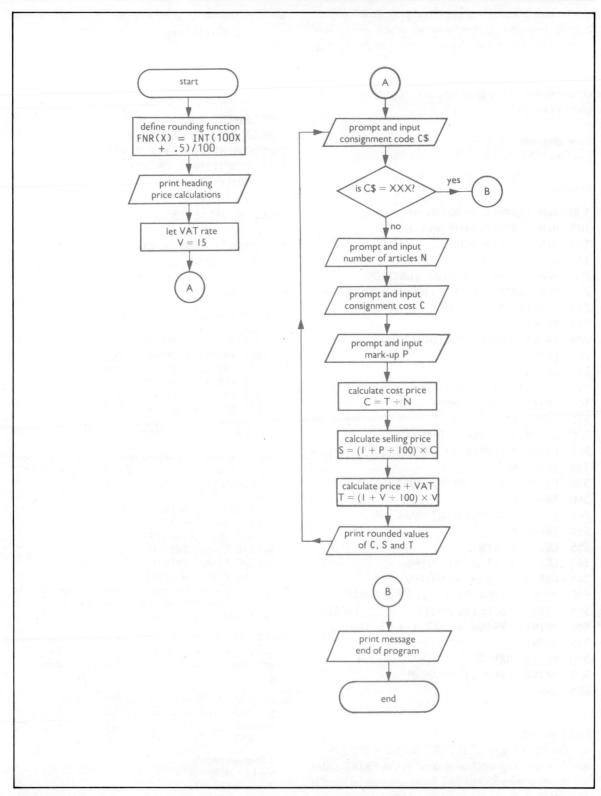

Figure 9F1   Flow diagram for example program 9F

6 Define a function to convert marks out of a given amount to percentages, rounded to the nearest whole percentage. The function requires two arguments, the mark and the total mark. Input a total mark, and a set of pupils' names and marks. Output the percentage corresponding to each mark.

7 The formula for the volume of the shape in figure 9F2 is:
$$V = \tfrac{5}{12} \times \pi \times D^3$$
V volume   **D** diameter
$\pi = 3.14159$

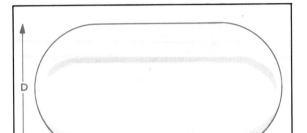

Figure 9F2 Exercise 9F, question 7

a) Define a function to calculate the volume, and print a table of volumes for diameters from 0.2 cm to 3 cm in steps of 0.2 cm.

b) Work out a formula for the surface area of the shape (it is a cylinder with a hemisphere at each end), define a function from the formula and include a column in the table for the surface area.

8 Define a function to convert German marks (DM) to pounds sterling, rounded to the nearest penny. Use the function in the following program:

Machine parts are imported to Britain from Germany. Each consignment is accompanied by an invoice with a list of part numbers, quantities and prices (in marks).

Input the date, current exchange rate from marks to pounds, and the number of different parts in the invoice. Then, for each part, input the part number, quantity and price (DM). Calculate the cost (cost = quantity × price) and convert it to pounds. Add up the total cost in marks, and convert it to pounds.

Print a suitable heading for the invoice, followed by columns for the part number, quantity price (DM), cost (DM) and cost (£). Print the total costs underneath.

9G End-of-chapter summary

This chapter has introduced the idea of a function, and shown how functions are implemented in Basic language. Both standard functions and user-defined functions have been discussed. The main points of the chapter are as follows:

- A function transforms one quantity (the argument) to another quantity (the value). A function may have more than one argument.

- Basic language contains a number of standard functions, and permits functions to be defined by users.

- Some common standard Basic functions are as follows:

LEN(X$)	produces the length of a string of characters.
MID$(X$, A, B)	produces a substring of string **X$**, of length **B** characters starting at the **A**th character.
VAL(X$)	produces the numeric value of the literal variable **X$**.
STR$(X)	produces a literal variable containing the same characters as the numeric variable **X**.
RND(X)	produces a random number in the range 0 to 1.
INT(X)	produces the whole number part of its argument.
ABS(X)	produces the absolute value of its argument.
SGN(X)	= +1 if **X** is positive = 0 if **X** is zero = −1 if **X** is negative
SQR(X)	produces the square root of its argument.
SIN(X), COS(X), TAN(X)	sine, cosine and tangent functions, with angles in radians.
ATN(X)	arc tan function, value in radians.

- User defined functions are declared by means of a **DEF** statement. The function name contains three letters, starting with **FN**. The **DEF** statement also contains a formula for evaluating the function.

Exercise 9G

This exercise covers topics introduced in this and previous chapters.

1 If A$ = "MKX 347W", B = −9.6, C = 0 and D = 3.9, write down the values of the following functions:
a) LEN (A$)
b) VAL (MID$ (A$, 5, 3))
c) STR$ (D)
d) RND (C)

e) `INT (B)`
f) `INT (ABS(B))`
g) `COS (C)`
h) `SQR (INT (D + 0.5))`
i) `SGN (B)`
j) `INT (B + 0.5)`

Draw flow diagrams and write programs for the tasks in questions 2 to 9. Validate input data where necessary, and pay attention to the layout of output. Choose suitable test data to check the running of the programs, and write user and programmer's documentation for them.

2 An approximate formula for the height of the tide above or below its average level is:

$$D = A \times \cos(2 \times \pi \times F \times T)$$

A maximum height above or below average (m)

F $= \dfrac{1}{12.25}$ (high tide every 12.25 hours)

T time (hours) since last high tide
D height of tide (m)
π = 3.14159

Input the time of a morning high tide (in hours and decimals of an hour: 9.5 for 09.30 hours), and a value of the maximum tide height A. Print a table of the height of the tide every quarter hour till next high tide. (Alternatively display a simple graph or bar chart of the height of the tide.)

3 An approximate formula for the length of a day (hours from sunrise to sunset) in Britain is:

$$D = 12 - 6 \times \cos\left(\frac{2 \times \pi \times N}{365}\right)$$

D length of day (hours)
N number of days since shortest day
π = 3.14159

Print a table, or display a graph, of lengths of days every seven days for a year, starting from the shortest day. (Use variable N as a loop counter from 0 to 365 in steps of 7.)

4 In order to be legally acceptable, a cheque must contain the amount in words and in figures. When a cheque is printed by a computer, the commonest technique is to have columns for the thousands, hundreds, tens and units of pounds, as illustrated in figure 9H1. Note that the pence does not have to be printed in words.

Input a date, the name of a person to whom a cheque is payable, and the amount. Print a cheque with the amount in words and figures, set out as in figure 9H1.

Figure 9H1 Exercise 9H, question 4

5 Packets of cornflakes are despatched in small, medium or large boxes, containing 24, 72 and 216 packets respectively. As much as possible of an order is packed in large boxes, the rest as far as possible in medium boxes and the remainder in small boxes, the last of which may not be full.

Input a set of orders, each comprising an order number and number of packets. For each order, work out the number of large, medium and small boxes needed. Output the results in a suitable table.

6 The possibility of a telephone call being received at an office switchboard in any minute is 0.3. Simulate an hour's operation of the switchboard by generating a random number for each minute, and registering a call if it is 0.3 or less. Output the minutes during which a call is received. Add up the total number of calls, and calculate the average number of calls per minute.

7 The formula for the range of a projectile is:

$$R = \frac{V^2}{G} \sin 2A$$

R range (m)
V speed on firing (m/sec)
G acceleration due to gravity (9.8 m/sec²)
A angle of firing (radians)

This formula can be used in a simple artillery game, the overall steps of which are as follows:

The range of a target is chosen at random (between 500 m and 5000 m).
The player decides on an angle of firing and fires.
The range of the shot is displayed, or some indication is given of how close it was to the target.
Firing continues until a shot lands within 5 m of the target.
Another target is chosen and its range displayed.
A simple method of scoring can be devised. It is also possible to depict the game graphically.

☐**8** The game 'Howzat' uses a dice to simulate a simplified version of a cricket match; it can also be played on a computer. The bowling of a ball is represented by throwing a dice:
1 means no score
2 means score 1 run
3 means score 2 runs
4 means score 4 runs
5 means score 6 runs
6 means 'Howzat'
If a 6 comes up, a dice is thrown again:
1 means bowled
2 means caught
3 means stumped
4 means run out
5 means leg before wicket
6 means not out
Use these ideas to simulate a cricket match, displaying a ball-by-ball commentary.

9 Convert a number from a Roman numeral to an ordinary base ten number.

10
Subprograms

The programs introduced in the previous chapters of this book are generally fairly short, and self-contained. Whenever longer programs are planned, or lines of code written for use by more than one program, the idea of a **subprogram** is essential. This chapter introduces the general concept of a subprogram and shows how subprograms are written in Basic. It concludes with a section on the overall structure of programs, an essential aspect of programming, especially when long programs are written.

10A   The idea of a subprogram

As its name implies, a subprogram is a part of a whole program. It is a portion of code, performing a specific function, to which control is transferred from another part of the program. (Transferring control to a subprogram is also known as **calling** a subprogram.) At the end of the subprogram, control returns to the point from which the subprogram was called. The idea of a subprogram is illustrated in figure 10A1. It is possible for a subprogram to be called from another subprogram.

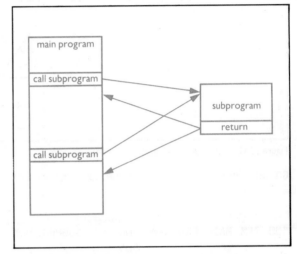

Figure 10A1   A subprogram

Another way of looking at subprograms is based on the fact that each subprogram in a program performs a specific function. A subprogram may be regarded as a 'building block' in the construction of a program. This view of subprograms is illustrated in figure 10A2. Note that the part of the program calling the subprograms is called the **main program**.

The way in which a whole program is built up from a number of subprograms is an important aspect of the **structure** of a program. This topic is discussed in section 10E.

10B   GOSUB and RETURN statements

The Basic statement which transfers control to a subprogram contains the word **GOSUB**, followed by the line number of the start of the subprogram. At the end of the subprogram, a statement containing the word **RETURN** transfers control to the statement after the

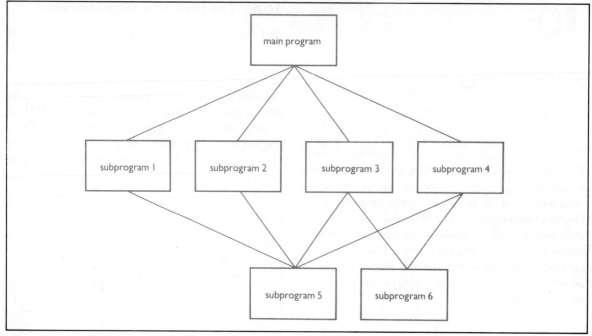

Figure 10A2   Subprograms as building blocks of a program

GOSUB statement which called the subprogram. For exampller:

Main Program
```
100  REM  MAIN  PROGRAM
  :
150  GOSUB  500
155  REM
180  GOSUB  500
185  REM
  :
```

Subprogram
```
500  REM  SUBPROGRAM
505  ...
  :
545  ...
550  RETURN
```

In this example, the first time the subprogram is called (from line 150), control returns to line 155. The second time the subprogram is called (from line 180), control returns to line 185.

Notice that there is no special statement to mark the start of a subprogram. It is strongly recommended that the start of a subprogram is *always* marked with a **REM** statement.

Example 10B

A travel agent has a program to print luggage labels for travellers. Two labels are printed, one for the outward journey, the other for the return journey. Input information is the names of the travellers and their outward and return addresses.

Method
In order to improve the appearance of the labels, a line is ruled at the top and bottom of each, as well as between the name and the address on each label. A subprogram is used to print the ruled line.

Variables

N$	name of traveller(s)
A1$, A2$, A3$	outward address (3 lines)
R1$, R2$, R3$	return address (3 lines)
J	loop counter

Flow diagram
See figure 10B1. Notice how a subprogram is represented.

Program
```
100  REM  EXAMPLE  PROGRAM  10B
105  REM  PRINT  LUGGAGE  LABELS
110  REM
200  REM  INPUT  NAME  AND  ADDRESSES
205  PRINT  " NAME " ;
210  INPUT  N$
215  PRINT  " DESTINATION  ADDRESS
                        (3  LINES) "
220  INPUT  A1$
225  INPUT  A2$
```

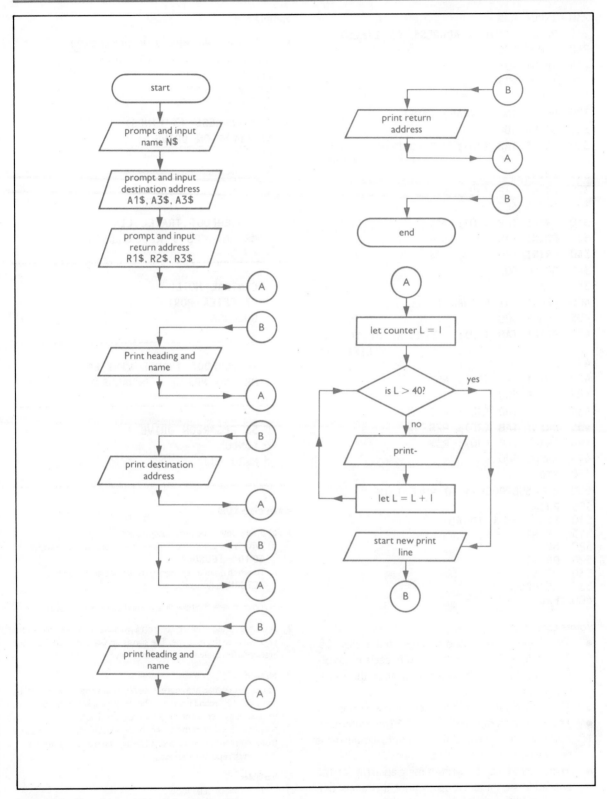

Figure 10B1 Flow diagram for example program 10B

```
230   INPUT A3$
235   PRINT "RETURN ADDRESS (3 LINES)"
240   INPUT R1$
245   INPUT R2$
250   INPUT R3$
255   REM
300   REM PRINT OUTWARD LABEL
305   GOSUB 500
310   PRINT TAB (10); "TENDERFOOT TRAVEL
                              LIMITED"
315   PRINT
320   PRINT TAB (10); N$
325   GOSUB 500
330   PRINT TAB (10); A1$
335   PRINT TAB (10); A2$
340   PRINT TAB (10); A3$
345   GOSUB 500
350   REM
400   REM PRINT RETURN LABEL
405   GOSUB 500
410   PRINT TAB (10); "TENDERFOOT TRAVEL
                              LIMITED"
415   PRINT
420   PRINT TAB (10); N$
425   GOSUB 500
430   PRINT TAB (10); R1$
435   PRINT TAB (10); R2$
440   PRINT TAB (10); R3$
445   GOSUB 500
450   STOP
500   REM SUBPROGRAM TO RULE LINE
505   PRINT
510   FOR L = 1 TO 40
515   PRINT "-";
520   NEXT L
525   PRINT
530   PRINT
535   RETURN
600   END
```

Points to notice

- The subprogram is called six times: from lines 305, 325, 345, 405, 425 and 445. On each occasion, control returns to the statement after the calling statement.
- The subprogram is written after the main program.
- The main program ends with a **STOP** statement. This halts the running of the program, although it is not the highest numbered statement.
- This program can be written using an array for the two addresses, and a loop to print the labels. See exercise 10B, question 3.

Sample run

```
NAME ? MR AND MRS J K DONALDSON
DESTINATION ADDRESS (3 LINES)
?  CENTRAL HOTEL
?  ST PETER PORT
?  GUERNSEY
RETURN ADDRESS (3 LINES)
?  56 EDGARSON DRIVE
?  LONDON
?  NW20 6JJ


-------------------------------------------

       TENDERFOOT  TRAVEL  LIMITED
       MR  AND  MRS  J  K  DONALDSON

-------------------------------------------

       CENTRAL  HOTEL
       ST  PETER  PORT
       GUERNSEY

-------------------------------------------

       TENDERFOOT  TRAVEL  LIMITED
       MR  AND  MRS  J  K  DONALDSON

-------------------------------------------

       56  EDGARSON  DRIVE
       LONDON
       NW20  6JJ

-------------------------------------------
```

Exercise 10B

1 a) Briefly define the term subprogram.
   b) What is the difference between the Basic instruction words **GO TO** and **GOSUB**?
   c) To which point in a program is control transferred by a **RETURN** statement?

Copy and complete the flow diagram and program for question 2.

2 A microprocessor which controls a machine is required to send two signals to the machine. The signals, an **ON** and an **OFF** signal, are sent alternately at 5 second intervals.

Method

The control signals are represented by displaying the words ON and OFF at 5 second intervals. The delay is caused by a loop of variable length, contained in a subprogram. The length of the loop is input at the start of the program; the value being determined by trial and error to give a 5 second delay. The main program is a loop which repeats indefinitely.

Variables

T   limit of delay loop
K   loop counter

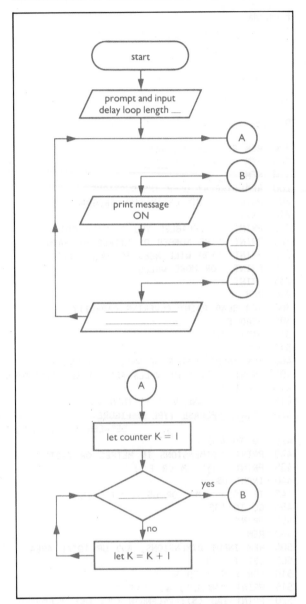

Figure 10B2 Flow diagram for exercise 10B, question 2

Flow diagram
See figure 10B2.

Program

```
100  REM EXERCISE 10B QUESTION 2
105  REM MACHINE CONTROL PROGRAM
110  REM
115  PRINT " DELAY LOOP LENGTH ";
120  _____
125  REM
200  REM MAIN CONTROL LOOP
205  GOSUB 300
210  PRINT " ON "
```

```
215  GOSUB ____
220  _____
225  GO TO ____
230  REM
300  REM DELAY LOOP SUBPROGRAM
305  FOR K = 1 TO ____
310  NEXT K
315  _____
400  END
```

Draw flow diagrams and write programs for the tasks in questions 3 to 5. Make sure that the links between the main program and the subprogram(s) are correct. Run the programs with suitable test data.

3 Rewrite example program 10B using an array to store the two addresses and a loop to control the printing of the two labels.

4 A pattern can be created on the screen by displaying rows of different characters in various combinations. Write a set of subprograms to print rows of characters or combinations of characters. Write a main program to create a pattern by calling the subprogram in a suitable sequence.

☐ **5** *Electronic funds transfer* (EFT) is the name given to the process of paying a sum of money directly from one bank account to another by accessing the computers of the banks concerned from a terminal. The first stage of a program to perform an EFT transaction is to validate the account numbers of the bank accounts concerned. The steps of this portion of the program are as follows:

Input the account number of the account from which the money is to be transferred.
Validate the account number, and re-enter it if necessary.
Input the account number of the account to which the money is to be transferred.
Validate the account number, and re-enter it if necessary.
Input the amount of the transaction.
Display a message confirming the transaction.

The validation is carried out in a subprogram which checks that the account number contains 8 numeric digits. It uses a check variable which is assigned the value 1 if the number is valid, and 0 otherwise.

Variables
A$ account number on input, and in validation subprogram
N1$ account number of account from which money is to be transferred
N2$ account number of account to which money is to be transferred
C Check variable in validation program
M sum of money transferred

10C Branching to subprograms

The previous section introduced the **GOSUB** statement which transfers control to a subprogram. Like the **GO TO** statement, the **GOSUB** statement may be thought of as an unconditional transfer of control. It is also possible to have a conditional transfer of control to a subprogram. This is achieved by the **IF...THEN GOSUB** statement. For example:

```
135  IF A = 0 THEN GOSUB 500
140  REM CONTINUE
```

calls the subprogram at line 500 if A = 0. Note that if the subprogram is called, control returns to line 140. If the subprogram is not called, control passes directly to line 140. In other words, line 140 is executed in either case.

Example 10C

A paint estimation program accepts as input the dimensions of one or more walls to be painted, and calculates the number of litres of paint required. The dimensions may be input in feet or in metres.

Method
The overall steps of the program are as follows:
Display user instructions
Read the covering capacity (square metres per litre) of the paint from data.
Input the number of walls to be painted.
Input the units (feet or metres) to be used.
Set the total wall area to zero.
For each wall, repeat:
Input length and height, converting from feet to metres if necessary,
Calculate the area of the wall and add it to the total.
Divide the total area by the covering capacity, rounding up to the next whole number, to get the number of litres needed.
Display the number of litres of paint needed.
The subprogram converts the dimensions from feet to metres if necessary.

Variables
C   covering capacity of the paint (litres per square metre)
N   number of walls to be painted
U$ units used for measurement (feet or metres)
T   total area to be painted (square metres)
D   input dimension, also used in conversion subprogram
L   length of wall (metres)
H   height of wall (metres)
A   area of wall (square metres)
P   number of litres of paint needed
W   loop counter

Formula
Converting the dimension D from feet to metres,
$D = D \div 3.2808$

Flow diagram
See figure 10C1.

Program

```
100  REM EXAMPLE PROGRAM 10C
105  REM PAINT ESTIMATOR
110  REM
200  REM DISPLAY USER INSTRUCTIONS
205  PRINT "PAINT ESTIMATION PROGRAM"
210  PRINT
215  PRINT "...ENABLES YOU TO FIND OUT"
220  PRINT "THE NUMBER OF LITRES OF PAINT"
225  PRINT "YOU WILL NEED TO PAINT ONE"
230  PRINT "OR MORE WALLS"
235  PRINT
240  REM
300  REM READ PAINT COVERING CAPACITY
305  READ C
310  DATA 17.0
315  REM
400  REM INPUT NUMBER OF WALLS AND UNITS
405  PRINT "HOW MANY WALLS ARE TO BE PAINTED";
410  INPUT N
415  IF N > 0 AND N < 11 THEN 430
420  PRINT "PLEASE TYPE A FIGURE
                        BETWEEN 1 AND 10";
425  GO TO 410
430  PRINT "DIMENSIONS IN METRES OR FEET?"
435  PRINT "TYPE M OR F";
440  INPUT U$
445  IF U$ = "M" OR U$ = "F" THEN 455
450  GO TO 435
455  PRINT
460  REM
500  REM INPUT DIMENSIONS, ADD UP TOTAL AREA
505  LET T = 0
510  FOR W = 1 TO N
515  PRINT "WALL"; W; ":"
520  PRINT TAB (5); "LENGTH ("; U$; ")";
525  INPUT D
530  IF U$ = "F" THEN GOSUB 700
535  LET L = D
540  PRINT TAB (5); "HEIGHT ("; U$; ")";
545  INPUT D
550  IF U$ = "F" THEN GOSUB 700
555  LET H = D
560  LET A = L*H
565  LET T = T + A
570  PRINT
575  NEXT W
580  REM
600  REM CALCULATE AND OUTPUT PAINT QUANTITY
615  LET P = INT (T/C + 1)
620  PRINT
```

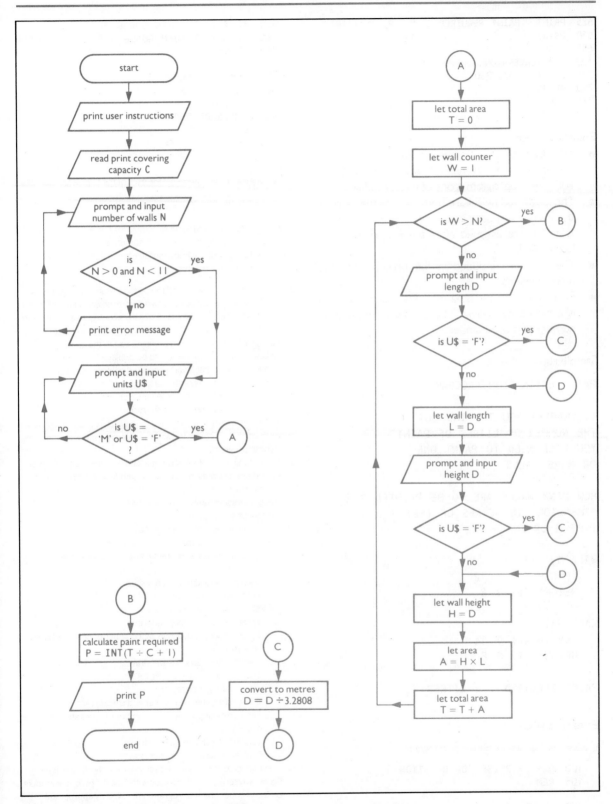

Figure 10C1 Flow diagram for example program 10C

```
625   PRINT  "PAINT  REQUIRED :  ";  P;  "LITRES"
630   PRINT
635   STOP
700   REM  CONVERSION  SUBPROGRAM
705   LET  D = D/3.2808
710   RETURN
715   END
```

Points to notice

- The program is written as a number of modules, each starting on a line number which is a multiple of 100. The subprogram is one of these modules.
- The length and height are both input as the variable **D**, which is also used in the subprogram. Variables **L** and **H** are assigned after the subprogram has been called.
- The units are included in the prompts for the measurements.
- Rounding up to the next whole number (line 615) is achieved by adding 1 before taking the whole number part of a number.

Sample run

```
PAINT  ESTIMATION  PROGRAM

...ENABLES  YOU  TO  FIND  OUT
THE  NUMBER  OF  LITRES  OF  PAINT
YOU  WILL  NEED  TO  PAINT  ONE
OR  MORE  WALLS

HOW  MANY  WALLS  ARE  TO  BE  PAINTED ?  2
DIMENSIONS  IN  METRES  OF  FEET ?
TYPE  M  OR  F ?  F

WALL  1:
    LENGTH  (F)  ?  12
    HEIGHT  (F)  ?  8

WALL  2:
    LENGTH  (F)  ?  14
    HEIGHT  (F)  ?  8

PAINT  REQUIRED :  2  LITRES
```

Exercise 10C

1 Consider the following portion of a program:

```
100   REM  EXERCISE  10C  QUESTION  1
105   REM
        ⋮
150   INPUT  A
```

```
155   IF  A > 10  THEN  GOSUB  300
160   IF  A < 1   THEN  GOSUB  400
165   PRINT  A
        ⋮
300   REM  SUBPROGRAM  1
305   LET  A = 10
310   RETURN
400   REM  SUBPROGRAM  2
405   LET  A = 1
410   RETURN
```

a) Dry run these statements for each of the following input values of A: 6, 10, 15, 0, −20, 0.99.

b) State briefly the overall effect of this portion of the program.

Draw flow diagrams and write programs for the tasks in questions 2 to 4. Pay particular attention to the links between the main program and the subprogram(s). Choose suitable test data to check the correctness of the programs.

2 Record the laps covered by the cars in a motor race, as follows:

The program responds to two commands, namely LAP and DISPLAY. The LAP command transfers control to a subprogram which requests the number of the car, and then increases its lap count by 1. The DISPLAY command causes the current number of laps covered by all the cars to be displayed.

It is suggested that an array be used to store the names of the drivers and the types of the cars, and another array be used to store the current lap counts. All the elements in the latter array are set to zero at the start of the race.

The main program contains a loop which repeats indefinitely, prompting for a command and transferring control to one of the two subprograms.

3 Most of the work of a cashier at a bank is concerned with three operations: deposits into accounts, withdrawals from accounts and cashing cheques. A program for a cashier to keep records of these operations requires three subprograms, as follows:

Deposit subprogram:
Enter account number and name.
Enter amount deposited, as a number of £20 notes, £10 notes, £5 notes, £1 notes and coins, as well as cheques and postal orders.
Calculate total amount deposited.
Add total cash to running total.
Withdrawal subprogram:
Enter account number and name.
Enter amount withdrawn, as a number of notes and coins (see above).
Calculate total amount withdrawn.
Subtract total from running total.
Cheque cashing subprogram:
Enter name, cheque number and cheque card number.
Enter amount paid out, as a number of notes and coins (see above).
Calculate total amount withdrawn.
Subtract total from running total.

In each case, the totals are calculated as a check against the figures written on the deposit or withdrawal slips, or the amount on the cheque. The subprograms are called by appropriate commands from a main program, which sets the running total to the 'float' at the beginning of the day, and outputs the running total at the end of the day.

This program may be modified to include other operations, and keep separate totals of the different denominations of notes, coins, cheques paid in and cheques cashed. Account numbers may be validated to ensure that they contain eight numeric digits.

□ **4** A machine which seals tin cans is controlled by a microprocessor. The machine has three modes of operation, depending on the type of can being sealed. Each mode requires a 10 second cycle of control signals, as follows:

Mode A:

second 1: control 4
second 2: control 1
second 5: control 6
second 8: control 3
second 10: control 1

Mode B:

second 1: control 3
second 2: control 1
second 4: control 5
second 8: control 4
second 10: control 1

Mode C:

second 1: control 4
second 3: control 2
second 5: control 1
second 6: control 3
second 7: control 2
second 8: control 3
second 10: control 1

Control is transferred to one of the three modes for two minutes (12 cycles) at a time.

Suggested method

It is suggested that the program is structured as shown in figure 10C2. The lowest-level subprogram causes a delay of 1, 2, 3 or 4 seconds depending on the value of a suitable variable. Control signals are simulated by messages displayed on the screen.

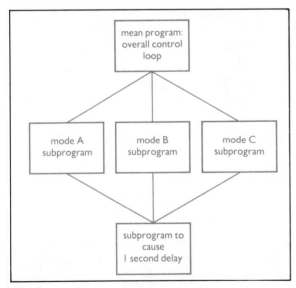

Figure 10C2 Suggested program structure for exercise 10C, question 4

10D Multi-way branches to subprograms

In section 4F, the `ON...GO TO` statement was introduced as a way of transferring control to one of a number of points in a program. In a similar way, one of a number of subprograms may be called from an `ON...GOSUB` statement. The `ON...GOSUB` statement contains a control variable, and a list of line numbers, which are the start line numbers of the various subprograms. For example:

`ON J GOSUB 500, 600, 700`

If `J` has the value 1, the subprogram starting at line 500 is called, if `J = 2` the second subprogram is called and if `J = 3` the third subprogram is called. Any other values of `J` will cause an error. Control returns from the subprogram to the statement after the `ON... GOSUB` statement.

Example 10D

A program to use a computer as a simple 'ready reckoner' works as follows:

A number is entered to choose between addition, subtraction, multiplication and division.
Two numbers are entered, and added, subtracted, multiplied or divided as required.
The result is displayed.
This process is repeated as often as required.

Method

The main program has a loop which prompts for the number which determines the type of operation. This number is validated, and then a subprogram for the required operation is called. There is a subprogram for each operation.

Variables

P   operation type
A   first number of sum
B   second number of sum
R   result of sum

Flow diagram

See figure 10D1.

Program

```
100  REM EXAMPLE PROGRAM 10D
105  REM READY RECKONER
110  REM
```

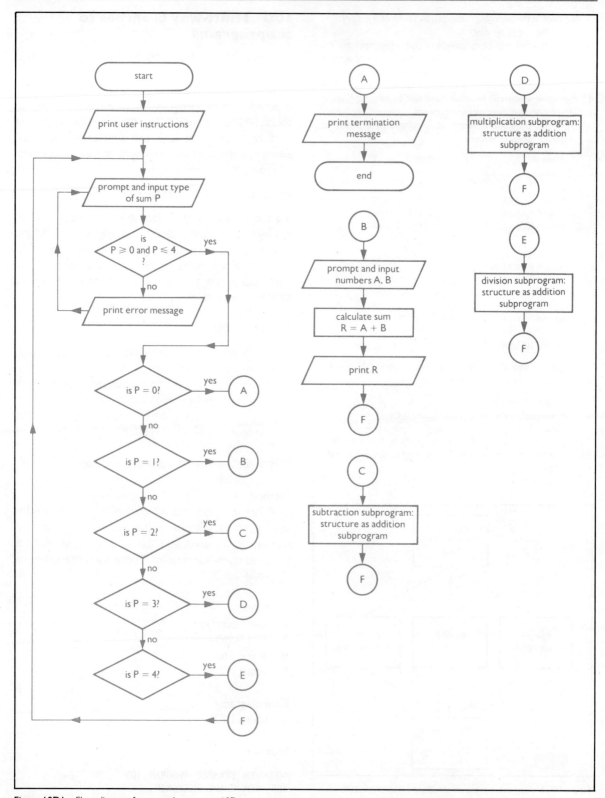

Figure 10D1 Flow diagram for example program 10D

```
200  REM DISPLAY INITIAL USER INSTRUCTIONS
205  PRINT "THIS PROGRAM MAKES YOUR COMPUTER"
210  PRINT "WORK AS A READY RECKONER"
215  PRINT
220  PRINT "WHEN ASKED...TYPE OF SUM?..."
225  PRINT
230  PRINT TAB(10); "TYPE 1 FOR ADDITION"
235  PRINT TAB(10); "TYPE 2 FOR SUBTRACTION"
240  PRINT TAB(10); "TYPE 3 FOR MULTIPLICATION"
245  PRINT TAB(10); "TYPE 4 FOR DIVISION"
250  PRINT
255  PRINT TAB(10); "TYPE 0 TO STOP THE PROGRAM"
260  PRINT
265  PRINT
300  REM MAIN CONTROL LOOP
305  PRINT
310  PRINT "TYPE OF SUM";
315  INPUT P
320  IF P >= 0 AND P <= 4 THEN 335
325  PRINT "TYPE A NUMBER BETWEEN 0 AND 4"
330  GO TO 310
335  IF P = 0 THEN 350
340  ON P GOSUB 400, 500, 600, 700
345  GO TO 305
350  PRINT
355  PRINT "READY RECKONER SIGNING OFF"
360  PRINT
365  STOP
400  REM ADDITION SUBPROGRAM
405  PRINT
410  PRINT "    ";
415  INPUT A
420  PRINT " + ";
425  INPUT B
430  LET R = A + B
435  PRINT " = "; R
440  RETURN
500  REM SUBTRACTION PROGRAM
505  PRINT
510  PRINT "    ";
515  INPUT A
520  PRINT " - ";
525  INPUT B
530  LET R = A - B
535  PRINT " = ";R
540  RETURN
600  REM MULTIPLICATION SUBPROGRAM
605  PRINT
610  PRINT "    ";
615  INPUT A
620  PRINT " × ";
625  INPUT B
630  LET R = A*B
635  PRINT " = "; R
640  RETURN
700  REM DIVISION SUBPROGRAM
705  PRINT
710  PRINT "    ";
715  INPUT A
720  PRINT " / ";
725  INPUT B
730  LET R = A/B
735  PRINT " = "; R
740  RETURN
800  END
```

Points to notice

- The four subprograms all follow an identical pattern of statements.
- The control variable P is validated before it is used in the **ON...GOSUB** statement.
- The structure of the program makes it easy to modify to include other operations. See exercise 10D question 2.

Sample run

```
THIS PROGRAM MAKES YOUR COMPUTER
WORK AS A READY RECKONER

WHEN ASKED...TYPE OF SUM?...

  TYPE 1 FOR ADDITION
  TYPE 2 FOR SUBTRACTION
  TYPE 3 FOR MULTIPLICATION
  TYPE 4 FOR DIVISION

  TYPE 0 TO STOP THE PROGRAM

TYPE OF SUM ? 3
     ? 17
  × ? 5
  =   85

TYPE OF SUM ? 2
     ? 39.61
  - ? 27.09
  =   12.52

TYPE OF SUM ? 0
READY RECKONER SIGNING OFF
```

Exercise 10D

1 Briefly explain, in your own words, how a multi-way branch to a subprogram is implemented in Basic language.
2 Modify example program 10D to include further operations such as calculating a percentage of a number, and increasing or decreasing a number by a percentage. Provide suitable prompts for the numbers input, and use the following formulae:

A% of B: $R = \dfrac{A \times B}{100}$ (R: result)

A% increase on B: $R = B \times \left(1 + \dfrac{A}{100}\right)$

A% decrease on B: $R = B \times \left(1 - \dfrac{A}{100}\right)$

Draw flow diagrams and write programs for the tasks in questions 3 to 5. Pay careful attention to the structure of the programs, especially the relationship between the main program and the subprograms. Validate input data where necessary, particularly where control variables for **ON...GOSUB** statements are input. Run the programs with suitable test data.

3 For a number of cars currently available, find out details such as name, price, fuel consumption, special features and optional extras. Use this information in a program which displays the names of the cars and then, when an appropriate number is entered to identify a particular car, displays the details of the car.

4 Select a number of cooking recipes and include them in a program which displays a list of the recipes available, and then displays a recipe according to a number which is entered.

☐ 5 A simple statistics program enables a user to carry out any of the following operations:
Enter a set of numbers.
Calculate the mean of the numbers.
Calculate the standard deviation of the numbers.
Calculate the range of the numbers (largest − smallest).
Calculate the frequency of the number (the number of times each number occurs in the set).

Formulae

$$M = \frac{S1}{N}$$

N number of numbers
S1 sum of the numbers
S2 sum of the squares of the numbers

$$D = \sqrt{\frac{S2}{N} - \left(\frac{S1}{N}\right)^2}$$

M mean
D standard deviation

10E Program structure

One of the most important aspects of the way a program is written is its **structure** − how the various parts of the program relate to each other. The quality of a program can always be judged by how clearly it is structured. Program structure is particularly important when a program is written by more than one person, and when a program must be easy to modify.

In common with most high-level languages, Basic has five elementary ways of creating the structure of a program. All five have already been introduced in various sections of this book; they are summarised below and illustrated in figures 10E1 to 10E5.

Sequencing
Sequencing is where one step or statement of a program follows another. Sequencing is achieved in Basic by the order of line numbers on program statements. See figure 10E1.

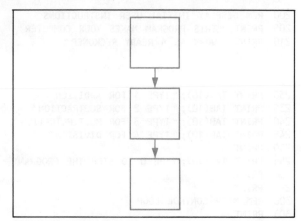

Figure 10E1   Program structure: sequencing

Branching
Branching is where control is transferred to one part of a program or another. Branching in Basic is achieved by combinations of **IF...THEN** and **GO TO** statements. Multi-way branching is also available via the **ON...GO TO** statement. See figure 10E2.

Looping
Looping is where a portion of a program is repeated. In Basic, a loop may be controlled by **FOR...TO** and **NEXT** statements, or by combinations of **IF...THEN** and **GO TO** statements. See figure 10E3.

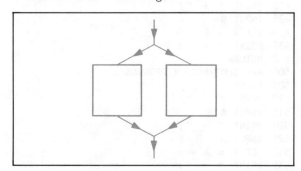

Figure 10E2   Program structure: branching

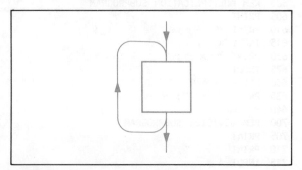

Figure 10E3   Program structure: looping

Nesting

Nesting is where one program structure is enclosed in another. Figure 10E4 illustrates nested loops and a branch enclosed in a loop.

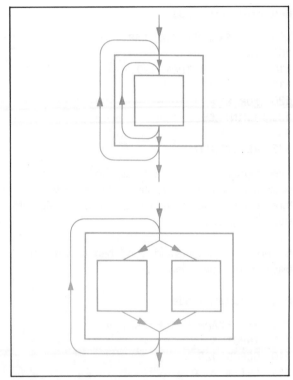

Figure 10E4 Program structure: nesting

Calling

Calling is where control is transferred to a subprogram, and then returns to the point from which it was transferred. See figure 10E5. The Basic **GOSUB** and **RETURN** statements are used to transfer control to and from a subprogram.

Combined structures

It is important to realise that the five ways of structuring a program described in the previous paragraphs are the *only* ones which should be used in constructing a program. Practices such as branching into or out of loops, branching to statements in a subprogram and the excessive use of **GO TO** statements should be avoided at all costs. What is required is a program structure which is clear, concise and as simple as possible under the circumstances. If a program has a number of subprograms, the relationship between the main program and the subprograms is very important. Programs which are as short as possible are not always well structured.

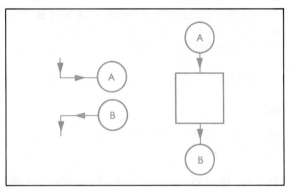

Figure 10E5 Program structure: calling

Example 10E

The four portions of program shown below are examples of poor program structure. In each case an improved version of the code is also written. It must be emphasised that the improved versions are not the only ones which could be written.

1   Input a maximum of ten numbers, which may be terminated earlier by a 0 input. The numbers are stored in an array **X(10)**.

Poorly structured code

```
100   REM EXAMPLE 10E PART 1A
105   FOR K = 1 TO 10
110   INPUT X(K)
115   IF X(K) = 0 THEN 125
120   NEXT K
125   REM CONTINUE
```

This version contains a branch out of a **FOR...NEXT** loop. This is poor program structure, and will 'clog up' the memory of most microcomputers with unwanted values of loop counters.

Better structured code

```
100   REM EXAMPLE 10E PART 1B
105   FOR K = 1 TO 10
110   INPUT X(K)
115   IF X(K) <> 0 THEN 125
120   LET K = 10
125   NEXT K
130   REM CONTINUE
```

Note that the improved version of the program uses the method for branching out of loops introduced in section 6G. It is also one statement longer.

2   Input the values of two variables, **A** and **B**. The values are valid if they are both in the range 1 to 10 (inclusive) and their sum does not exceed 15.

As there are too many conditions for a single `IF...THEN` statement, a combination is required.

Poorly structured code

```
100  REM EXAMPLE 10E PART 2A
105  INPUT A, B
110  IF A >= 1 AND B >= 1 THEN 120
115  GO TO 135
120  IF A <= 10 AND B <= 10 THEN 130
125  GO TO 135
130  IF A + B <= 15 THEN 145
135  PRINT " INVALID INPUT—PLEASE REPEAT "
140  GO TO 105
145  REM CONTINUE
```

This version of the program contains an excessive number of **GO TO** statements. It is generally preferable to express the conditions as ones for the inputs to be invalid.

Better structured code

```
100  REM EXAMPLE 10E PART 2B
105  INPUT A, B
110  IF A < 1 OR A > 10 THEN 130
115  IF B < 1 OR B > 10 THEN 130
120  IF A + B > 15 THEN 130
125  GO TO 140
130  PRINT " INVALID INPUT—PLEASE REPEAT "
135  GO TO 105
140  REM CONTINUE
```

This version of the program is easier to understand, and saves a **GO TO** statement.

3   A string of characters, stored in the variable **C$** is to be output a number of times, according to the variable **N**. If **N = 0**, the string is still to be output once.

Poorly structured code

```
100  REM EXAMPLE 10E PART 3A
105  INPUT N
110  IF N = 0 THEN 120
115  FOR K = 1 TO N
120  PRINT C$
125  IF N = 0 THEN 135
130  NEXT K
135  CONTINUE
```

This version of the program contains a branch into and a branch out of a loop. On any compiled version of Basic it will cause an error.

Better structured code

```
100  REM EXAMPLE 10E PART 3B
105  INPUT N
110  IF N > 0 THEN 120
115  LET N = N + 1
120  FOR K = 1 TO N
125   PRINT C$
130  NEXT K
135  REM CONTINUE
```

The improved version amends the value of **N** if necessary before the loop starts. However, this structure cannot be used if the original value of **N** is required later in the program.

4   Input two numbers and round them to two decimal places before continuing.

Poorly structured code

```
100  REM EXAMPLE 10E PART 4A
105  INPUT X
110  GOSUB 125
115  LET A = X
120  GO TO 135
125  LET X = INT (X * 100 + 0.5)/100
130  RETURN
135  INPUT X
140  GOSUB 125
145  LET B = X
150  REM CONTINUE
```

A subprogram is used to round the numbers to two decimal places. However, the subprogram is enclosed in the main program, and is 'bypassed' by a **GO TO** statement.

Better structured code

```
100  REM EXAMPLE 10E PART 4B
105  INPUT X
110  GOSUB 200
115  LET A = X
120  INPUT X
125  GOSUB 200
130  LET B = X
```

```
135  REM CONTINUE
  :
  :
200  REM ROUNDING SUBPROGRAM
205  LET X = INT (X * 100 + 0.5)/100
210  RETURN
```

In this version of the program, the subprogram is clearly separated, and the start marked by a **REM** statement.

Exercise IOE

I a) Briefly define the term program structure.
   b) Why is program structure important?
   c) Are short programs always well structured?
   d) Basic language has been criticised for its lack of facilities to assist the structuring of programs, and the fact that it is easy to write badly structured programs in Basic. Give your opinion on this question. If possible include portions of programs as examples of the points you make.

Rewrite the portions of programs in questions 2 to 5, in each case improving the structure.

2 A table, stored in array **N(20)** is searched to see if an element is equal to variable **X**. If so, the index of the corresponding array element is output.

```
100  REM EXERCISE 10E QUESTION 2
105  FOR K = 1 TO 10
110  IF N(K) = X THEN 130
115  NEXT K
120  PRINT "NUMBER NOT FOUND"
125  GO TO 135
130  PRINT "ELEMENT"; K
135  REM CONTINUE
```

3 A variable **M** is input and validated. It must be an integer in the range 48 to 57 or 65 to 90.

```
100  REM EXERCISE 10E QUESTION 3
105  INPUT M
110  IF M = INT(M) THEN 120
115  GO TO 130
120  IF M >= 48 AND M <= 57 THEN 140
125  IF M >= 65 AND M <= 90 THEN 140
130  PRINT "INVALID INPUT, PLEASE
                            RE-ENTER"
135  GO TO 105
140  REM CONTINUE
```

4 Generate 20 pairs of random numbers, each in the range 1 to 10, and output the sum of each pair.

```
100  REM EXERCISE 10E QUESTION 4
105  RANDOMIZE
110  FOR K = 1 TO 10
115  GOSUB 140
120  GOSUB 150
125  LET S = A+B
130  PRINT S
```

```
135  NEXT K
140  LET A = INT (10 * RND (1)) + 1
145  RETURN
150  LET B = INT (10 * RND (1)) + 1
155  RETURN
200  REM CONTINUE
```

5 Given three numbers, stored as variables **A**, **B** and **C**, sort them in order so that the largest is variable **A** and the smallest variable **C**.

```
100  REM EXERCISE 10E QUESTION 5
105  INPUT A, B, C
110  IF A > B AND A > C THEN 160
115  IF B > A AND B > C THEN 200
120  LET T1 = C
125  IF B > A THEN 145
130  LET T2 = A
135  LET T3 = B
140  GO TO 240
145  LET T2 = B
150  LET T3 = A
155  GO TO 240
160  LET T1 = A
165  IF B > C THEN 185
170  LET T2 = C
175  LET T3 = B
180  GO TO 240
185  LET T2 = B
190  LET T3 = C
195  GO TO 240
200  LET T2 = B
205  IF A > C THEN 230
210  LET T2 = C
220  LET T3 = A
225  GO TO 240
230  LET T2 = A
235  LET T3 = C
240  LET A = T1
245  LET B = T2
250  LET C = T3
255  PRINT A, B, C
260  REM CONTINUE
```

IOF End-of-chapter summary

This chapter has introduced the idea of a subprogram, and shown a number of ways in which subprograms can be used. The general idea of program structure, which relates to a number of techniques introduced in several chapters, has also been discussed. The main points of the chapter are as follows:

● A subprogram is a portion of a program, performing a specific function, to which control is transferred from another part of the program and from which control is returned to the point from which it was called.

- The portion of a program which calls the subprograms is called the main program.
- The Basic statement which transfers control to a subprogram contains the word **GOSUB**, followed by the line number of the start of the subprogram.
- At the end of a subprogram, the word **RETURN** transfers control to the statement after the **GOSUB** statement which called the subprogram.
- It is strongly recommended that the start of a subprogram is always marked with a REM statement.
- The five elementary ways of creating the structure of a program are sequencing, branching, looping, nesting and calling. These must be combined to form a program which has a clear, concise structure, as simple as possible under the circumstances.

Exercise 10F

This exercise covers topics introduced in this and previous chapters.

1 Consider the following program:

```
100  REM EXERCISE 10F QUESTION 1
105  INPUT X, N
110  ON N GOSUB 200, 300, 400
115  PRINT X
120  STOP
200  REM ROUND TO NEAREST INTEGER
205  LET X = INT (X + 0.5)
210  RETURN
300  REM ROUND TO NEAREST THOUSAND
305  LET X = INT (X/1000 + 0.5)*1000
310  RETURN
400  REM ROUND TO NEAREST MILLION
405  LET X = INT (X/1000000 + 0.5)*1000000
410  RETURN
500  END
```

a) Dry run the program for each of the following sets of input

   X = 10.9,   N = 1
   X = 3572,   N = 2
   X = 8370000, N = 3
   X = 5936.4,   N = 1
   X = 5936.4,   N = 2
   X = 350,   N = 4

b) What input values will cause the program to fail?

c) Include suitable validation of input to prevent the program from failing.

d) Briefly describe the overall effect of the program.

2 Rewrite the program shown below, correcting the errors and improving the structure where necessary. The program inputs a literal variable and prints the characters it contains on separate lines, in a vertical column.

```
100  REM EXERCISE 10F QUESTION 2
105  INPUT C$;
```

```
110  LET L = LEN$(C$)
115  FOR K = 0 TO L
120  GOSUB 135
125  PRINT M$
130  NEXT L
135  LET M$ = MID(C$, K, 1))
140  RETURN
145  END
```

Draw flow diagrams and write programs for the tasks in questions 3 to 5. Pay particular attention to the structure of the programs. Use suitable test data to check the working of the programs, and write programmer's and user documentation for them.

3 Store, in suitable arrays, tables of the names of a number of places and the road distances between them. Then input the names of pairs of places and, if they are both in the table, output the distances between them.

Suggested method

Use a one-dimensional literal array for the names of the places, and a two-dimensional numeric array for the distances. Use the same order of places in both arrays. Use a subprogram to search the names array for the index numbers of the two places input (see section 8D for the method) and use these index numbers to locate the distance in the distances array.

4 Below is a simple subprogram which will 'scramble' the letters in a word. The word is stored in variable **W$** and the scrambled word is returned in the same variable.

```
900  REM SCRAMBLER SUBPROGRAM
905  LET L = LEN(W$)
910  FOR K = 1 TO 5
915  LET T$ = ""
920  FOR J = 1 TO L
925  LET U$ = MID$ (W$, J, 1)
930  IF RND (1) > 0.5 THEN 945
935  LET T$ = T$ + U$
940  GO TO 950
945  LET T$ = U$ + T$
950  NEXT J
955  LET W$ = T$
960  NEXT K
965  RETURN
```

Use this subprogram in a program which stores a set of words in an array, and then presents the words, scrambled, on the screen. The user has a number of attempts to type the unscrambled word. Devise a suitable method of scoring.

☐ 5 Write a program which enables you to carry out physics or chemistry calculations by supplying numbers which are then substituted into the appropriate formula. In the main program, display a 'menu' of the available formulae, one of which is called up by a suitable input. In the subprogram for each formula, display the formula, together with definitions and units of all the variables, and prompt for the input of the required variables. Evaluate the formula and display the result, before returning to the 'menu'. Structure your program so that it can be enlarged to accommodate additional formulae.

11
Graphics

Graphics is one of the fastest growing application areas of computing. The display of graphs, maps, diagrams, animated cartoons etc., very often in colour, enhances many existing uses of computers, and is opening up a large number of new application areas.

Unfortunately, writing programs to produce graphics displays is somewhat difficult, for two reasons. The first is that a diagram, graph or map contains a large amount of information, often needing a considerable amount of processing. The second is that versions of Basic differ very widely in the techniques used for graphs. Accordingly, the objectives of this chapter are fairly limited. They are to introduce a few very common graphics techniques, and show how they can be used in simple applications. The first few sections do not use any special graphics facilities; they rely entirely on techniques already introduced. The remaining sections introduce some graphics subprograms which can be used as 'building blocks' for a wide range of applications. They are written in the version of Basic most commonly used in schools – Research Machines Extended Basic Version 5. Equivalent subprograms in other versions of Basic are not too difficult to write. The programs introduced in this chapter do not require colour or high-resolution graphics, but the ideas introduced here can be extended if these facilities are available.

11A Some general ideas about graphics

Graphics is concerned with displaying characters or shapes on the screen of the computer. Although the screen appears, when clear, as a blank area, it must be thought of as a grid of small spaces, as shown in figure 11A1. For the purposes of this chapter, each space is the size which can be occupied by one character, which may be a letter or number, or, on some computers, a special graphics character. On most computers, the screen 'grid' has between 20 and 25 rows and 40 columns. If high-resolution graphics is used, the grid spaces are considerably smaller.

For almost all graphics work, it is necessary to number the spaces on the grid according to their row and column. The method of numbering used in this chapter is the same as the method of co-ordinates on a graph, and is illustrated in figure 11A2.

11B Graphics using the TAB function

The **TAB** function, introduced in section 5D, counts the number of character positions from the start of a line to the start of the character(s) to be output. For example:

```
PRINT TAB (16); " GRAPHICS "
```

leaves 16 character positions before displaying the word GRAPHICS. Even if a computer has no special graphics facilities, the **TAB** function can be used to produce graphs, diagrams, maps and pictures. This section shows how it is done.

Example 11B

Display a simplified diagram of a plant cell.

Method
The first step is to draw, on squared paper corresponding to a screen 'grid', a simple sketch of a plant cell. The sketch is then converted into a set of suitable shapes, displayed at appropriate positions. See figure 11B1. This is by far the most important step in writing the program, and generally requires more than one attempt to obtain a satisfactory result.

The second step is to decide on the structure of the program. In this case, a simple sequence of **PRINT** statements, one for each line of the diagram, is quite adequate. Reading the labels into an array at the start improves the appearance of the program, and makes modifications easier. As the program structure is so simple, there is no need for a flow diagram.

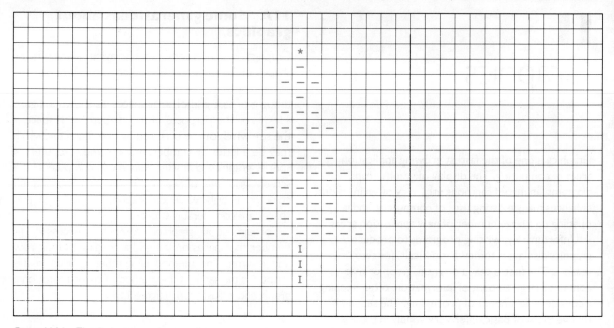

Figure 11A1   The display screen of a computer

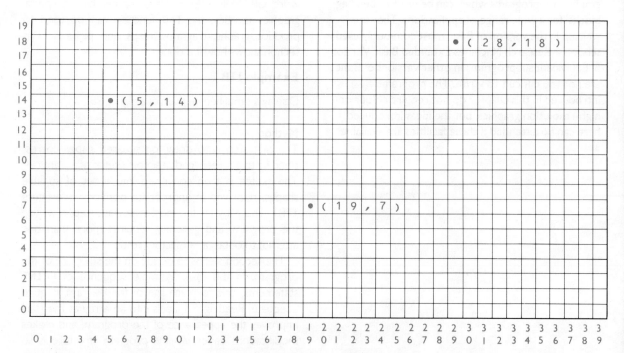

Figure 11A2   The co-ordinates of positions on a display screen

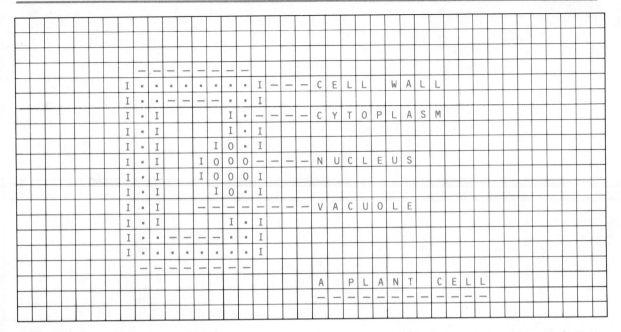

Figure 11B1 Diagram for example program 11B

Variables

L$(5) array of labels
K loop counter

Program

```
100  REM EXAMPLE PROGRAM 11B
105  REM DISPLAY DIAGRAM OF PLANT CELL
110  DIM L$(5)
200  REM READ LABELS ARRAY
205  FOR K = 1 TO 5
210  READ L$(K)
215  NEXT K
220  DATA "CELL WALL"
225  DATA "CYTOPLASM"
230  DATA "NUCLEUS"
235  DATA "VACUOLE"
240  DATA "A PLANT CELL"
245  REM
300  REM DISPLAY DIAGRAM
305  PRINT
310  PRINT
315  PRINT
320  PRINT TAB (8);  "--------"
325  PRINT TAB (7);  "I........I---";L$(1)
330  PRINT TAB (7);  "I..----..I"
335  PRINT TAB (7);  "I.I    I.----";L$(2)
340  PRINT TAB (7);  "I.I    I.I"
345  PRINT TAB (7);  "I.I    I0.I"
350  PRINT TAB (7);  "I.I    I000----";L$(3)
355  PRINT TAB (7);  "I.I    I000I"
360  PRINT TAB (7);  "I.I    I0.I"
```

```
365  PRINT TAB (7);  "I.I  --------";L$(4)
370  PRINT TAB (7);  "I.I    I.I"
375  PRINT TAB (7);  "I..----..I"
380  PRINT TAB (7);  "I........I"
385  PRINT TAB (8);  "--------"
390  PRINT TAB (20); L$(5)
395  PRINT TAB (20); "------------"
400  PRINT
405  END
```

Points to notice

- There is one **PRINT** statement for each line of the diagram.
- The **TAB** function determines the number of character spaces before the start of each line.
- This program can be modified in a number of ways; one possibility is to replace the labels with numbers, and then request the user to key the name corresponding to each number.

Sample run

A sample run of the program produces a display similar to figure 11B1.

Exercise 11B

1 Figure 11B2 shows a simplified map of Africa.
  a) Write a program to produce the outline shown in the diagram.
  b) Modify your program to include various geographical features (cities, mountains, rivers etc.). Do not include too much detail.

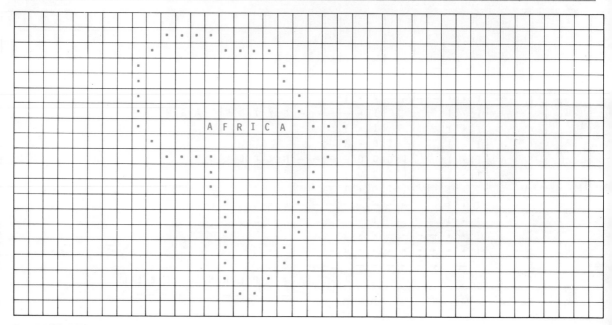

Figure 11B2   Diagram for exercise 11B, question 1

2   Select a suitable map to form the basis of a graphics display. (Suggestions: Australia, North or South America, the UK.)
   a) On a tracing of the map, draw a 'grid' to represent the display screen of the computer, with 40 columns and between 20 and 25 rows of rectangles.
   b) Write suitable characters into the grid rectangles, to represent coastal outlines, cities, mountains, rivers etc.
   c) Write any labels which are required, one character per grid rectangle.
   d) Write a program to display the simplified map you have created.
3   Select a suitable biology diagram similar to the one used in example program 11B. (Suggestions: simple diagrams of organs such as the lungs or kidneys, schematic diagrams of blood circulation, digestion etc.) Follow the steps of example program 11B to produce a simplified display of the diagram.
4   Figure 11B3 shows some typical components of an electric circuit. Use these symbols, or improved versions using graphics characters on your computer, to produce displays of various circuit diagrams.
5   A number of companies have distinctive symbols, called **logos**, to identify them. Prominent examples are British Rail, Granada TV, Mercedes Benz and IBM. Use the methods introduced in this section to produce displays of one or more of these logos.

11C   Histograms

Histograms are a very simple but effective way of displaying numerical information. This section shows how histograms can be produced without any special graphics facilities. The only restriction is that the 'bars' of a histogram are horizontal, rather than vertical, as is generally the case. Later sections in this chapter introduce techniques which can be used to produce vertical histograms.

Example 11C

Input the attendance figures for a form for the ten school sessions in a week. Display a histogram of them. The maximum attendance in the form is 30.

Method

An array is used to store the names of the sessions (MON AM, MON PM...FRI PM). The attendances are input into another array. The main steps of the program are as follows:
   Read session names into array.
   Prompt and input form name and date of first day of week.
   For each session repeat:
       Prompt and input attendance.
   Display heading of histogram.
   For each session, repeat:
       Display session name.
       For each pupil present, repeat:
           Display histogram symbol '+'.

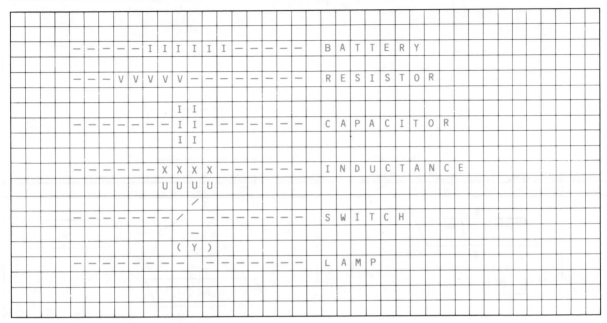

Figure 11B3   Diagram for exercise 11B, question 4

Note that nested loops are used in the histogram. The outer loop works down the rows, the inner loop displays the symbols in each 'bar'.

Variables

S$(10)	array of session names
A(10)	array of attendances
D$	date of first day of week
F$	form name
I, J, K, L	loop counters

Flow diagram

See figure 11C1.

Program

```
100  REM EXAMPLE PROGRAM 11C
105  REM FORM ATTENDANCE HISTOGRAM
110  DIM S$(10), A(10)
200  REM READ SESSION NAMES INTO ARRAY
205  FOR I = 1 TO 10
210  READ S$(I)
215  NEXT I
220  DATA "MON AM", "MON PM"
225  DATA "TUE AM", "TUE PM"
230  DATA "WED AM", "WED PM"
235  DATA "THU AM", "THU PM"
240  DATA "FRI AM", "FRI PM"
245  REM
300  REM INPUT ATTENDANCES ETC
305  PRINT "ATTENDANCE HISTOGRAM"
310  PRINT
315  PRINT "FORM";
320  INPUT F$
325  PRINT "DATE OF START OF WEEK";
330  INPUT D$
335  PRINT
340  PRINT "ENTER ATTENDANCES FOR"
345  PRINT "EACH SESSION"
350  PRINT
355  FOR J = 1 TO 10
360  PRINT S$(J);
365  INPUT A(J)
370  NEXT J
375  PRINT
380  REM
400  REM DISPLAY HISTOGRAM
405  PRINT "FORM";F$
410  PRINT
415  PRINT "ATTENDANCE FOR WEEK";
420  PRINT "COMMENCING";D$
425  PRINT
430  FOR K = 1 TO 10
435  PRINT S$(K);"   ";
```

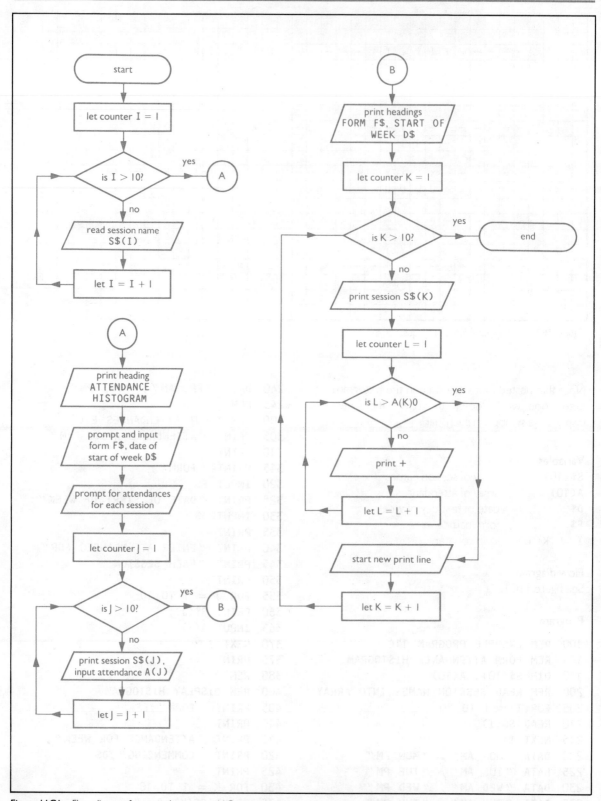

Figure 11C1 Flow diagram for example program 11C

```
440  FOR L = 1 TO A (K)
445  PRINT "+";
450  NEXT L
455  PRINT
460  NEXT K
465  PRINT
470  PRINT
475  PRINT
480  END
```

Points to notice

- The array element **A(K)** is the limit of the inner nested loop which displays the symbols making up the 'bars' of the histogram.
- Line 455 has the effect of starting a new print line.

Sample run

ATTENDANCE HISTOGRAM

FORM ? <u>3JM</u>
DATE OF START OF WEEK ? <u>30/11/81</u>

ENTER ATTENDANCES FOR
EACH SESSION

```
MON AM ? 20
MON PM ? 18
TUE AM ? 21
TUE PM ? 20
WED AM ? 17
WED PM ? 17
THU AM ? 19
THU PM ? 18
FRI AM ? 21
FRI PM ? 21
```

FORM 3JM

ATTENDANCE FOR WEEK COMMENCING 30/11/81

```
MON AM ++++++++++++++++++++
MON PM ++++++++++++++++++
TUE AM +++++++++++++++++++++
TUE PM ++++++++++++++++++++
WED AM +++++++++++++++++
WED PM +++++++++++++++++
THU AM +++++++++++++++++++
THU PM ++++++++++++++++++
FRI AM +++++++++++++++++++++
FRI PM +++++++++++++++++++++
```

Exercise IIC

1   Consider the segment of program shown below. Assume that the array **A** contains the values 100, 150, 175, 225, 150.

```
100  REM EXERCISE 11C QUESTION 1
105  DIM A(5)
110  REM LOAD VALUES INTO A
195  INPUT S
200  FOR K = 1 TO 5
205  PRINT K; TAB(8); ":";
210  FOR L = 1 TO A(K)/S
215  PRINT "*";
220  NEXT L
225  PRINT
230  NEXT K
235  REM CONTINUE
```

a) Dry run this program for values of **S** of 5 and 25.
b) What effect does variable **S** have on the output?
c) Why is a variable such as **S** necessary?

Draw flow diagrams and write programs for the tasks in questions 2 to 8. Pay careful attention to the layout of the output and check your programs against the original data to ensure that they are correct.

2   The average weekly earnings of full-time manual workers in the UK, during the ten years up to 1978 were as follows:

Year	Average men's wage (£)	Average women's wage (£)
1969	24.83	12.11
1970	28.05	13.99
1971	30.93	15.80
1972	35.82	18.30
1973	40.92	21.16
1974	48.63	27.01
1975	59.58	34.19
1976	66.97	40.61
1977	72.89	44.31
1978	83.50	50.03

Reference: *Facts in Focus*, Central Statistical Office (Penguin/HMSO) reproduced with the permission of the Controller of Her Majesty's Stationery Office.

Display one or more histograms of these figures, or of figures derived from them, such as the difference between men's and women's wages. Use a suitable scale, for example '*' = £5.

3   The numbers of people killed in road accidents, per 100 000 of population, in the nine EEC countries in 1977 were as follows:

Country	Persons killed per 100 000 population in road accidents (1977)
Britain	12
Belgium	26
Denmark	16
France	27
West Germany	24
Ireland	18
Italy	16
Luxembourg	31
Netherlands	19

Reference: *Facts in Focus*, Central Statistical Office (Penguin/HMSO) reproduced with the permission of the Controller of Her Majesty's Stationery Office.

Display a histogram of these figures.

4 The consumer price index figures for Britain for the period 1973 to 1978 were:

1973:	69	1976:	116
1974:	81	1977:	135
1975:	100	1978:	146

These figures mean that an article costing 100 pence in 1975 would, on average, have cost 69p in 1973 and 146p in 1978. Display a histogram of these figures, using a suitable scale.

5 The following figures give indications of the relative access of people from different parts of the world to communication media:

	Daily newspapers (copies per 100 people)	Radios (sets per 100 people)	TV (sets per 100 people)	Telephones (sets per 100 people)
World	10.5	18.5	6.3	6.8
Asia	4.2	3.7	1.2	1.4
Europe	25.8	28.0	15.9	12.0
Africa	1.1	4.4	0.2	0.9
South America	6.5	15.1	4.0	2.7
North America	23.8	102.3	28.5	52.7
USSR	29.5	34.2	9.6	14.1
Oceania	29.6	21.0	17.1	26.5

Reference: John McHale, *World Facts and Trends* (Collier)
Display histograms of some or all of these figures.

6 If the inflation rate remains constant, the price of an article over a number of years will follow the formula:

$$P = N \left(1 + \frac{R}{100} \right)^T$$

P price (£) after T years   **N** price now (£)
R inflation rate (%)   **T** time (years)

Input values of N and R, and display a histogram of the price of the article over the next fifteen or twenty years.

7 Counting frequencies for histograms
A very useful enhancement to a histogram plotting program is a facility for counting the frequencies from the 'raw' data, before displaying the histogram. The basis for such a facility is shown below. It is a program segment which inputs a sequence of numbers in the range 1 to 10, and counts the number of 1's, the number of 2's etc, storing the results in the array **N(10)**. It assumes that all the elements of **N(10)** have been set to zero, and does not validate the input. Input is terminated by the number −1.

```
300  REM EXERCISE 11C QUESTION 7
305  REM COUNT FREQUENCIES FOR HISTOGRAM
310  INPUT X
315  IF X = −1 THEN 330
320  LET N(X) = N(X) + 1
325  GO TO 310
330  REM CONTINUE
```

Incorporate this program segment, suitably modified, in the following program:

The number of children in the family of each pupil in a class is recorded. These figures are input and the numbers of families with 1 child, 2 children . . . up to 7 children are counted. A histogram is displayed of the result.

8 Input a set of heights, measured in centimetres, of the members of your class, and count the number in each of the following intervals:
less than 130 cm
130 cm to 145 cm
146 cm to 160 cm
more than 160 cm

(See section 4D for a method of sorting the heights into the groups.) Plot a histogram of the results.

11D   Plotting points

The simplest graphics facilities provided by most computers enable a point to be plotted at any required position on the screen. The point can contain a character, or a special graphics symbol, and can, in many computers, be of a chosen colour. By plotting a series of points, maps, pictures and graphs can be built up. All the displays discussed in sections 11B and 11C can be produced by the method of plotting points introduced here. Furthermore, these displays can be animated, as new plotted points overwrite old ones, causing the display to appear to move.

In this section, two graphics subprograms are introduced, written for Research Machines 380 Z Computers, using Extended Basic Version 5. The first switches the computer into **graphics mode**. In this mode, the top 20 lines of the screen are for graphics displays, and the bottom four for ordinary text, which is 'scrolled' up in the usual way. The second subprogram enables a character or graphics symbol to be plotted at a point, identified by its row and column, as shown in figure 11A2. These two subprograms are used in the example program and the exercises which follow. Writing equivalent subprograms for other microcomputers is fairly straightforward.

Switch to graphics mode and clear screen
A subprogram which switches the computer to graphics mode and clears the screen is as follows:

```
700  REM GRAPHICS MODE, CLEAR SCREEN
705  REM RML EXTENDED BASIC VERSION 5
710  GRAPH
715  RETURN
```

Plot character on screen
A subprogram which plots a character at a required point on the screen is as follows:

Variables

C$ character
X, Y   co-ordinates of screen position

```
800  REM PLOT CHARACTER ON SCREEN
805  REM RML EXTENDED BASIC VERSION 5
810  REM C$ : CHARACTER
815  REM X, Y : SCREEN CO-ORDINATES
820  REM WRAP AROUND
825  LET X1 = X - INT(X/40)*40
830  LET Y1 = Y - INT(Y/20)*20
835  PLOT X1*2, Y1*3, C$
840  RETURN
```

Note that the X and Y co-ordinates must be in the ranges 0 to 39 and 0 to 19 respectively. If they are outside these ranges, they will be 'wrapped around'. For example, an X value of 45 will be plotted as 5.

Whenever this subprogram is used, the variables X, Y and C$ must have values assigned in the main program before the subprogram is called.

Example 11D

Input a map or a diagram as a set of co-ordinates, and the characters to be displayed at the co-ordinates. Display the map or diagram from this information.

Method

The first stage of the process is to prepare a 'grid' of the map or diagram, as discussed in section 11B. From this grid, a set of co-ordinates and characters is written down. Figure 11D1 shows a suitable diagram, for which the co-ordinates and characters are as follows:

15, 10, −	20, 10, −	17, 5, −
14, 9, <	18, 9, (	18, 5, −
15, 9, 0	19, 9, <	16, 4, =
16, 9, >	20, 9, 0	17, 4, =
17, 9,)	21, 9, >	18, 4, =
15, 8, −	20, 8, −	19, 4, =
15, 7, X	20, 8, X	etc.
16, 6, (	19, 8,)	

These sets of data are input into arrays. When input is complete, the computer switches to graphics mode and displays the picture they create. The overall steps of the program are as follows:

    Repeat:
        Input X co-ordinate, Y co-ordinate and character into arrays,
    Until end-of-input marker received or points arrays full.
    Change to graphics mode.
    Repeat:
        Plot character from co-ordinates in arrays,
    Until end-of-input marker or array limit reached.

A suitable end-of-input marker is the set of values 40, 20, X.

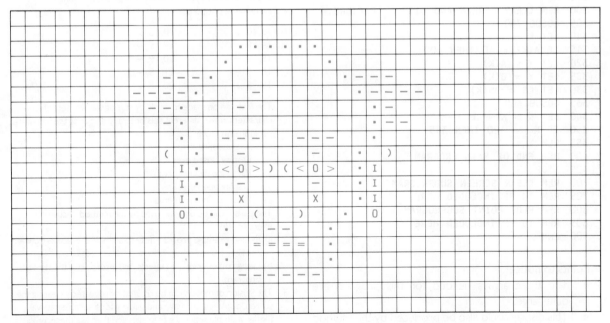

Figure 11D1   Diagram for example 11D

Variables

A(120)   array of X co-ordinates
B(120)   array of Y co-ordinates
D$(120)   array of characters to be plotted
X   X co-ordinate of character being plotted
Y   Y co-ordinate of character being plotted
C$ character being plotted
K   array index

Flow diagram

See figure 11D2.

Program

```
100  REM EXAMPLE PROGRAM 11D
105  REM DISPLAY PICTURE BY PLOTTING POINTS
110  DIM A(120), B(120), D$(120)
115  REM
200  REM INPUT POINTS TO BE PLOTTED
205  PRINT "FOR EACH POINT, TYPE"
210  PRINT "X CO-ORDINATE"
215  PRINT "Y CO-ORDINATE"
220  PRINT "CHARACTER OR GRAPHICS SYMBOL"
225  PRINT "END INPUT WITH 40, 20, X"
230  LET K = 1
235  INPUT A(K), B(K), D$(K)
240  IF A(K) = 40 THEN 300
245  LET K = K + 1
250  IF K > 120 THEN 260
255  GO TO 235
260  PRINT "NO MORE POINTS CAN BE STORED"
265  PRINT "THE PICTURE SO FAR IS..."
270  REM
300  REM CLEAR SCREEN AND DISPLAY PICTURE
305  GOSUB 700
310  LET K = 1
315  IF A(K) = 40 THEN 400
320  LET X = A(K)
325  LET Y = B(K)
330  LET C$ = D$(K)
335  GOSUB 800
340  LET K = K + 1
350  IF K <= 120 THEN 315
355  REM
400  REM END OF MAIN PROGRAM
405  STOP
700  REM CLEAR SCREEN SUBPROGRAM
705  REM TO BE INCLUDED HERE
800  REM PLOT POINT SUBPROGRAM
805  REM TO BE INCLUDED HERE
900  END
```

Points to notice

- The three arrays needed for this program are quite large.
- This display could also be produced by the method introduced in section 11B. However, the technique introduced here permits the display to be animated, as discussed in exercise 11D, question 2.
- The main program is written in a version of Basic which does not include any special graphics facilities. It is **machine-independent**, in the sense that it will run on a number of different types of computer. Different versions of the subprograms starting at lines 700 and 800 need to be written for computers other than the 380 Z.

Sample run

A sample run of the program produces a display similar to figure 11D1.

Exercise 11D

1 a) Write down a set of co-ordinates from figure 11B2.
   b) Use the data from part (a) and example program 11D to produce a display of figure 11B2.
   c) Run example program 11D with data corresponding to displays of your own.

2 The display generated by example program 11D can be animated by the technique described below:
   The eyes of the face are created by the following characters:

15, 10, –	20, 10, –
14, 9, <	19, 9, <
15, 9, 0	20, 9, 0
16, 9, >	21, 9, >
15, 8, –	20, 8, –

   A pair of closed eyes can be created by the following characters at the same positions:

15, 10, .	20, 10, .
14, 9, –	19, 9, –
15, 9, –	20, 9, –
16, 9, –	21, 9, –
15, 8, .	20, 8, .

   The face can be made to 'blink' by storing the two sets of characters in two different sets of arrays, and using the following program structure:
   Repeat indefinitely:
       Display closed eyes.
       Pause for short interval.
       Display open eyes.
       Pause for longer interval.
   The pauses can be programmed by the method discussed in exercise 10B.
   a) Extend example program 11D to animate the face as outlined above.
   b) Design other animation effects, and incorporate them into the program.

3 The illusion of motion can be created by repeatedly clearing the screen, displaying an image and pausing for a suitable interval. Design a simple sequence of images and then use the techniques

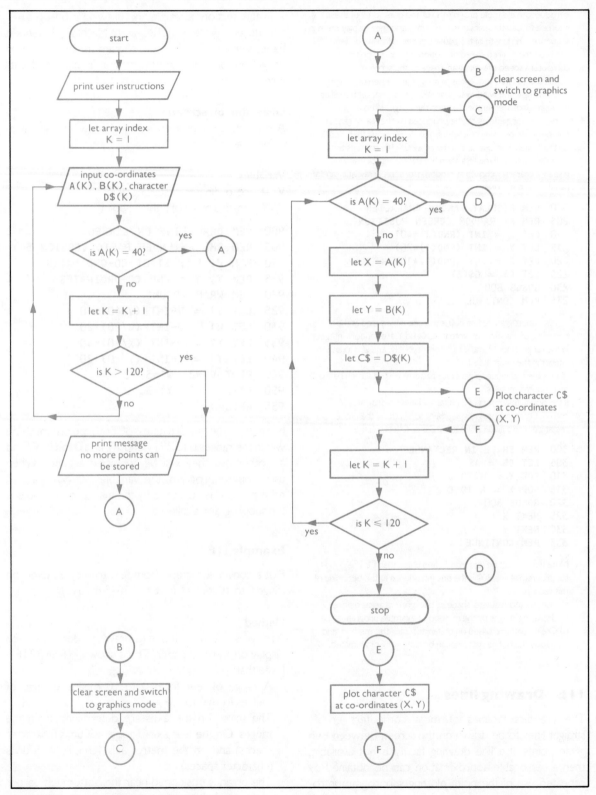

Figure 11D2 Flow diagram for example program 11D

introduced in example program 11D and question 2 of this exercise to load these images into arrays and then display them in sequence. The length of the pause between displays depends partly on the desired speed of motion, and partly on the computer's speed of writing an image to the screen.

Some suggested sequences of images are: a person running, a tree waving in the wind, waves breaking and a rocket travelling through space. Remember to keep the images simple.

4 Very interesting effects can be produced by the use of random numbers in generating characters, and determining their position on the screen. For example, if the array G$(10) contains ten suitable graphics characters, then the statements below will display a character chosen at random from this array, at a random position on the screen:

```
200  REM DISPLAY RANDOM CHARACTER
205  REM AT RANDOM SCREEN POSITION
210  LET X = INT (RND(1)*40)
215  LET Y = INT (RND(1)*20)
220  LET Z = INT (RND(1)*10) + 1
225  LET C$ = G$(Z)
230  GOSUB 800
235  REM CONTINUE
```

The subprogram at line 800 is the one introduced at the beginning of this section. Note that X and Y are random integers in the ranges 0 to 39 and 0 to 19 respectively, and Z is a random integer in the range 1 to 10.

Use this technique to generate patterns on the screen based on random numbers.

5 If the opposite corners of a rectangle have co-ordinates (A, B) and (C, D), then a program segment to 'shade in' the entire rectangle with a given character A$ is as follows:

```
300  REM SHADE IN RECTANGLE
305  LET C$ = A$
310  FOR Y = B TO D
315  FOR X = A TO C
320  GOSUB 800
325  NEXT X
330  NEXT Y
335  REM CONTINUE
```

Note that A must be less than C, and B less than D. The subprogram at line 800 is the one introduced at the beginning of this section.

a) Use this technique to 'shade in' background areas before displaying images by the method of example program 11D.

b) Create patterns based on rectangles using this method, and display them. The patterns can be stationary or animated.

11E Drawing lines

The graphics facilities of most computers enable straight lines to be drawn on the screen between two given points. If a line drawing facility is not available, then a reasonable approximation can be obtained by repeated use of the point plotting subprogram introduced in the previous section.

In this section, a simple line drawing subprogram is introduced, written in Research Machines Extended Basic Version 5. The subprogram is then used in programs to display graphs, diagrams, plans and patterns.

Draw line on screen

A subprogram which draws a line between two given points is as follows:

Variables

V, W   co-ordinates of starting point
X, Y   co-ordinates of finishing point

```
900  REM DRAW LINE ON SCREEN
905  REM RML EXTENDED BASIC VERSION 5
910  REM V, W : START CO-ORDINATES
915  REM X, Y : END CO-ORDINATES
920  REM WRAP AROUND
925  LET V1 = V-INT (V/40)*40
930  LET W1 = W-INT (W/20)*20
935  LET X1 = X-INT (X/40)*40
940  LET Y1 = Y-INT (Y/20)*20
945  PLOT V1*2, W1*3, 2
950  LINE X1*2, Y1*3, 2
955  RETURN
```

Note that the co-ordinates of both points must be within the ranges 0 to 39 (V and X), and 0 to 19 (W and Y), otherwise they will be 'wrapped around'. When using this subprogram, the variables V, W, X and Y must have values assigned by the main program before the subprogram is called.

Example 11E

Plot a conversion graph from feet to metres, over the range 0 to 10 feet. (1 foot = 0.3048 metres).

Method

As always, the first step is to draw the desired screen display on squared paper. This is shown in figure 11E1. Note that:

A range of feet from 0 to 10 means a range of metres from 0 to 3.

The scales on the axes are determined from the ranges. On the feet axis, 1 foot = 3 units (character spaces) and on the metres axis 1 metre = 5 units (character spaces).

The origin is positioned near the bottom left corner of the graph. It has co-ordinates 3, 2.

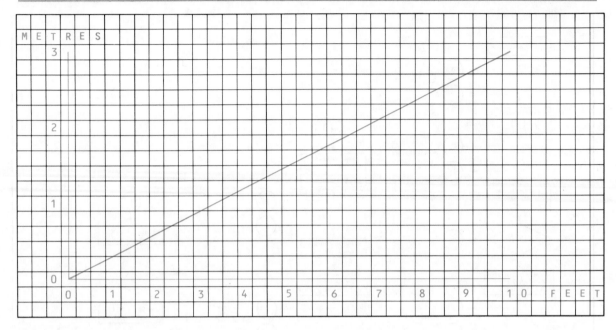

Figure 11E1 Diagram for example 11E

The overall steps of the program are as follows:
  Switch to graph mode and clear the screen.
  Draw the line for the feet axis.
  Plot the numbers on the feet axis.
  Label the feet axis.
  Draw the line for the metres axis.
  Plot the numbers on the metres axis.
  Label the metres axis.
  Draw the line for the graph.

The most efficient way to display the labels and numbers on the axes is to use a subprogram which extracts one character at a time from the word or number and uses the character plotting subprogram to display it. The label display subprogram needs the co-ordinates of the starting position of the label and the text of the label.

Variables

V, W, X, Y	co-ordinates of points, used by plotting and line drawing sub-programs
C$	character used by point plotting subprogram
L$	label
V1, W1, X1, Y1	'wrapped around' values of co-ordinates
I, J, K	loop counters

Flow diagram
See figure 11E2.

Program

```
100  REM EXAMPLE PROGRAM 11E
105  REM FEET-TO-METRES CONVERSION GRAPH
110  REM
150  REM ENTER GRAPHICS MODE, CLEAR SCREEN
155  GOSUB 700
160  REM
200  REM DRAW FEET AXIS
205  REM FROM (3, 2) TO (33, 2)
210  LET V = 3
215  LET W = 2
220  LET X = 33
225  LET Y = 2
230  GOSUB 900
235  REM
250  REM PLOT NUMBERS ON FEET AXIS
255  REM FROM (3, 1) TO (33, 1)
260  FOR I = 0 TO 10
265  LET X = 3*I+3
270  LET Y = 1
275  LET L$ = MID$ (STR$(I), 2,
                         LEN(STR$(I))-1)
280  GOSUB 600
285  NEXT I
290  REM
300  REM LABEL FEET AXIS
305  REM AT (36, 1)
310  LET X = 36
```

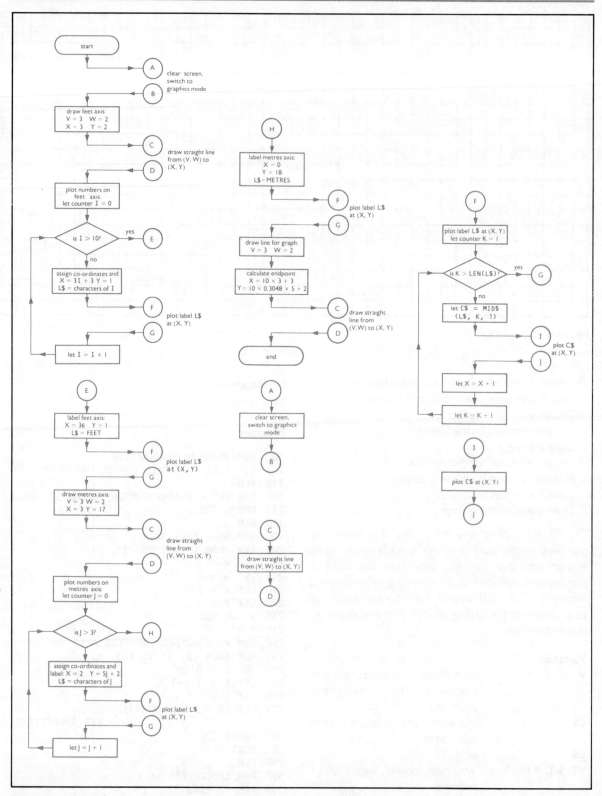

Figure 11E2 Flow diagram for example program 11E

```
315   LET Y = 1
320   LET L$ = "FEET"
325   GOSUB 600
330   REM
350   REM DRAW METRES AXIS
355   REM FROM (3, 2) TO (3, 17)
360   LET V = 3
365   LET W = 2
370   LET X = 3
375   LET Y = 17
380   GOSUB 900
385   REM
400   REM PLOT NUMBERS ON METRES AXIS
405   REM FROM (2, 2) TO (2, 17)
410   FOR J = 0 TO 3
415   LET X = 2
420   LET Y = 5*J+2
425   LET L$ = MID$ (STR$(J), 2,
                        LEN (STR$(J))-1)
430   GOSUB 600
435   NEXT J
440   REM
450   REM LABEL METRES AXIS
455   REM AT (0, 18)
460   LET X = 0
465   LET Y = 18
470   LET L$ = "METRES"
475   GOSUB 600
480   REM
500   REM DRAW LINE FOR GRAPH
505   REM ORIGIN (3, 2)
510   LET V = 3
515   LET W = 2
520   REM CALCULATE ENDPOINT
525   REM AT 10 FEET
530   LET X = 10*3+3
535   LET Y = 10*0.3048*5+2
540   GOSUB 900
545   REM
550   STOP
600   REM SUBPROGRAM TO DISPLAY LABEL
605   REM USES POINT PLOTTING SUBPROGRAM
610   REM X, Y : CO-ORDS OF START OF LABEL
615   REM L$ : LABEL
620   FOR K = 1 TO LEN(L$)
625   LET C$ = MID$(L$, K, 1)
630   GOSUB 800
635   LET X = X+1
640   NEXT K
645   RETURN
700   REM CLEAR SCREEN SUBPROGRAM
705   REM TO BE INCLUDED HERE
800   REM POINT PLOT SUBPROGRAM
805   REM TO BE INCLUDED HERE
900   REM LINE DRAWING SUBPROGRAM
905   REM TO BE INCLUDED HERE
999   END
```

Points to notice

- The calculation of the endpoint of the graph is based on the following principles:

    The X co-ordinate corresponds to the value 10 feet. Since 1 foot = 3 units, and the origin has X co-ordinate 3, the X co-ordinate is:

    $$X = 10 \times 3 + 3$$

    The Y co-ordinate corresponds to the value (10 × 0.3048) metres. Since 1 metre = 5 units and the origin has Y co-ordinate 2, the Y co-ordinate is:

    $$Y = 10 \times 0.3048 \times 5 + 2$$

- Lines 275 and 425 assign a number in character form to the variable L$. Since the **STR$** function includes a leading space for the sign of the number, this must be removed by the **MID$** function. A leading space would cause the numbers to be positioned wrongly.

- The program is independent of the graphics facilities of any particular type of computer.

Sample run

A sample run of this program produces a display similar to figure 11E1.

Exercise 11E

1 Modify the scales and labels in example program 11E to produce one or more of the following conversion graphs:

   a) Pounds to kilograms, over the range 0 to 10 pounds.
   (1 pound = 0.495 kg)

   b) Pints to litres, over the range 0 to 10 pints.
   (1 pint = 0.568 litre)

   c) Inches to centimetres, over the range 0 to 12 inches.
   (1 inch = 2.54 cm)

   d) A graph for converting currency, using up-to-date exchange rates.

2 Plot the graph of the function:

   $$Y = 20 - 2X$$

   for values of X from 0 to 10. Draw the line for the graph by calculating the Y co-ordinate at the two endpoints (X = 0 and X = 10).

3 A graph which is not a straight line can be drawn by plotting a set of individual points close to each other, or by drawing short straight line segments between points close to each other. The following segment of program can be used for the latter method. It assumes that a function F of variable E is to be plotted, and:

   The origin has co-ordinates **(P, Q)**

   The range of values **E** is from **A** to **B** in steps of **C**.

   The function to be plotted has been defined in a **DEF** statement as **FNF**.

   The scale on the **E** axis is one E unit = **S** character spaces.

   The scale on the **F** axis is one F unit = **T** character spaces.

   The line drawing subprogram described at the start of this section is used.

```
300  REM CURVE PLOTTING SEGMENT
305  REM PLOT FUNCTION F OF
310  REM VARIABLE E, OVER
315  REM RANGE A TO B
320  REM ORIGIN AT (P, Q)
325  LET V = A*S+P
330  LET W = FNF(A)*T+Q
335  FOR E = A*C TO B STEP C
340  LET X = E*S+P
345  LET Y = FNF(E)*T+Q
350  GOSUB 900
355  LET V = X
360  LET W = Y
365  NEXT E
370  REM CONTINUE
```

Use this program segment, or a modified version of it, to plot one or more of the graphs below. Use the method of example program 11E to draw and label the axes. It is essential to draw the axes on squared paper before writing the program, even if the curve is not plotted.

a) F = 1/E for values of E from 0.5 to 10 in steps of 0.5. Set out the axes as for example program 11E, except that the vertical scale is 1 unit of F = 3 character spaces.

b) F = E^2 for values of E from −2 to +2 in steps of 0.25. The origin is at (20, 2) and the scales are: E : 1 unit = 8 character spaces, F : 1 unit = 4 character spaces.

c) F = sin (E) for values of E from 0 to 6.284 radians (0 to 360 degrees). The origin is at (2, 10) and the scales are: E : 1 unit = 5 character spaces, F : 1 unit = 8 character spaces.

4 The height of the cable of a suspension bridge at a distance D metres from one end of the main span is:

$$H = \frac{D \times (D - 100)}{50} + 55$$

The span is 100 m long and 55 m high at each end.
Use this information to plot a graph of the cable.

5 In addition to plotting graphs, the line drawing subprogram can be used to draw patterns, diagrams and plans. For example, if the opposite corners of a rectangle have co-ordinates (A, B) and (C, D), then a program segment to draw the rectangle is as follows:

```
300  REM DRAW RECTANGLE
305  LET V = A
310  LET W = B
315  LET X = A
320  LET Y = D
325  GOSUB 900
330  LET V = C
335  LET W = D
340  GOSUB 900
345  LET X = C
350  LET Y = B
355  GOSUB 900
360  LET V = A
365  LET W = B
370  GOSUB 900
```

The subprogram at line 900 is the one introduced at the start of this section. Note that the lines of the rectangle are not drawn in order around the rectangle, as this would lengthen the program considerably.

a) Use this program segment, possibly as a subprogram, to create patterns based on rectangles, or to draw diagrams or plans incorporating rectangles.

b) Write similar program segments to draw triangles, pentagons, hexagons, stars etc. Use these program segments to display patterns or diagrams.

11F   End-of-chapter summary

This chapter has discussed some general ideas relating to computer graphics, and introduced a few techniques for simple graphics operations. The main points of the chapter are as follows:

● A major difficulty with computer graphics is that different types of computers have different instructions for graphics operations. This problem is dealt with here by using subprograms for various graphics operations and calling them from a main program that is independent of the graphics facilities of the particular computer.

● A considerable amount of graphics can be produced without any special graphics facilities.

● When graphics displays are being designed, the screen of the computer must be imagined as a 'grid' of small rectangular spaces. For the purposes of this chapter, each space is the size which may be occupied by one character, but the spaces can be smaller if higher resolution graphics are available.

● The spaces on the screen 'grid' are identified by co-ordinates, numbered from an origin (0, 0) at the bottom left of the screen.

● A point can be plotted by specifying its co-ordinates and the character to be displayed, and then calling the plotting subprogram provided.

● A straight line can be drawn by specifying the co-ordinates of the start and endpoints, and then calling the line drawing subprogram provided.

● A curved line can be drawn by a sequence of short straight lines between points on the curve.

Exercise 11F

This exercise covers all the techniques introduced in this chapter. In several cases, the questions are deliberately 'open-ended', providing suggestions which can be followed up in a variety of ways. It is worth remembering that an essential ingredient of any graphics display is imagination.

1 A portion of a program which displays an ellipse is shown below. The equations are actually for a circle, but an ellipse is formed

because the 'grid' spaces on a screen are rectangular and not square. The method is the one introduced in exercise 11E, question 3.

Variables

P, Q	co-ordinates of centre of circle
R	radius of circle, in grid units
A	angle of rotation around the circle as it is being displayed.
V, W, X, Y	co-ordinates of start and end points of short straight-line segments.

```
300   REM DISPLAY "ELLIPSE"
305   REM BASED ON CIRCLE
310   REM CENTRE (P, Q)
315   REM RADIUS R
320   LET V = R+P
325   LET W = Q
330   FOR A = 0.01 TO 6.284 STEP 0.01
335   LET X = R*COS(A) + P
340   LET Y = R*SIN(A) + Q
345   GOSUB 900
350   LET V = X
355   LET W = Y
360   NEXT A
365   REM CONTINUE
```

The subprogram at line 900 is the one introduced in section 11E.

a) Incorporate this segment in a simple program which inputs values of **P**, **Q** and **R**, switches to graphics mode and displays an ellipse.

b) By multiplying the Y co-ordinate by a suitable scale factor (in the range 0.5 to 1.5), change the ellipse into a circle.

c) Use the ellipse or circle drawing segment as a subprogram in a program which draws patterns or diagrams.

2 Make a survey of the number of occupants in the cars passing in a road over a period of time. Input these numbers (end marked 0) and count the number of cars with 1 occupant, the number with 2 occupants . . . up to 8 occupants. Display a histogram of the result.

Modification

Calculate the percentage of the total with each number of occupants. Plot the percentages instead of the frequencies in the histogram.

3 Make a survey of the ages of the cars passing in a road over a period of time by recording the last letter of their registration numbers. Use these letters to determine the ages. Input the ages (end marked − 1) and count the numbers in the groups:
   less than 2 years old
   2 to 5 years old
   6 to 10 years old
   more than 10 years old
Display a histogram of the results.

Modification

Write part of the program to convert the registration letters to ages. Use the method of searching a table introduced in section 8D.

☐ 4 Write a general histogram program which can be used for a variety of purposes. Labels of axes, scales, symbols to be plotted etc, must all be input at the start.

5 The program segment introduced in question 1, which produces a circle or ellipse, can be modified to produce a spiral as follows:
   The loop limit in line 330 is replaced by 25.136. This gives a spiral of four revolutions.
   The term **R** in lines 335 and 340 is replaced by **R*A/25.136**. This makes the spiral 'grow' from the centre to a final radius **R**.

a) Write a program to input the co-ordinates of the centre and outside radius of a spiral, and display it.

b) Incorporate one or more spirals in programs which produce various patterns.

6 Suggestions for further graphics programs:
The graphics techniques introduced in this chapter can be used for a wide variety of applications. Some suggestions are:
Histograms of:
   distances of homes from school
   months of birthdays
   amounts of pocket money
   favourite colours
   countries visited on holiday
   types of house heating
   favourite school subject
   political party supported
   football team supported
   use of local agricultural land
Displays of:
   a clock face, showing the right time
   the Eiffel Tower
   animated cartoons, possibly with moving text
   railway track layouts
   house plans
   simplified maps
   boards on which to play games

12
File handling

One of the most useful features of computers is their ability to store and access large quantities of information very rapidly. This information is stored in **files**, on **backing store**, generally magnetic disks or tapes. Large quantities of information stored in this manner are known as **data banks** or **databases**.

This chapter introduces a few simple techniques for storing and retrieving data using files. As in the case of graphics, file handling facilities differ somewhat from one type of computer to another. Accordingly, the programs in this chapter are written in Research Machines Extended Basic Version 5, and are intended for use with disk files. However, the methods of file handling discussed here are fairly general, and only minor modifications need to be made to the programs for cassette tape files, or for other versions of Basic.

The three example programs introduced in this chapter all relate to one application – a simple pupil records system in a school. It is hoped that they will give some initial guidance to pupils or teachers planning such a system.

12A   The idea of a file

A file is any organised collection of data, on a permanent form of storage which can be accessed by a computer. A file consists of a number of **records**, each of which in turn contain a number of data items. All the records in a file have the same structure.

A number of operations can be carried out on a file, but this chapter concentrates on just two, namely **writing** data to a file, and **reading** data from a file. These two operations do, however, form the basis of a wide variety of file handling applications.

12B   Writing data to a file

The operation of storing data on a magnetic tape or disk file is known as **writing** data to a file. In most Basic language systems, there are three steps to the operation:

Creating a file, giving it a name and making it ready for writing.
Writing the data, one record at a time.
Closing the file.

These steps are quite straightforward, and the new instructions they require (for creating and closing the file) are very simple. Writing the records is done by a modified form of the **PRINT** statement.

Example 12B

Create a pupil records file, containing the following information for each pupil: name, sex, date of birth, form. The file must be able to contain any number of records.

Method

As a variable number of records are required, a loop terminated by an end-of-data marker is the most obvious method. The overall steps of the program are as follows:

Prompt and input date, file name and file title.
Open the file, giving it the name input.
Write file title and date to the file.
Repeat, until end-of-data marker input:
   Input pupil name, sex, date of birth and form.
   Write these to the file.
Close the file.

Notice that the data is written to the file as soon as it is input; it is not all stored in the computer memory first. Thus the file can (in theory) be larger than the available computer memory space.

Variables

D$	date	**F$**	file name
T$	file title	**N$**	pupil name
S$	sex	**B$**	date of birth
M$	form		

A suitable end-of-data marker is an asterisk (*) for each data item.

Flow diagram

See figure 12B1.

Program

```
100  REM EXAMPLE PROGRAM 12B
105  REM CREATE PUPIL RECORDS FILE
110  REM
115  PRINT "PUPIL RECORDS SYSTEM — FILE
                              CREATION"
120  PRINT
125  PRINT "DATE";
130  INPUT D$
135  PRINT "FILE NAME";
140  INPUT F$
145  PRINT "FILE TITLE";
150  INPUT T$
155  PRINT
160  REM
200  REM CREATE AND NAME FILE
205  CREATE #10, F$
210  PRINT #10, T$, D$
215  PRINT "INPUT NAME, SEX, DATE OF BIRTH"
220  PRINT "AND FORM OF EACH PUPIL"
225  PRINT
230  PRINT "END INPUT WITH *, *, *, *"
235  PRINT
240  INPUT N$, S$, B$, M$
245  PRINT #10, N$, S$, B$, M$
250  IF N$ <> "*" THEN 240
255  REM CLOSE FILE
260  CLOSE #10
265  PRINT
270  PRINT "FILE"; F$; "COMPLETE"
275  PRINT
280  END
```

Points to notice

- Notice the difference between the file name and the file title: the file name identifies the file to the computer, while the file title is part of the first record of the file, providing a more detailed identification.
- The file *must* be closed at the end of the program, otherwise it cannot be accessed.
- Lines 210 and 245 each write a record to the file.

In the first case, the record contains two data items, in the second case it contains four data items.
- This program is an example of a 'repeat until' loop.

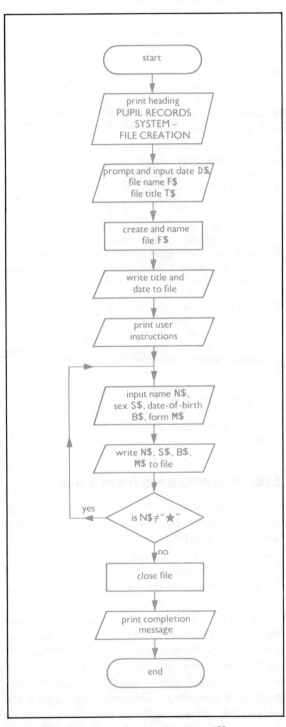

Figure 12B1 Flow diagram for example program 12B

Exercise 12B

1 a) In your own words, briefly describe the nature and structure of a file.
   b) What are the three overall steps involved in storing data on a file?

Write programs to create some or all of the files below. If necessary modify or extend the information stored. Pay particular attention to the heading information (file title, etc.) and to the structure of a record. The files created here will be used in later exercises in this chapter. The programs may be extended to allow input data to be checked and corrected if necessary, before being written to the file.

2 Create a foreign language dictionary file. A record contains an English word and the equivalent word in the foreign language. More than one foreign language may be included in the same file.
3 Create a more comprehensive pupil records file, containing, for example, pupil's addresses and optional subjects.
4 Create a library book index file, containing the author's name, title, serial number and subject classification of each book in the library.
5 Create an appointments file to be used, for example, by a doctor. The file contains the appointment times and patients' names.
6 Create a file which could be used by an estate agent, containing records for a number of properties for sale. Each record contains a reference number, address of the property, type of house, brief details and price.
7 Create an examination results file, containing a record for each candidate. Each record consists of a name, candidate number and a number of subject names, together with their grades. Either use the same number of subjects for each candidate, or include the number of subjects in the record, after the candidate number.
8 Question 2 of exercise 2D concerned a program to input the data for an entry into a school Accident Record Book. Extend this program to allow the user to check the information, and correct items if necessary, and then store it on a file. Allow the user to input, check and store a number of records during one run of the program.

12C   Reading data from a file

Having learned how to write data to a file, the obvious next step is to find out how to read data from a file. Reading from a file has two overall steps:
   Opening the file for reading.
   Reading the records of the file.
On some computers, the file must be closed after reading.

   The most important general point to be made about reading from a file is that records are read in the same order as they were written to the file. Furthermore, all the data items in a record must be read before the next record is read. In most cases this requires that the structure of the program which reads from a file is the same as that of the program which wrote the data to the file.

Example 12C

Read the data from a pupil records file created by example program 12B and display or print it.

Method

It is important that the overall structure of this program be exactly the same as that of the file creation program, example program 12B. Accordingly, the overall steps of the program are as follows:
   Prompt and input the name of the file to be read.
   Open the file for reading.
   Read and display file title and date created.
   Repeat, until end-of-file marker reached:
      Read from file pupil name, sex, date of birth and form.
      Display this information.
The variable names do not have to be the same as those for the file creation program. Accordingly, the set shown below are used.

Variables

A\$	date file created	L\$	file name
I\$	file title	P\$	pupil name
X\$	sex	E\$	date of birth
R\$	form		

Flow diagram
See figure 12C1.

Program

```
100   REM EXAMPLE PROGRAM 12C
105   REM READ PUPIL RECORDS FILE
110   REM
115   PRINT  "PUPIL RECORDS SYSTEM—FILE
                                   ACCESS "
120   PRINT
125   PRINT  "NAME OF FILE TO BE READ";
130   INPUT L$
135   REM
200   REM OPEN FILE FOR READING
205   OPEN #10, L$
210   INPUT #10, I$, A$
215   PRINT
220   PRINT  "FILE TITLE:"; I$
225   PRINT  "DATE CREATED:"; A$
230   PRINT
235   PRINT  "NAME"; TAB(20);  "SEX";
240   PRINT TAB(25);"DATE OF"; TAB(35);"FORM"
245   PRINT TAB(25);  "BIRTH"
```

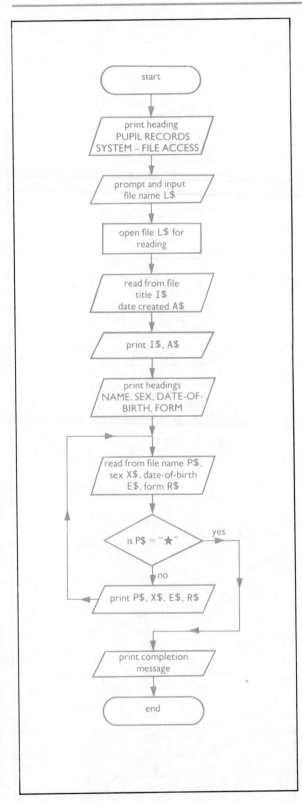

Figure 12C1 Flow diagram for example program 12C

```
250  INPUT #10, P$, X$, E$, R$
255  IF P$ = "*" THEN 270
260  PRINT P$; TAB(20); X$; TAB(25); E$;
                                  TAB(35); R$
265  GO TO 250
270  PRINT
275  PRINT "FILE"; L$; "COMPLETE"
280  PRINT
285  END
```

Points to notice

- Records are read from the file in exactly the same order as they were written.
- The program structure is identical to that of example program 12B, except that the end-of-file marker is not printed.

Exercise 12C

1 a) Describe in your own words, the steps required to read data from a file.
   b) Can the data in a file be accessed in any order?
2 For each of the files created by a program in exercise 12B, write a program to access the data in the file and print or display it. Pay particular attention to the layout of the output. Use suitable test data to check that data stored in the file is actually recovered.
3 **Updating** a file is a process which involves changing some or all the data stored in a file. In Basic this requires creating a new copy of the file to store the updated information. The overall steps of a simple file updating program are as follows:
   Create a file to store updated information.
   Open the existing version of the file.
   For each record in the existing file, repeat:
      Read a record from existing version of file.
      Display the record.
      If the record is to be changed, then input new values for all data items.
      Write the record to the new version of the file.
   The updating process may be extended to allow records to be deleted, or new records to be inserted.
   Write program(s) to update one or more of the files created in exercise 12B. Note that the structure of the new version of the file must be *exactly* the same as that of the old version. Use a program from question 2 of this exercise to check the new version of the file.

12D Information retrieval

In many computer applications involving large files of data, it is necessary to access selected items of the data. The selected data satisfies one or more conditions. Applications of this nature are given the name **information retrieval** systems.

This section uses files created earlier in this chapter as the basis of simple information retrieval systems.

Example 12D

Using the pupil records file created by example program 12B, print or display a list of all the pupils in a given form.

Method

Since the program must access the entire file, its overall structure closely resembles that of example program 12C. The difference is in the fact that only records matching the given form are displayed. Accordingly, the overall structure of the program is as follows:

Prompt and input the name of the file to be read.

Prompt and input the name of the form to be printed.

Open file for reading.

Repeat, until end-of-file marker reached:

Read from file pupil name, sex, date of birth and form.

If the form matches the given form, then print or display this information.

The variable names are the same as those for example program 12C, with the addition of:

Q$ form requiring list to be printed.

Flow diagram

See figure 12D1.

Program

```
100  REM EXAMPLE PROGRAM 12D
105  REM DISPLAY FORM LIST
110  REM FROM PUPIL RECORD FILE
115  PRINT "PUPIL RECORDS SYSTEM—FORM LIST"
120  PRINT
125  PRINT "NAME OF FILE TO BE READ";
130  INPUT L$
135  PRINT "FORM TO BE LISTED";
140  INPUT Q$
145  REM
200  REM OPEN FILE FOR READING
205  OPEN #10, L$
210  INPUT #10, I$, A$
215  PRINT
220  PRINT "FORM"; Q$
225  PRINT
230  PRINT "NAME"; TAB(20); "SEX";
235  PRINT TAB(25); "DATE OF BIRTH"
240  PRINT
```

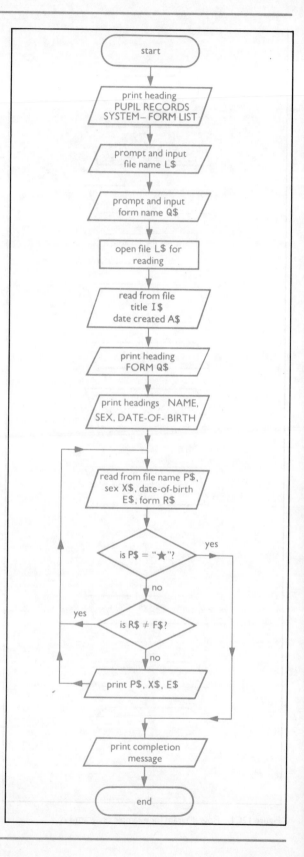

Figure 12D1   Flow diagram for example program 12D

```
245  INPUT #10, P$, X$, E$, R$
250  IF P$ = "*" THEN 270
255  IF R$ <> Q$ THEN 245
260  PRINT P$; TAB(20); X$; TAB(25); E$
265  GO TO 245
270  PRINT
275  PRINT "END OF FORM"; Q$; "LIST"
280  PRINT
285  END
```

Points to notice
- The structure of this program is almost identical to that of example program 12C.
- The file title and date created are read from the file even though they are not used (line 210).
- The condition in line 255 is for not displaying the record. This simplifies and shortens the program.

Exercise 12D

1 a) What is meant by information retrieval?
   b) Name some applications of information retrieval.
2 Modify example program 12D, by the insertion of a few extra lines, to print a list of only girls, or only boys in the form.
3 Write a program, using the pupil records file, to accept as input the name of a particular pupil and then locate and print the record for that pupil. If the pupil name cannot be found, a suitable message is displayed.
4 Write a program to look up a word in the foreign language dictionary file (exercise 12B, question 2). The word can be in English or in the foreign language and, if it is found in the file, the translation of the word is displayed.
5 Using the library book file (exercise 12B, question 4), write a program to list the titles of all the books written by a particular author. The author's name is input at the start of the program.
6 Using the estate agent's file (exercise 12B, question 6) write a program to list the details of all houses in a given price range. The limits of the price range are input at the start of the program.

12E End-of-chapter summary

This chapter has introduced the idea of a file, and demonstrated some simple file handling techniques in Basic language. The topics introduced in this chapter are not the only file handling operations carried out in practice, but relatively complex operations such as sorting and merging files must wait for a more advanced course. The main points of the chapter are as follows:
- A file is an organised collection of data, on a permanent form of storage which can be accessed by a computer.
- A file consists of a number of records, which in turn contain a number of data items.

- The operation of storing information on a file is known as writing data to a file. Accessing information from a file is known as reading data from a file.
- The file handling statements in Research Machines Extended Basic Version 5 introduced in this chapter are as follows:

CREATE #10, F$ create a file named **F$** and open it for writing.

PRINT #10, A, B$ write a record to a file, containing data items **A** and **B$**.

CLOSE #10   close a file at the end of writing.

OPEN #10, F$ open file **F$** for reading.

INPUT #10, A, B$ read a record from a file, containing data items **A** and **B$**.

Note that, at any one time, only one file may be open for reading and one for writing.

Exercise 12E

1 Summarise, in your own words, the Basic language file handling facilities which have been introduced in this chapter.

Draw flow diagrams and write programs for the tasks outlined in questions 2 to 5. If necessary modify, or extend the program specifications according to your requirements. Use suitable test data to check the workings of your programs, and write programmer's documentation and user guides for them.

2 Write a set of three programs to create, update and display a 'desk diary' file. The file should cover a week, and contain the date of each day of the week, and the day, time and place of all the appointments for the week. If required, also write an information retrieval program to display all the appointments for a particular day of the week.
3 Create a set of twelve files containing twelve pages of a calendar, one for each month. Use the same program to create all twelve files. Identify the files by the names of the months to which they refer. Write a program to accept from the user the name of a month, and then access the file for that month and display it.
☐4 The Prestel information access service enables 'pages' of information to be displayed on a TV screen reaching the user via a telephone line from a central computer. One 'page' is the contents of a TV screen. The user controls the system via a simple numeric keypad. At the foot of each page are instructions for accessing other pages by pressing appropriate keys. The overall structure of the pages is shown in figure 12E1. Such a structure is known as a **tree**.
　Choose a suitable topic, and write a number of 'pages' of information about the topic. Match the 'pages' to the size of the screen of your computer. The pages must form a tree structure like figure 12E1, and each page must contain instructions for accessing pages lower down, or going back to the previous page. Devise a scheme for naming the 'pages' according to the tree structure.

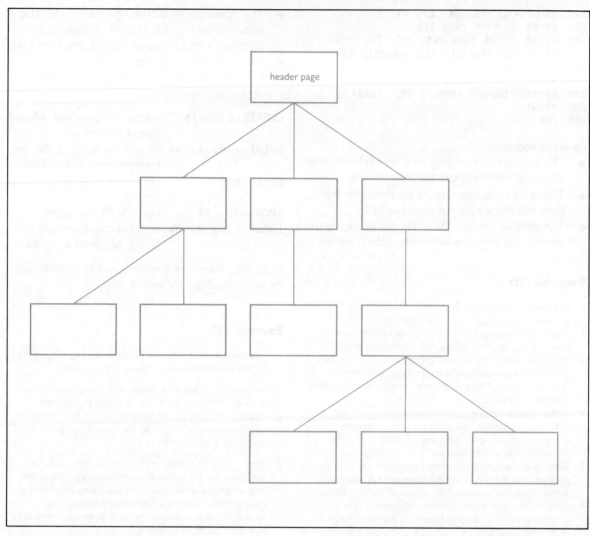

header page

Figure 12E1   Diagram for exercise 12E, question 4

Write a program to create a number of files, each storing one 'page' of information. In addition to the lines which are displayed, it is advisable to store some extra information such as the title of the page, the date it was created and the characters which transfer control to other pages. Also write a program to display a 'page' that has been stored.

Write a Prestel-type program which displays the 'page' at the 'top' of the tree, and then allows the user to work through the 'pages', following the instructions on each 'page' to access another one.

Some suggested topics for the 'pages' are: news items, sports information, recipes, notes on a school subject, a local entertainments guide, notes for repairing a bicycle or motorbike or a travel guide.

5   Some further suggestions for files and file handling programs are:

A personal telephone directory file, containing names, addresses and telephone numbers.

A personal accounts file, containing records of money received and spent. A file of this nature could also be used for a sports club or youth club.

A stock file for a shop, containing the numbers, names, prices and possibly stock levels.

A bus or train timetable file which can be accessed to find the times of buses or trains to a given destination.

A set of files, each storing the information for one graphics display.

13
Projects

This chapter provides suggestions for programs which may be used either as projects for Computer Studies Examinations, or simply as substantial, useful programming exercises. The programs are designed to be realistic and useful, without being too long. They require a fairly thorough knowledge of most of the programming techniques introduced in this book.

Before embarking on a project program, one or two words of advice and caution are essential:

Plan your project carefully before you start writing the program.
Think carefully about the situation in which your program will be used. Who will use it, and what will they use it for? Write down the answers to these questions.

Write down an outline of your program, and check it carefully, before drawing detailed flow diagrams and writing segments of program.
Whether your program is long or short, it is important to decide on the overall design, and the structure of the program, before writing any parts of it. Pay particular attention to subprograms and their relation to the main program.

If at all possible, write and test parts of your program separately before combining them into a single program.
This is particularly important if your program has subprograms, or uses graphics or file handling facilities.

Test your program with as wide a variety of test data as possible.
Make sure that every logical path in your program is followed, and a wide variety of test data, including 'awkward' values, is used.

Write clear, concise documentation for users and programmers.
In many cases, the documentation is as important as the program in marking the project.

Project program 1: Landing the LEM

The lunar excursion module (LEM) is 1000 m above its landing site on the moon, descending at 100 m/s, accelerating due to the moon's gravity at 2 m/s^2. The mass of the LEM is 2000 kg, plus 500 kg of fuel. Its retro-rockets can develop up to 50 0000 newtons of thrust, at which 50 kg/s of fuel are used up. At lower thrusts, proportionally less fuel is used.

If the speed of the LEM is less than 5 m/s on touchdown, then a successful landing has been made. If the speed is more, or the fuel runs out, then the LEM has crashed . . . .

The objective of the program is to simulate landing the LEM, accepting a value of the retro-thrust from the 'pilot' each second until touchdown. The most effective output is a simple graphics display of the craft, and current values of certain key quantities, updated once a second. The numberic keys 0 to 5 are 'polled' once a second, and the value of the key currently being pressed is multiplied by 10000 to determine the current thrust. A method of 'polling' the keyboard is outlined below.

The calculations which simulate the motion of the LEM are as follows:

Thrust
If k is the value of the key pressed, then the thrust F is calculated by the formula
$$F = k \times 10000$$
$\quad$ F $\quad$ thrust (newtons)
$\quad$ k $\quad$ value of key depressed

Deceleration
The deceleration a (m/s^2) is calculated from Newton's law of motion
$$a = \frac{F}{m} - 2$$
$\quad$ a $\quad$ deceleration (m/s^2)
$\quad$ m $\quad$ LEM mass (kg)

The -2 term is due to the moon's gravity.

Speed
The change in speed in a one second interval is numerically equal to the deceleration. In other words
$$v^n = v - a$$
$\quad$ v^n $\quad$ new speed (m/s)
$\quad$ v $\quad$ old speed (m/s)

Altitude
The change in altitude in a one second interval is numerically equal to the speed. In other words
$$h^n = h - v$$
$\quad$ h^n $\quad$ new altitude (m)
$\quad$ h $\quad$ old altitude (m)

Fuel used

The amount of fuel used is calculated from the fact that at 50 000 N thrust, 50 kg/s of fuel are used. Accordingly, the amount of fuel used in one second at a thrust F is

$$u = \frac{F}{50\,000} \times 50 \qquad u \quad \text{fuel used (kg)}$$

Fuel left

The amount of fuel left is reduced by the amount used

$$f^n = f - u \qquad \begin{array}{ll} f^n & \text{new amount of fuel left (kg)} \\ f & \text{old amount of fuel left (kg)} \end{array}$$

Mass

In a one second interval, the mass of the LEM is reduced by the amount of fuel used.

$$m^n = m - u \qquad \begin{array}{ll} m^n & \text{new LEM mass (kg)} \\ m & \text{old LEM mass (kg)} \\ u & \text{fuel used (kg)} \end{array}$$

Using this information, an outline of the LEM landing simulation is as follows:

Initialise mass, altitude, speed and fuel left.
Repeat:
    Display LEM at current altitude.
    Get thrust value from keyboard.
    If there is fuel left, calculate thrust, else thrust is zero.
    Calculate the deceleration, new speed, new altitude, fuel used, new fuel left and new mass.
    Pause to use up rest of one second interval.
Until touchdown.
    If speed on touchdown is less than 5 m/s then safe landing, else crash . . . .

The simplest method of obtaining the thrust value from the keyboard is to use the **GET** function. In Research Machines Extended Basic Version 5, the statement

```
150 LET J = GET (0)
```

will test the keyboard, and assign to **J** the ASCII code of the key currently being pressed, or the value 0 if no key is being pressed. Since the ASCII codes of the required keys (0 to 5) are 48 to 53, the following sequence of statements will assign to the variable **K** a value in the range 0 to 5 according to the key pressed:

```
155 IF J < 48 OR J > 53 THEN 170
160 LET K = J-48
165 GO TO 175
170 LET K = 0
175 REM CONTINUE
```

Note that variable **K** is assigned the value of 0 if no key is pressed or if an invalid key (outside the range 0 to 5) is pressed.

Project program 2: Keeping accounts

The only proper way to look after money – whether it is your own, or belongs to an organisation like a youth club – is to keep accounts. An account is a record of money received and money spent, and the difference between the two amounts. Keeping accounts on a computer has the added benefit of accuracy, neatness and ease of keeping up to date.

Figure 13.1 illustrates a simple, but very useful, method of keeping accounts. It shows one month's accounts for a youth club. The account has:

A title (St Mary's Church Youth Club General Account)
A date for the whole account (November 1981)
A number of entries, each containing the following information:
    date,
    description,
    amount,
    the letters CR for money received
      or   DR for money spent,
    the balance, showing the up-to-date amount in the account. It is calculated by adding the amount received to, or subtracting the amount spent from the previous balance.
The first entry is the balance brought forward from the previous month.
The last entry shows the balance to be carried forward to the next month.

Accounts like this are best kept on a file on a cassette tape or magnetic disk. You will need to write several programs for the accounting system:

A program to create the file for an account, giving it a title, date and filling in the amount brought forward.

A program to update the account, allowing one or more entries to be typed, and calculating the balance after each entry.

A program to display or print an account.

A program to close an account, calculating and displaying the balance to be carried forward.

Note that when an account is updated, a new version of the file is created. It must then be renamed to have the same name as the previous version of the file, which is erased in the process.

70

St. Marys Church Youth Club

Account for December 1981

DATE	DESCRIPTION	AMOUNT		BALANCE
02/12/81	Balance brought forward	27.93	CR	27.93
02/12/81	Subscriptions	1.60	CR	29.53
02/12/81	Sale of refreshments	3.09	CR	32.62
08/12/81	Purchase of refreshments	14.82	DR	17.80
09/12/81	Subscriptions	1.30	CR	19.10
09/12/81	Sale of refreshments	2.74	CR	21.84
16/12/81	Subscriptions	1.50	CR	23.34
16/12/81	Sale of refreshments	3.34	CR	26.68
16/12/81	Collection for Christmas party	13.02	CR	39.70
19/12/81	Food for Christmas party	21.11	DR	18.59
19/12/81	Decorations	6.20	DR	12.39
23/12/81	Collection at Christmas party	5.13	CR	17.52
30/12/81	Subscriptions	0.90	CR	18.42
30/12/81	Sale of refreshments	2.11	CR	20.53
30/12/81	Balance carried forward	20.53	DR	0.00

Figure 13.1   A youth club account

Project program 3: Stock records

Wherever large quantities of goods are kept, it is essential to keep accurate, up-to-date records of them. The programs outlined below are designed to do just that. They can be used for a school stockroom or for a warehouse.

The permanent record of the stock is kept on a **stock file**. For each item, it records the stock number, description, number in stock, minimum stock level and re-order quantity. Several programs are needed to keep the stock file up to date.

A program to create a stock file, and input initial values of all the information.

A program to add records for new stock items, or delete records for items no longer stocked.

A program to record stock movements, and update the stock file. It starts by reading the file from backing store, and then allows the user to enter information for stock received or despatched. For each stock movement, the stock number and number of items received or despatched are entered. The new stock level is calculated and displayed. If it is below the minimum stock level, a message is displayed, reminding the user to order more, and showing the re-order quantity. At the end of the program run, the updated information is copied onto a new version of the stock file.

A program to print or display an entire stock file.

Project program 4: Magazine subscriptions

A simple computerised system for dealing with magazine subscriptions uses a file to store the following information for each subscriber: subscriber number, name, address, number of copies paid for. A number of programs are required, for the following tasks:

Create a subscriber file, and store a number of subscriber records.

Edit the subscriber file, deleting records and inserting records for new subscribers.

Printing a set of address labels for an issue of the magazine, and reducing the number of copies paid for by one.

Writing a subscription reminder letter to all subscribers whose number of copies paid for is less than a certain number (say 4).

Recording the payment of subscriptions for a certain number of issues, updating the records of the subscribers who have paid.

Project program 5: Air traffic control

The objective of this program is to simulate the radar display screen of an air traffic controller, and allow the controller to guide a number of aircraft towards a runway.

The program presents a graphics display of the radar screen, using a suitable scale, with the control tower at the centre, and showing the outline of the runway. A few key compass directions are shown. The display is updated every ten seconds or so. See figure 13.2.

Aeroplanes appear, at suitable intervals, at random positions on the edge of the screen. An aeroplane is indicated by a suitable character, perhaps flashing on and off, and an identification number, course bearing, altitude and speed. At any one time there may be up to five aeroplanes on the screen.

Every ten seconds the controller has the opportunity to give an instruction to an aircraft. This is done by entering the identification number of the aircraft, and a new course bearing, altitude and speed.

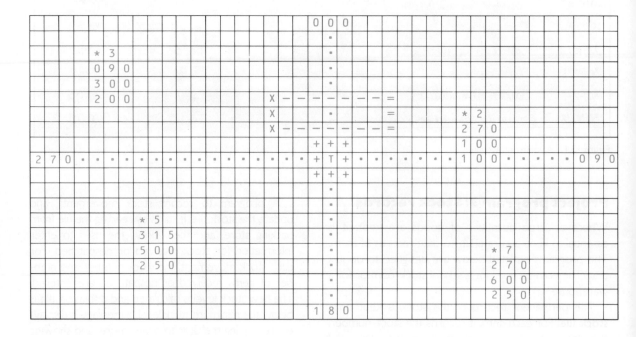

Figure 13.2   A traffic controller's display screen

During the ten second interval between screen displays, the new positions of the aircraft are calculated from their speeds and bearings, as shown below. An aeroplane which has been instructed to change course at the start of the interval is assumed to have a speed and bearing (and altitude) of half way between the old and the new values.

If the speed of an aircraft is the variable **V** (metres per second) and its bearing is the angle **B** (measured clockwise from North, which is the y-axis on the screen), then:

change in x co-ordinate (metres) = $V \times T \times \sin B$
change in y co-ordinate (metres) = $V \times T \times \cos B$

where **T** is 10 for a second interval. (Remember that the angle must be in radians for the **SIN** and **COS** functions.)

If an aeroplane reaches a *landing zone* in line with the end of the runway with the correct bearing, speed and altitude, then it is assumed to have landed safely, and is removed from the screen.

Project program 6: School records

Computerised records can be of great assistance to many aspects of school administration. The files and programs discussed in this project form an outline of a simple but potentially very useful school records system.

One or more files are used to store the following information for each pupil: name, sex, date of birth, home address, year, form, optional subjects. Programs are written for each of the following operations:

Create a pupil records file, giving it a suitable heading and storing a number of records on it.

Edit a pupil records file, inserting, updating and deleting records.

Display or print all the records in a file.

Select pupil records according to specified conditions (e.g. year = 4 and sex = M) and display or print some or all of the data items in the selected records.

The three program examples in chapter 12 illustrate a very simple pupil records system.

Project program 7: Standing in a queue

Whether it is people waiting for a bus, cars at a junction or aeroplanes waiting to land, queues are an important,

and often annoying, part of our daily lives. A program which simulates the behaviour of a queue accordingly has a number of uses. It is best combined with a graphics display showing the current number of people (or cars or aeroplanes . . .) in the queue.

People arrive at the back of a queue at random intervals. If, on average, A people arrive per minute, then the probability of a person arriving in a one second interval is A/60. Similarly, if people leave the queue at random intervals, on average B per minute, then the probability of a person leaving the queue in a one second interval is B/60. Using this information, the change in the length of a queue can be simulated by the portion of a flow diagram shown in figure 13.3.

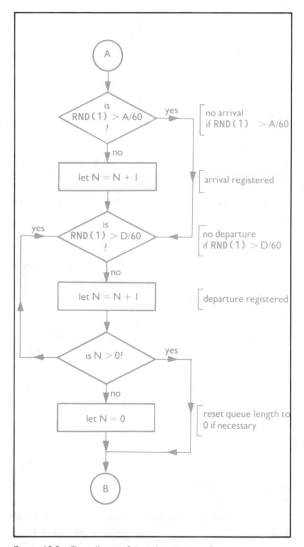

Figure 13.3 Flow diagram for project program 7

A random number in the range 0 to 1 is selected. If it is greater than A/60, then no arrival is said to have taken place. Another random number is used to determine if anyone has left the queue. The updated queue length is then passed to the graphics portion of the program. The effects of different values of A and B can be investigated over a period of time.

The technique introduced here can be extended to simulate a number of queues, such as at a supermarket, or a road junction, as outlined in project program 12.

Project program 8: Population growth

This project introduces a method for studying the growth of the population of a country or region, using a very simple mathematical formula.

If there are no restrictions on the growth of a population, the formula shown below can be used to calculate its change in numbers from one year to the next:

$g = kp$

p   size of population   k   growth factor
g   growth of population in one year

For example, if the population is 50 million, and the growth rate 2% (k = 0.02), then:

$g = 0.02 \times 50 = 1$ million

The growth is 1 million, and thus the population at the start of the next year is 51 million. This calculation can be repeated for a number of years, as shown in the table below.

Time (years)	Population (millions)	Growth (millions)
0	50	0.02 × 50 = 1
1	51	0.02 × 51 = 1.02
2	52.02	0.02 × 52.02 = 1.04
etc.		

If the size of the population of a country or region at a certain time is known, together with its growth rate, its size can be calculated for a number of future years by using this method repeatedly. Figures from the table below can be used, or more up-to-date ones from other sources.

Country or region	Population (1970) (millions)	Growth rate (% per year)
Britain	56.0	0.5
USA	205.2	1.0
France	51.1	0.6
West Germany	58.6	0.6
India	554.6	2.6
China	759.6	1.8
USSR	242.6	1.0
Kuwait	0.7	8.3
Kenya	10.9	3.1
Peru	13.6	3.1
Africa	344.0	2.6
Asia	2056.0	2.3
North America	228.0	1.1
South America	283.0	2.9
Europe	462.0	0.8
Western industrial states	705.0	1.01
Eastern industrial states	369.0	0.96
Non-industrial states	2560.0	2.40
World	3632.0	2.0

Reference: John McHale: *World Facts and Trends* (Collier).

Note that the growth rate (% per year) must be divided by 100 to obtain the growth factor used in the formula.

Project program 9: The solar system

The orbits of the planets around the Sun are approximately circular. Their radii, together with their times for a complete revolution, are listed in the table below:

Inner planets	Orbital radius (million miles)	Period of revolution (days)
Mercury	36	86
Venus	67	225
Earth	93	365
Mars	142	687

Outer planets	Orbital radius (million miles)	Period of revolution (years)
Jupiter	483	12
Saturn	886	29
Uranus	1783	84
Neptune	2793	165
Pluto	3666	248

Use this information in a program which performs some or all of the following operations:

1 Calculate the circumference of each orbit:

$c = 2\pi r$ $\qquad \pi = 3.14159$
$\qquad\qquad$ r $\quad$ orbit radius
$\qquad\qquad$ c $\quad$ circumference

2 Calculate the orbital speed of each planet in miles per hour:

$v = c \div t$ $\qquad$ v $\quad$ orbital speed (mph)
$\qquad\qquad$ c $\quad$ circumference (miles)
$\qquad\qquad$ t $\quad$ period of revolution (hours)

3 Calculate the angle through which each inner planet has turned in three months (92 days):

e.g. $\quad$ Venus completes 360° in 225 days

so in 92 days it does $\dfrac{92}{225} \times 360 = 147°$

4 Calculate the angle through which each outer planet has turned in one year.

5 Display a diagram of the positions and motion of some or all of the planets, using suitable scales for distance and time.

Project Program 10: Wage slips

Producing weekly wage slips for workers who are paid at an hourly rate is a task frequently carried out by computer. The system described below makes use of a *wages file* as well as information typed at the keyboard.

The information required to produce a wage slip is shown in the table below. Information which stays constant from one week to the next is stored in a wages file. Other information is typed at the keyboard.

From wages file	Variable name
Name	**N\$**
Works number	**W**
Ordinary pay rate	**R**
Overtime pay rate	**S**
Weekly tax-free allowance	**A**

From keyboard	
Ordinary hours worked	**H**
Overtime hours worked	**V**

Three programs are required, to carry out the following operations:

Create a wages file, with a record for each worker.

Update a wages file, inserting, deleting and amending records.

Produce weekly payslips, working through the wages file record by record, and accepting the ordinary and overtime hours worked by each worker from the keyboard. The following calculations are carried out:

Gross pay:	$G = H \times R + V \times S$
Taxable pay:	$X = G - A$
Income tax:	$T = 0.30 \times X$
National Insurance contribution:	$I = 0.06 \times X$
Nett pay:	$P = G - T - I$

A wage slip is printed for each worker, showing this information, as well as the input information in a suitable layout.

Note that the income tax calculation shown here is correct provided that the taxable pay is less than £225. More detailed income tax calculations are shown in project program 13.

Project program 11: Library records

A simple but very useful record system for a school library can easily be created using the programming techniques introduced in this book. The system is based on a *book record file*, containing a record for each book with the following information:

Author's surname
Author's first name or initials
Title
Publisher
Year of publication
International standard book number (ISBN)
Subject reference number
Sequence number

Programs are required for the following operations:

Create a book record file and enter a number of records.

Edit a book record file, inserting, deleting and updating records.

Print all or part of the book record file.

An information retrieval system, allowing a user to:

Display information on all the books written by a certain author.

Display information on all the books with a certain subject reference number.

Display information on all the books containing a certain word in their titles.

Find out if the library has a book with a certain title.

Project program 12: Simulating a road junction

The objective of this program is to simulate the behaviour of a road junction controlled by traffic lights, as shown in figure 13.4. The simulation determines the number of cars in each of the four queues at any time. It may be used to determine the phasing of the traffic lights which keeps these queues as short as possible.

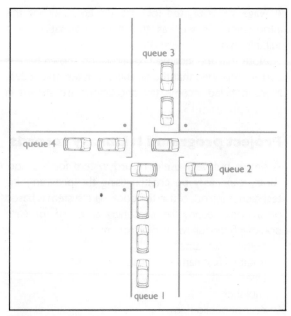

Figure 13.4 A road junction

The traffic lights are green for a number of seconds for queues 1 and 3, and then green for a different number of seconds for queues 2 and 4. When the lights are green for a particular queue, it is assumed (for simplicity) that one car per second passes through the junction and out of the queue.

It is suggested that the following variables be used:

N(4) the number of cars in each queue

P(4) the probability of a car arriving during a one second interval in each queue (suggested range 0.1 to 0.7)

F(4) the colours of the lights in each direction: $+1$ for green, -1 for red.

S(2) the number of seconds green in each direction (only values for queues 1 and 2 are required).

The following program structure is suggested:

1 Input initial values of **N**, **P**, **F** and **S**, and the number of cycles to be simulated.

2 An outer loop counts the number of cycles to be simulated.

3 A middle loop counts the number of seconds for the current phase. The loop limit will be **S(1)** or **S(2)** depending on which set of lights is green.

4 An inner loop counts the four queues. In the inner loop, a random number in the range 0 to 1 is selected. If it is less than the arrival probability for the particular queue, then the queue length is increased by 1. If the lights are green for the particular queue, and the queue length is greater than 0, the queue length is decreased by 1.

5 At the end of the middle loop, the phases are altered (by multiplying the values of **F** by -1) and the middle loop limit changed from **S(1)** to **S(2)** or vice versa.

Either a table is displayed of the queue lengths at the end of each phase, or an animated diagram based on figure 13.4 is shown, being updated as the queue lengths change.

A measure of the efficiency of the system is the overall average queue length. This is the total of all four queue lengths every second, added up for the duration of the simulation, and divided by the total number of seconds simulated.

Project program 13: Income tax

Income tax in Britain is calculated from a person's total earnings over a year (called *gross income*). A certain part of this income (called the *allowance*) is tax free. The allowance is deducted from a person's gross income to obtain their *taxable income*. Each person is allocated a *tax code*, which is one tenth of their allowance.

The percentage of taxable income paid in tax varies according to the band in which the income falls. The income bands for 1981–82 are shown in the table below (they are likely to change in future years):

Percentage	Taxable income (£)(1981–82)
30%	1 to 11 250
40%	11 251 to 13 250
45%	13 251 to 16 750
50%	16 751 to 22 250
55%	22 251 to 27 750
60%	over 27 750

The personal allowances for 1981–82 are as follows:

Allowance	1981–82 (5)
Single person	1375
Married man	2145
Wife's earned income	1375
Age – single person	1820
Age – married man	2895
Additional personal	770
Widow's bereavement	770
Blind person	360
Blind couple	720

Additional allowances are given for children, mortgage interest payments, certain insurance premiums and a small number of other expenses.

An example of an income tax calculation is as follows:

gross income: £18000   tax code: 235

Taxable income = gross income − 10 × tax code
= 18000 − 2350 = £15650

Income tax:

30% of first	£11250 =	£3375
40% of next	£ 2000 =	£ 800
50% or remaining	£ 2400 =	£1200
total income tax		= £5375

Write a program to input the gross income and tax code for a number of people, and calculate and output their income tax.

Project program 14: Installing central heating

If a house is to be heated at a constant temperature above its surroundings, heat will be lost from all the outside surfaces: ground floor, outer walls, windows, outside doors and roof. Heat will also be lost by ventilation – warm air from the inside will have to be exchanged for cold air from the outside. All the heat being lost must be continuously replaced by the central heating system. In order to determine the heating capacity of the central heating system (measured in kilowatts), this rate of heat loss must be calculated.

Heat lost by conduction through surfaces

The heat loss through a surface depends on the nature of the surface, its area and the temperature difference from one side to the other:

$$\text{heat loss (watts)} = U \times \text{area (m}^2) \times \text{temperature difference (}^\circ\text{C)}$$

where U (watts per m^2 per $^\circ$C) is a measure of the conductivity of the material. Required values of U are shown in a table below.

Heat loss by ventilation

The rate of ventilation is measured by the number of air changes per hour. It requires 0.2 watts to heat one cubic metre of air by 1°C in one hour, so:

$$\text{heat loss (watts)} = \text{volume of air} \times \text{number of air changes per hour} \times \text{temperature difference (}^\circ\text{C)} \times 0.2$$

Write a program to calculate the total rate of heat loss from a house, such as the one shown in figure 13.5. It is suggested that the following steps be used:

1 Store the U values in an array.
2 Display user instructions.
3 For the house design chosen, input the required lengths and calculate the total area of: ground floor, walls, windows, doors, roof.
4 Calculate the total volume of the house.
5 Input an outside temperature, a required inside temperature, and the number of air changes per hour.
6 Using the appropriate U values, calculate the heat loss through each surface.
7 Calculate the heat loss through ventilation.

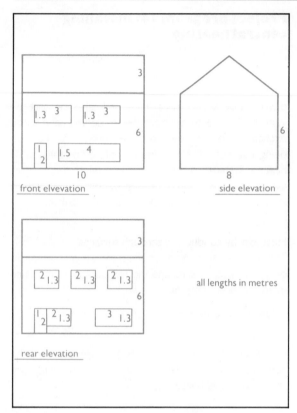

Figure 13.5   Home plan for project program 14

8 Calculate the total rate of heat loss (and change from watts to kilowatts). This is equal to the total heating capacity required of the central heating system.

Steps 5 to 8 may be repeated for different weather conditions, inside temperature and ventilation requirements. The effect of insulating the walls and roof, and double glazing the windows can also be investigated.

Table of U values

Surface	U (watts per m^2 per °C)
ground floor	1.14
cavity wall	1.93
window	5.68
door	2.41
tiled roof	3.32
insulated cavity wall	0.48
insulated ceiling or roof	0.90
double glazed windows	2.84

Project program 15: Sorting

Many computer applications require numbers or literal data items to be sorted in numerical or alphabetical order. Although sorting large sets of data is an extremely slow and complicated task, there are a number of fairly simple methods for sorting small sets of data. These include the **selection sort**, which is introduced here. The method is as follows:

Compare the first number with each subsequent number. If any subsequent number is larger than the first one, interchange the numbers. At the end of this series of comparisons, the largest number will be first.

Compare the second number with each subsequent number, interchanging as above. This series of comparisons will end with the second largest number second.

Continuing this process as far as the second last number will put all the numbers in order.

Example

The numbers 6, 8, 3 and 9 are sorted by the method outlined above. ⌐⇄ denotes a comparison and ⇅⌐ an interchange.

```
first number    →6↩    →8    →8↩    9    largest number
compared:     ↳8↩    6     6       6    now first
                 3    →3    3       3
                 9     9   ↳9↩    8

second           9     9     9         second largest
number                →6   →6↩    8    number now
compared:     ↳3    3     3         second
                 8   ↳8↩    6

third number     9     9               numbers now
compared:        8     8               in order
              →3↩    6
              ↳6↩    3
```

It is suggested that the numbers (or words) to be sorted are stored in an array. An outer loop is used to select each number in turn, and an inner nested loop to compare the subsequent numbers.

The sorting program may be modified to sort associated sets of data, such as names and percentages, where the names can be sorted in alphabetical order, or the percentages in numerical order.

Project program 16: Hangman

The popular game of 'hangman' is great fun to play, and has a number of educational benefits. The game has a number of variations, and is fairly easy to program, provided that some graphics facilities are available. A program for a simple variation of the game has the following steps:

Choose a word at random from a stored list, and display a number of dashes, one for each letter of the word.

The user keys in a letter. If it is contained in the word, it is displayed in place of the dashes at the appropriate position(s).

If the letter is not in the word, another portion of the scaffolding is displayed on the screen. Another letter is keyed in.

If the user completes the word before the scaffolding is finished, he or she escapes. Otherwise . . . see figure 13.6.

Project program 17: Organising sports day

Organising a school sports day is a considerable task. A computer can be of great assistance in two key areas – keeping records of the competitors for each event, and recording results on the day, as each event takes place.

An outline for a set of programs to carry out these tasks is as follows:

A *competitor file* is created for each event. It contains:

Name of event.

Name and distance of time of current record holder.

Names and houses of competitors.

A program is needed to create a competitor file, and one is required to access a file and print or display the information on it.

A *result recording* program is required, which runs for the duration of the sports day. It must carry out the following operations:

Open a *house points* file, setting the total points for each house to zero, or to some values from previous events.

Repeat, until all events are complete:

Input the results for an event: the name, house and distance or time of the competitors coming first, second and third.

Update the scores for each house, display or print them and write them to the house points file.

Read the competitor file for the event and write the information together with the results, to an *event result* file. If the record has been broken, enter the new record and holder's name.

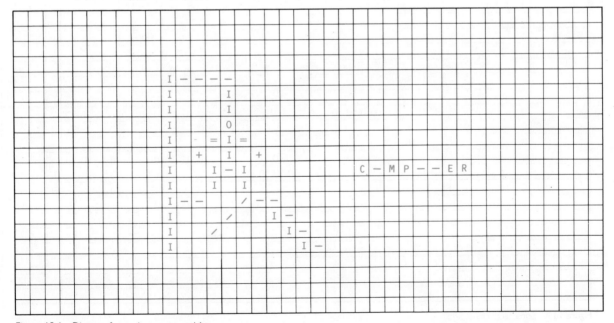

Figure 13.6   Diagram for project program 16

Programs are required to read and print the house points file and the event results files.

It goes without saying that these programs must be tested very thoroughly before sports day, as a failure on the day would be serious indeed.

Project program 18: Displaying large characters

A number of computer applications require large letters or numbers to be displayed on the screen of a computer. As long as some graphics facilities are available, it is not too difficult to write a subprogram to display a large character, or string of large characters, at a given screen position. One possible approach is as follows:

Decide on the size for a character. Either five rows by three columns or (preferably) seven rows by five columns on a screen 'grid' are recommended.

Draw the characters on squared paper. Either use ordinary characters, or special graphics symbols if they are available. Figure 13.7 shows some examples, using seven rows and five columns.

Store the symbols which make up each large character as literal data items in an array. The symbols for one large character are placed in a single string, row by row, from top to bottom. Examples of the '1' and '2'

characters from figure 13R1 are shown below (. represents a space):

```
C$(1)= " ..0...00....0....0....0....0..00000 "
C$(2)= " .000.0...0....0...0...0...0...00000 "
```

Write a subprogram which accepts a character to be displayed and the co-ordinates of the top left corner. The array element for the large character is accessed and 'scanned' character by character. The point plotting subprogram from section 11D is used to plot each character at the required position.

Project program 19: A careers information system

With the nature, training required and employment prospects of many careers changing very rapidly, a valuable aid to careers counselling is a computer-based careers information system. A simple version of such a system is outlined in this project.

The system is based on a *careers file*, containing at least the following information for each career:

Career title.
Brief job description.
Aptitudes and abilities needed.
Qualifications needed.
Recommended school subjects at CSE, O or A level.

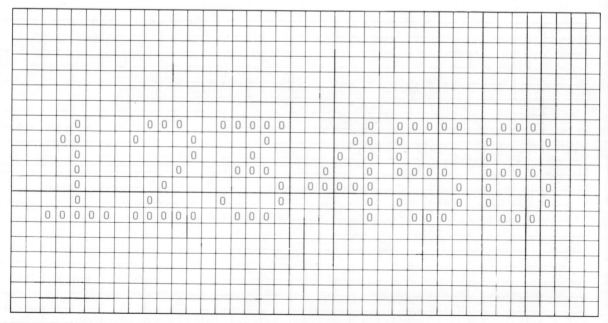

Figure 13.7   Some large characters

Expected salary range.

General employment prospects.

Some local employers.

Sources of further information.

Three programs are required, namely:

A program to create a careers file, entering records for a number of careers.

A program to update a careers file, deleting, inserting and editing records in it.

A program to access selected records and display or print them. Records can be selected by title, qualification or school subject(s).

Project program 20: Computer art

Chapter 11 introduced a number of ideas and techniques of computer graphics. These can be used to produce a wide variety of graphics displays. This project provides a few more suggestions, particularly for computers which have a printer. The suggestions are presented by means of an example, the picture *Reflections* shown in figure 13.8.

To accommodate the width of a typical printer, the picture is 80 characters wide and 40 lines deep. The picture is produced one line at a time, the array **S$(80)** storing the characters to be printed in the line.

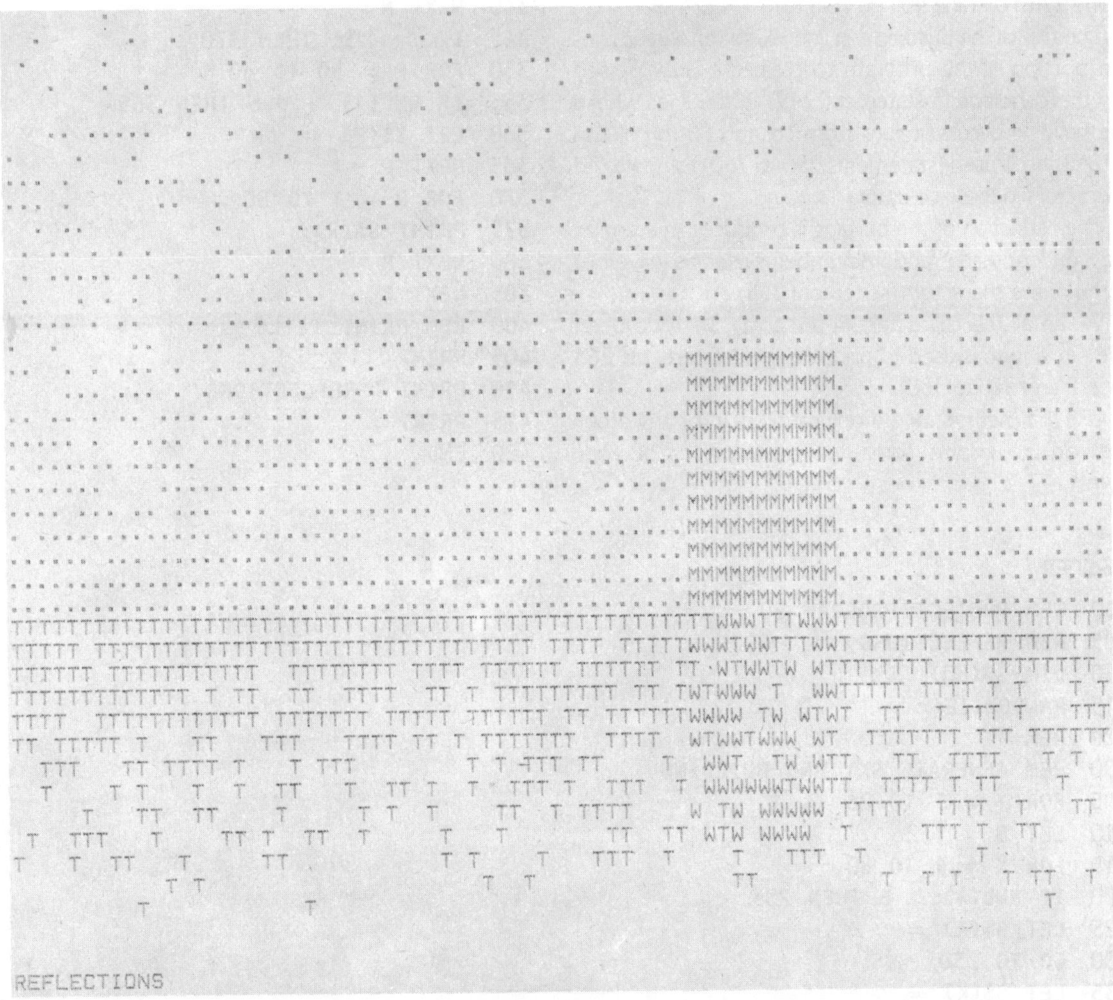

Figure 13.8   Reflections

The program which produced the picture *Reflections* is shown below. Is overall steps are as follows:

The horizon is between lines 26 and 27, counting from the top. A loop counter **Y** works down the first 26 lines, while counter **Z** covers lines 27 to 40.

The backgrounds are generated by random numbers. The sky is either a space or a dot, with the probability of a dot going from 1/26 at the top to 1 in line 26. The achieve this, a variable **B** has the value Y/26. (**B** is 1/26 in line 1 and 26/26 = 1 in line 26.) A counter **K** works across each line, and for each character position, a random number between 0 and 1 is compared with **B** (statement 210). If it is greater than **B**, the character is a blank; otherwise it is a dot.

The water background uses a similar method, with the probability of the character being a T going from 1 in line 27 to 0 in line 40.

The top of the building is in line 16, so for earlier lines the portion of the program to creater it is by passed (by the condition in statement 245). In the lines where the building occurs, it runs from column 50 to column 60. A loop is used (statements 250 to 260) to make the characters in these columns M's.

The reflection of the building is produced in a similar way, except that a random number is used to leave out some of the characters (statement 355).

When all the characters in the array **S$** have been filled in, a loop is used to print the line (statements 265 to 275 and 370 to 380).

Use this method, or a modification of it (or any other method) to inspire computer masterpieces of your own.

```
250  FOR L = 50 TO 60
255  LET S$(L) = "M"
260  NEXT L
265  FOR M = 1 TO 80
270  PRINT S$(M);
275  NEXT M
277  PRINT
280  NEXT Y
300  REM GENERATE WATER AND REFLECTION
305  FOR Z = 27 TO 40
310  LET B = (40-Z)/13
315  FOR N = 1 TO 80
320  IF RND(1) > B THEN 335
325  LET S$(N) = "T"
330  GO TO 340
335  LET S$(N) = "  "
340  NEXT N
345  IF Z > 36 THEN 370
350  FOR P = 50 TO 60
355  IF RND(1) > 0.6 THEN 365
360  LET S$(P) = "W"
365  NEXT P
370  FOR R = 1 TO 80
375  PRINT S$(R);
380  NEXT R
385  NEXT Z
400  REM PRINT TITLE
405  PRINT
410  PRINT "REFLECTIONS"
415  PRINT
420  END
```

Program

```
100  REM PROJECT PROGRAM 20
105  REM REFLECTIONS
110  DIM S$(80)
115  RANDOMIZE
120  REM
200  REM GENERATE SKY AND BUILDING
205  FOR Y = 1 TO 26
210  LET B = Y/26
215  FOR K = 1 TO 80
220  IF RND(1) > B THEN 235
225  LET S$(K) = "."
230  GO TO 230
235  LET S$(K) = "  "
240  NEXT K
245  IF Y < 16 THEN 265
```

14

Revision Exercise

All the questions in this exercise are taken from past Examination Papers in Computer Studies at CSE or O-level. A list of abbreviations of the names of the Examination Boards is shown below. These abbreviations are used to identify the questions in the exercise.

Examination Boards which have supplied Past Examination Papers are as follows:

Abbreviation   Name
O-level
AEB   Associated Examining Board
JMB   Joint Matriculation Board
OLE   Oxford Delegacy of Local Examinations
SUJB   Southern Universities' Joint Board
UCLES   Universities of Cambridge Local Examination Syndicate
UL   University of London
WJEC   Welsh Joint Education Committee (CSE and O-Level)

CSE
ALSEB   Associated Lancashire Schools Examining Board
EAEB   East Anglian Examination Board
EMREB   East Midlands Regional Examination Board
LREB   London Regional Examining Board
NWREB   North-West Regional Examinations Board
SEREB   South-East Regional Examinations Board
SREB   Southern Regional Examinations Board
SWEB   South Western Examinations Board
WMEB   The West Midlands Examinations Board
YREB   Yorkshire Regional Examinations Board

1 Work through the flowchart in figure 14.1 using the data given, showing the contents of the stores in a copy of the table provided. Write the results in the output blank.

ALSEB 78

2 In an imaginary country the amount of income tax a man pays in a year is worked out using the information and calculations shown in the flowchart (figure 14.2). The data input are: salary (S); personal code (A) = 1 for single man and 2 for a married man; number of children less than 11 years (B); number of children ages 11 years or over (C); the amount of mortgage interest paid by a man buying his own house (M).
   a) (i) To what allowance is a single man who has no mortgage entitled?
      (ii) How much tax would this man pay if his annual income was 2400?
   b) What is the tax paid by a married man earning 6000 who has four children (ages 13, 9, 7 and 5) and who pays 750 per year mortgage interest?
   c) The government decide that everybody must pay more tax. Which single box in the flowchart would you alter? How would you alter it?
   d) In order to encourage people to have more children the government have decided that those married men who have 5 or more children shall not pay any income tax. In order to do this is it necessary to add some extra boxes to the flowchart. Which boxes would you add, what would be written in them, and where would you put them?

ALSEB 79

3 a) You have a series of records whose fields contain the following information: nationality; sex; age; height; hair colour; name and address. From these records draw up a flow chart to print out a list of the names and addresses of British men 25 years old, over 5ft 8 inches tall and with fair hair.
   b) Carefully read through the flowchart (figure 14.3) and then draw up the results of dry running it with the given data.

ALSEB 80

4 Your Computer Studies group has decided to run a project to find which type of television programme (i.e. sport, plays, etc) is most popular.

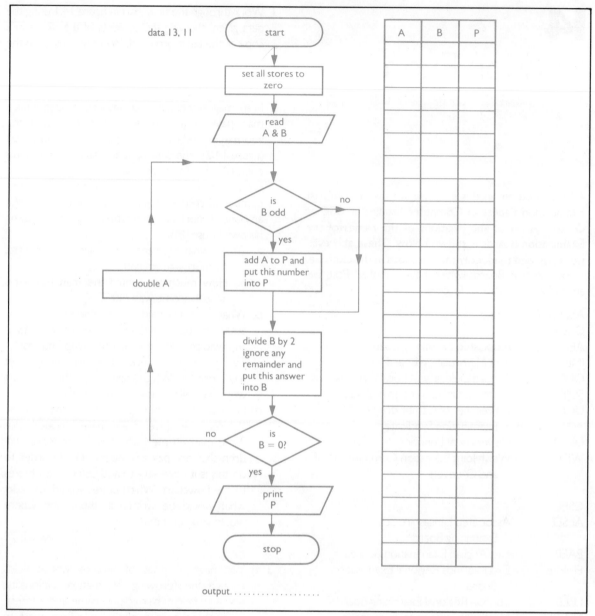

data 13, 11

start

set all stores to zero

read A & B

is B odd — no

yes

add A to P and put this number into P

double A

divide B by 2 ignore any remainder and put this answer into B

no — is B = 0?

yes

print P

stop

output. . . . .

A	B	P

Figure 14.1 Diagram for exercise 14, question 1

a) Design a questionnaire to obtain the information you require.
b) Draw a flowchart and give any other documentation which you feel is necessary in preparation for writing your program. (The actual program is NOT required).

ALSEB 81

5 Complete the diagram in figure 14.4 which gives an algorithm for using a television set by writing in appropriate phrases chosen from the list

Stop	Switch on	Change channel
Start	Programme finished?	Watch programme
Switch off	TV switched on?	Correct channel?
	Another programme?	

EAEB 80

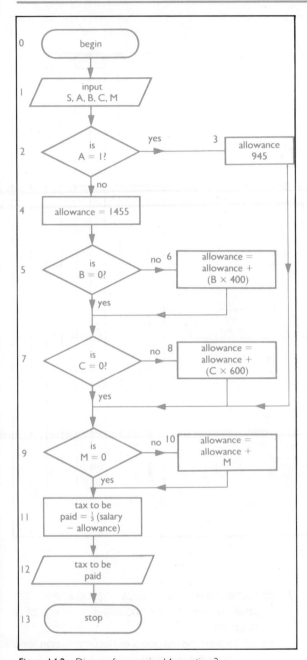

Figure 14.2   Diagram for exercise 14, question 2

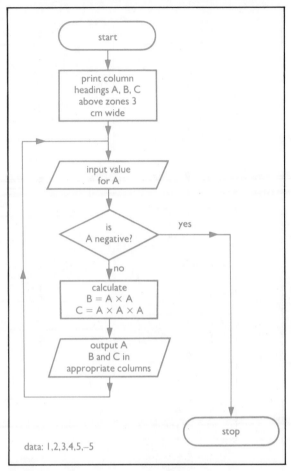

data: 1,2,3,4,5,–5

Figure 14.3   Diagram for exercise 14, question 3

6 The instruction **VAL(CHAR)** converts a numeric character in **CHAR** to its face value. It also converts the character X to 10. Thus if **CHAR** CHAR holds the character 2 then **VAL(CHAR)** = 2.

The instruction **INT** truncates values to integers. Thus **INT(7.76)** = 7 and **INT(13/5)** = 2.

The flowchart in figure 14.5 gives a method of testing strings. The strings consist of either five

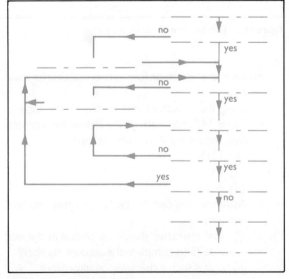

Figure 14.4   Diagram for exercise 14, question 5

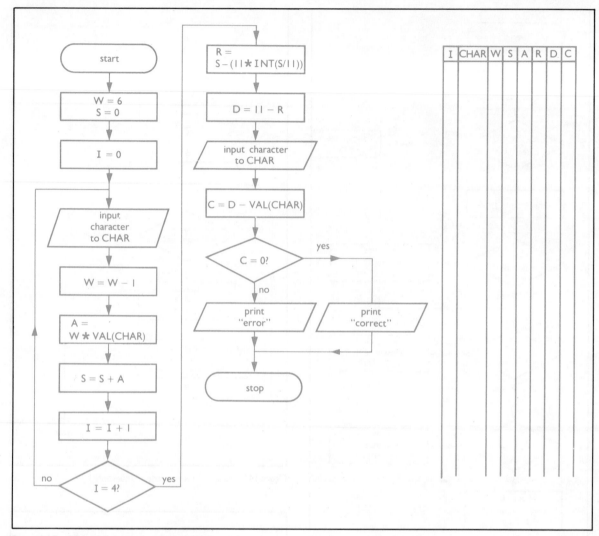

Figure 14.5   Diagram for exercise 14, question 6

numeric characters or four numeric characters and an X.

a) Using the flowchart and a copy of the table in figure 14.5 test each string below for correctness and state if it is correct or incorrect.
   (i) 22152
   (ii) 04166
   (iii) 8400X

b) Assuming a string to be a customer account number,
   (i) what character should be placed at the end of 3675 to complete the account number?
   (ii) what is such a character usually called?

EAEB 81

7 a) Outline the various steps a programmer can take to ensure the successful working of a program.
   b) (i) Explain the purposes of documentation for a computer program.
      (ii) Outline the main features that should appear in any documentation.

EMREB 81

8 a) (i) Explain the term 'rogue value'.
      (ii) Why are 'rogue values' used?
   b) Draw a flowchart to find and output the largest of a set of positive numbers, terminated by a negative number. Produce a trace table for your

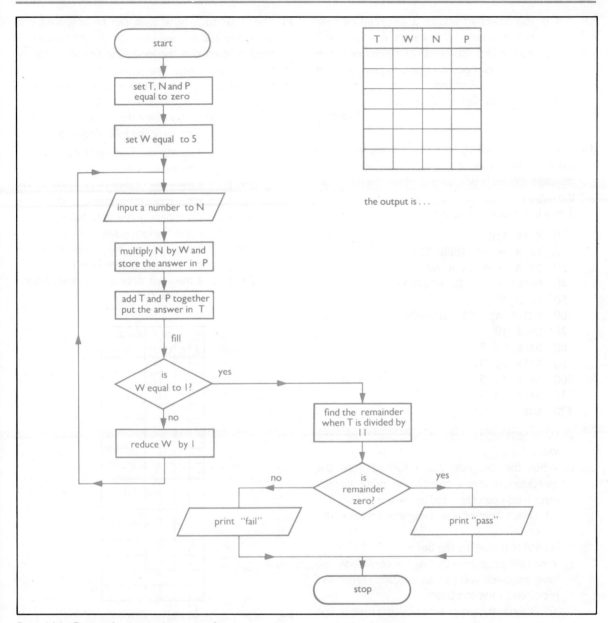

Figure 14.6 Diagram for exercise 14, question 9

flowchart using the sequence of numbers 4, 3, 1, 5, 2, −99 as your data.

EMREB 81

9 a) Dry run the flowchart (figure 14.6) using the numbers 2, 1, 0, 3 and 2 as data.

Complete one row of a copy of the table each time you pass the point labelled FILL. Write down the output beneath the table.

b) A company uses five-digit codes for its employee numbers (for example: 21032).

The flowchart (figure 14.6) can be used to validate these codes. This is done by using the five digits of the code as data (for example: to validate the code 21032 the data would be 2, 1, 0, 3, 2).

(i) Explain what is meant by 'validate'.

(ii) Why is data validation necessary?

(iii) The flowchart applies a weighted modulo 11 test to five-digit numbers. If 3, 1, 6 and 2 are the first four digits of a number which passes this modulo 11 test, explain how the last digit is calculated.

The last digit should be ___.

LREB 80

10 A student was asked to write a program which would accept pairs of numbers and print out a message for each pair stating which number was the bigger.

This is the student's program:

```
10   READ A;B
20   IF A = -1 THEN 120
30   IF A > B THEN 60
40   PRINT B;  " IS BIGGER"
50   GOTO 10
60   PRINT A;  " IS BIGGER"
70   GOTO 10
80   DATA 5, 7
90   DATA 7, 5
100  DATA 3, 3
110  DATA -1
120  END
```

a) What technique has the student used to stop the loop?

b) When the program was returned from the computer centre a compilation error (syntax error) had been reported by the computer.

  (i) Which line of the program contains this error?

  (ii) What should the line be?

c) When the program including the correction you have suggested was run, an execution error was reported by the computer.

  (i) Dry run the program to discover which line has caused the error.

  (ii) Write down any changes which are needed to correct this error.

d) When the program including both your suggested corrections was run again, a logical error occurred.

  (i) What is meant by a logical error?

  (ii) Dry run the program to discover which line has caused the error.

  (iii) Write down any changes which are needed to correct this error.

LREB 81

11 The door to a bank vault can be unlocked only when the alarm is switched off. At least two keys must be turned in the lock. One of these must be the manager's key. The deputy manager and the chief cashier each have a key as well. At least one of these must also be turned in the lock.

a) Complete a copy of the truth table in figure 14.7 for this situation using the following codes.

A = 1   if the alarm is switched ON. (otherwise A = 0)

C = 1   if the chief cashier has turned his key in the lock. (otherwise C = 0)

D = 1   if the deputy manager has turned his key in the lock. (otherwise D = 0)

M = 1   if the manager has turned his key in the lock. (otherwise M = 0)

V = 1   if the vault door is unlocked. (otherwise V = 0)

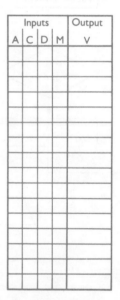

Figure 14.7   Diagram for exercise 14, question 11

b) Draw a logic network for operating the vault door (using inputs A, C, D, M and producing output V).

c) Copy and complete the following BASIC program so that it outputs the correct value of V (you may assume that each value input will be either 0 or 1).

```
10   INPUT A, C, D, M
20   IF A <> 0 THEN _____
30   IF M <> 0 THEN _____
```

```
40  IF C = 1 THEN _____
50  IF D = 1 THEN _____
60  LET V = 0
70  GOTO 90
80  LET V = 1
90  PRINT V
100 STOP
110 END
```

NREB 81

12 The flowcharting instructions in figure 14.8 placed in the correct order would produce an output of 1, 3, 6, 10, 15. There is one instruction too many.
 a) Design a flowchart using all instructions except one to produce the required outputs.
 b) Copy and complete the table below to show that the required output is produced.

A	B	OUTPUT A

NWREB 79

13 a) Study carefully the flowchart in figure 14.9. The flowchart is intended to produce the outputs 1, 4, 9, 16, 25, 36, 49, 64, 81. However, errors have been made in its construction.
   (i) What output would be obtained from the flowchart as shown?

(ii) Redraw the flowchart to produce the required output.
 b) Using the logic system in figure 14.9, construct a truth table showing all possible outputs for A, B, C. Indicate, in columns X and Y, all possible outputs.

NWREB 80

14 The flowchart in figure 14.10 shows a game between two players. The game consists of throwing two pennies.
 a) Study the flowchart and write down the rules of the game.
 b) Using the flowchart above as a guide, construct a new flowchart for a game between two players in which the game can be won using the rules below.

Rules
The first player throws a die and tosses a coin. If the die gives an even number or the coin is a head then the player wins, otherwise the next player takes his turn, and so on, until the game is won.

NWREB 81

15 Using the information given below draw a flowchart to find out if a patient should be charged for medicines prescribed by a doctor:
  If patient is aged under 16 — No charge.
  If patient is a woman aged over 59 — No charge.
  If patient is a man over 64 — No charge.
  All other patients must pay for their medicines.

SEREB 78

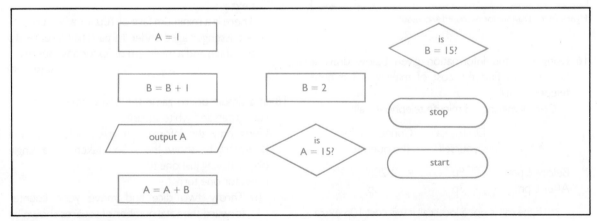

Figure 14.8 Diagram for exercise 14, question 12

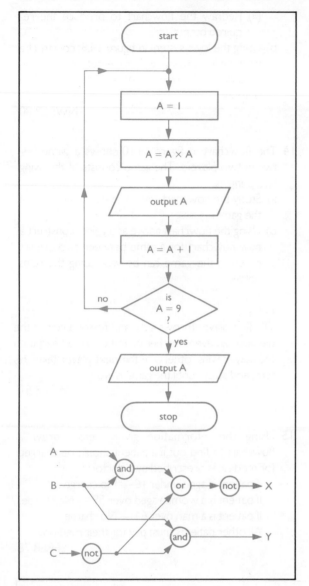

Figure 14.9 Diagram for exercise 14, question 13

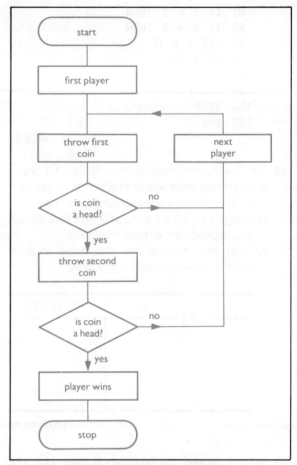

Figure 14.10 Diagram for exercise 14, question 14

16 Using only the information given below draw a flowchart to find the cost of making a 3 minute telephone call.

Cost of making a 3 minute telephone call

	Dialling call yourself	Connected by the operator
Before 6 pm	9p	20p
After 6 pm	3p	6p

If the call is not a local call it will cost 10p extra.

SEREB 79 II

17 Using only the information given below draw a flowchart to find the cost of making a bus journey.

A passenger aged 60 or over travels free.

The fare is calculated at the rate of 2p per stage. (A stage is a journey from one bus stop to the next.)

There is a minimum fare of 10p for any journey.

A passenger aged under 14 pays half fare, i.e. 1p per stage and a minimum of 5p for any journey.

SEREB 80

18 In a simple board game the board consists of only red, green and white squares.

Using only the information given below draw a flowchart to show the action taken by a single player having just one turn.

Rules for one turn

(i) Throw two dice and move your counter forward the total number of squares shown by both dice.

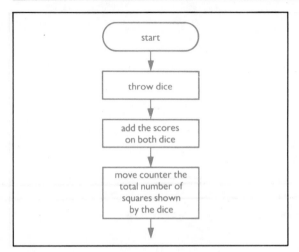

Figure 14.11   Diagram for exercise 14, question 18

(ii) Each time your counter ends up on a red square, move it back 2 squares.
(iii) Each time your counter ends up on a green square move it forward 2 squares.
(iv) Your turn only finishes when the counter ends up on a white square unless you threw 12, in which case you must throw the dice again.

Begin your flowchart with the boxes shown in figure 14.11.

SEREB 81

19 Draw a flowchart which illustrates how to make a telephone call. Below, to help you, are listed the tones with their meanings.
    Dialling tone : a continuous purring.
    Ringing tone : a repeated burr-burr.
    Engaged tone : a repeated single note.
    Number unobtainable : a steady high note.

SREB 79

20 a) Dry run the flow diagram in figure 14.12 by filling in a copy of the table below. The test data, which represents the lengths of sides of triangles is 2, 2, 1; 3, 4, 5; 2, 3, 4.

C	X	Y	Z	A	A^2	$X^2+Y^2+Z^2$	PRINT OUT

b) The three sets of data items are insufficient to test the flow diagram fully. Suggest additional numbers which complete the testing.
c) What is the section above the dotted line on the flow diagram designed to do?

SREB 79

21 What is a subroutine and why is it used? (Illustrate your answer with either a diagram or a flowchart or a simple program.)
    What is the difference between a user-written subroutine and a standard function?

SREB 80

22 Draw a flowchart to represent the following statement about the cost of insurance for a motorbike.

'The cost of annual insurance for a motorbike will be £15 for full insurance cover or £10 otherwise. If the driver has passed the driving test and is under 25 years of age, the cost will be increased by £5. If the driver has not passed the driving test and is under 25 years of age, the cost will be increased by £10. If the driver has had an accident during the last 3 years, a further £5 is added to the cost of insurance.'

SREB 81

23 a) The input to a program is a series of numbers representing hours worked by a firm's employees. For each input the program is to calculate and output the wages at a basic wage rate of 150p per hour. For example, for input 42 the wage would be calculated from 42 × 150p. The data is to be terminated by a negative number.
    Draw a flow diagram for this program.
    b) Draw another flow diagram to show how your program in part (a) could allow for overtime according to the following rules.
    Hours worked over 40 but less than 48: paid at 250p per hour.
    Hours worked over 48: paid at 350p per hour.
    E.g., three employees working 38, 45 and 52 hours would earn:
        (i) (38 × 150)p
       (ii) (40 × 150) + (5 × 250)p
      (iii) (40 × 150) + (8 × 350)p

SWREB 80

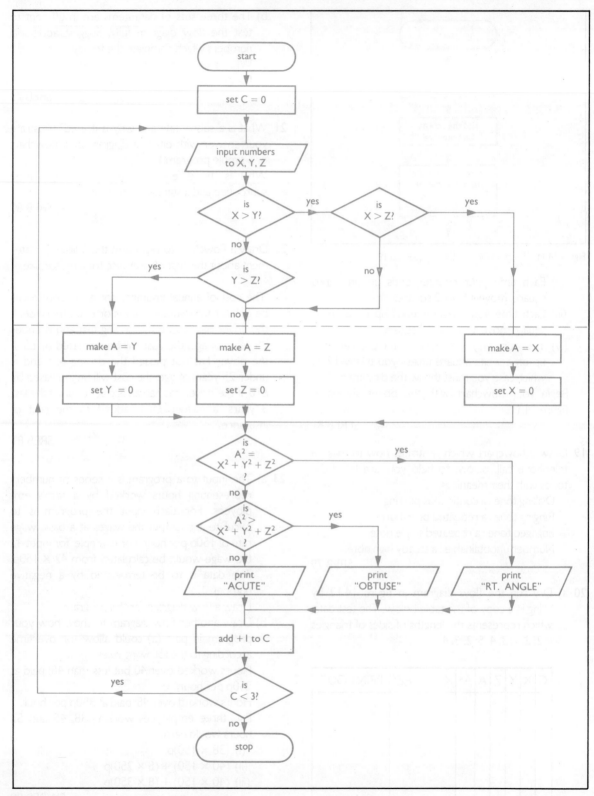

Figure 14.12 Diagram for exercise 14, question 20

24 A warehouse uses a computer in its stock-control system. The record for each item shows its code number and the quantity of that item in the warehouse.

For example, if the first two records read from the file were 1033, 1000 and 4166, 200, this would show that there were 1000 items with code number 1033 and 200 items with code number 4166 in stock in the warehouse.

When a customer orders goods from the warehouse, his order is input as two numbers:
(i) the code number of the item he wants to buy.
(ii) the quantity of that item he needs.
A series of orders from a customer is terminated by a negative code number.
Output is to be a table under headings:

Item code no.	Quantity ordered	Quantity sold	Quantity left in stock

Note: (i) the 'quantity left in stock' can never be negative so the program must test whether the quantity which a customer orders is greater than the quantity stocked in the warehouse.
(ii) The file must be kept up to date so that when stock is sold, the quantity left in the warehouse must be output to the file.
(iii) You need not make allowance for the input code number not being present in the file.
a) If the first two records in the file are as described above and the data sets (i) 1033, 600 and (ii) 4166, 400 are input, what would be the outputs?
b) Draw a flow diagram for this system.

SWREB 80

25 Consider the flowchart in figure 14.13.
a) Dry run this flowchart for the data sets:
(i) 3, 1, 5, 2
(ii) 3, 1, 6, 2
b) Using any high-level language, write a program from the above flowchart.
c) Modify your program to repeat the process for 12 data sets (this modification should take the form of replacement and insertion lines).

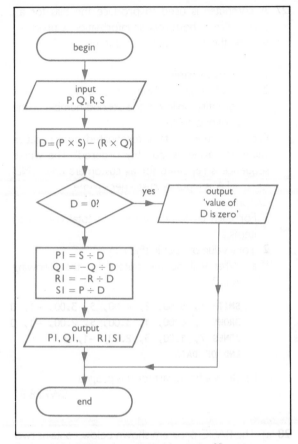

Figure 14.13 Diagram for exercise 14, question 25

d) What would happen if the decision D = 0? was left out and a data set which made D = 0 was input?

SWREB 80

26 The approximate time T taken for the swing of a pendulum can be found using the formula

$$T = 0.2\sqrt{L}$$

where T is the time in seconds and L is the length of the pendulum in centimetres.
a) Draw a flowchart for a program to input a value of L and output a value of T.
b) A computer is to be used to output:
(i) a table of values of L and T for values of L from 50 cm to 150 cm in steps of 5 cm,
(ii) the value of L which produces a value of T closest to 2 seconds.
Draw a flowchart for this program.

SWREB 81

27 A computer is used to produce the bills for a certain firm. The following information is processed and the bills produced as output.

Input:

1 Customer's name.
2 A series of pairs of numbers (the first number is the quantity ordered; the second number is the price of one item).

Each customer's data is terminated by a negative value appearing as 'quantity ordered'. The whole sequence is repeated for all customers until 'END OF DATA' is input as 'customer's name'.

Output:

1 For each customer, name and total cost of all items.
2 Total value of sales in that run.

 a) What will be the output for the following input?

```
SMITH 6, 5.00, 2, 4.00, 5, 3.00, -1, 0
BROWN 2, 6.00, 1, 3.00, 5, 2.00, -1, 0
JONES 7, 1.00, 3, 2.00, -1, 0
END OF DATA
```

 b) Draw a flowchart for this program.

SWREB 81

28 a) The BASIC program shown below contains two compilation and two execution errors. Copy the program, (i) correcting the lines with compilation errors, and (ii) inserting the lines to overcome the execution errors.

```
10   REM MULTIPLICATION TABLE PROGRAM
20   READ N
30   FOR C = 1 TO 12
40   P(C) = C x N
50   PRINT C, "X", N, "=" P(C)
60   NEXT C
999  END
```

 b) The BASIC program shown below involves subroutines.

```
10   REM PROGRAM USING SUBROUTINES
20   READ A, B, C
30   DATA 28, 6, 2
40   GOSUB 200
50   PRINT A, B, R
60   LET A = R
70   LET B = C
80   GOSUB 200
```

```
90   PRINT A, B, R
100  STOP
200  LET X = A/B
210  LET Y = INT(X)
220  LET Z = Y*B
230  LET R = A-Z
240  RETURN
999  END
```

(Note – function **INT** returns the next integer below X.)

 (i) What are the outputs for this data?
 (ii) Explain why this is an example showing poor use of subroutines.
 (iii) Rewrite the programs so that your program does the same job without using subroutines.

SWREB 81

29 a) Use the extra boxes given to complete the flowchart in figure 14.14 so that it describes the following program.

The input to the program is the price of an item costing less than 50p. The output gives the number of coins and their value which are to be given in change for a 50p piece. The program makes sure that the number of coins given in change is the smallest possible. All prices are in whole numbers of pence and $\frac{1}{2}$p coins are not used.

 b) How would you alter the program so that it would give the correct change when less than 50p but more than the cost was offered?

WMEB 78

30 When a problem has to be solved using a computer there are several stages that the solution must pass through. Figure 14.15 shows the first two boxes and the last two boxes of a flowchart describing these stages. Complete the flowchart to show the stages which have been missed out. Remember that during the development of a successful program several tests have to be made. Include details of these tests in your flowchart.

WMEB 78

31 There are N numbers each having a value less than 999 and they are stored in cells X_1, X_2, X_3, ... X_N. An algorithm copies these numbers into cells Y_1, Y_2, Y_3 ... Y_N in the following way.

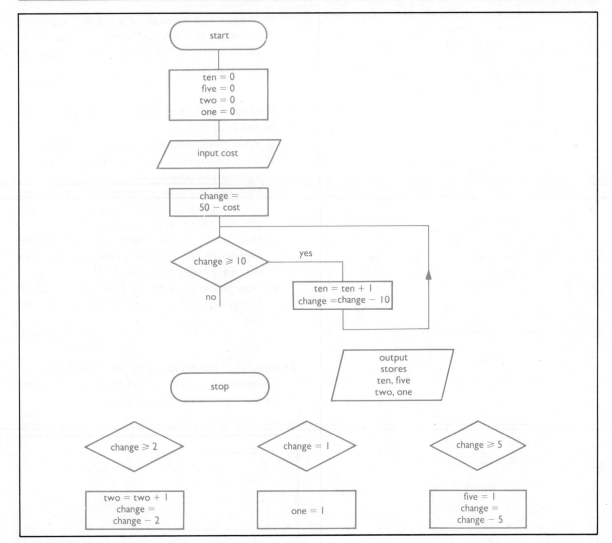

Figure 14.14   Diagram for exercise 14, question 29

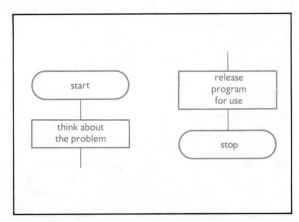

Figure 14.15   Diagram for exercise 14, question 30

The algorithm looks through the list of numbers in cells $X_1 \ldots X_3$ and picks out the smallest number. It writes this number into Y_1.

Then it looks through the list again and finds the next smallest number which it writes to Y_2.

The algorithm continues to look through the list. Each time it finds the smallest remaining number and writes it to the next position in the list $Y_1 \ldots Y_N$.

When all the numbers have been moved from $X_1 \ldots X_N$ into $Y_1 \ldots Y_N$ the algorithm is stopped.

A flowchart for this algorithm is shown in figure 14.16. Notice that the boxes have been labelled BOX 1 to BOX 8.

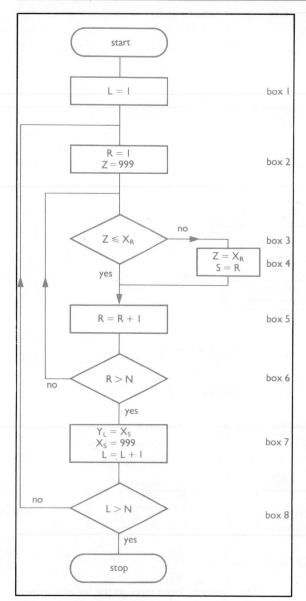

Figure 14.16   Diagram for exercise 14, question 31

a) When the algorithm stops what can you say about the order of the numbers in $Y_1 \dots Y_N$?

b) What is the purpose of the small loop of constructions which uses BOX 3, BOX 4, BOX 5 and BOX 6?

c) Explain carefully why the instruction $X_8 = 999$ in BOX 7 is necessary.

d) Describe exactly how the algorithm knows when all the numbers have been moved from $X_1 \dots X_N$ into $Y_1 \dots Y_N$.

e) Mention one example of a practical application in which this kind of operation has to be performed on a file and say why it is necessary in this particular case.

WMEB 79

32 Read the flowchart in figure 14.17 and then answer the following questions.

a) What causes the algorithm to leave the loop?

b) Describe carefully what is printed when the algorithm is obeyed.

c) How would you alter the flowchart so that the number of non-negative numbers in the input data was printed after the value of SUM?

d) How would you alter the flowchart so that the average of the positive numbers in the input data was printed instead of SUM?

e) How would you alter the flowchart so that the largest of the input numbers was also printed out?

WMEB 79

33 Rearrange boxes in figure 14.18 and draw in connecting lines with arrows to build a flowchart for sorting numbers into ascending order. .

WMEB 80

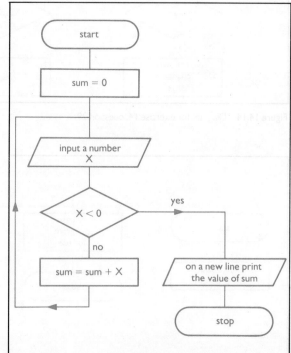

Figure 14.17   Diagram for exercise 14, question 32

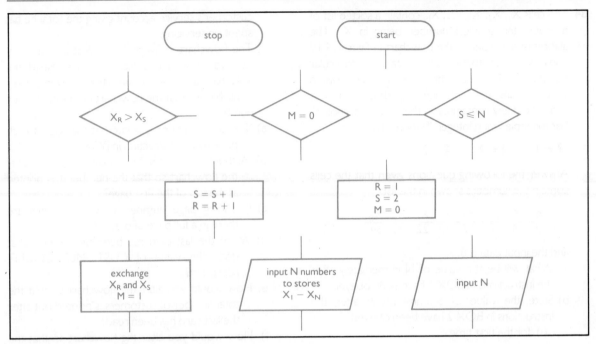

Figure 14.18   Diagram for exercise 14, question 33

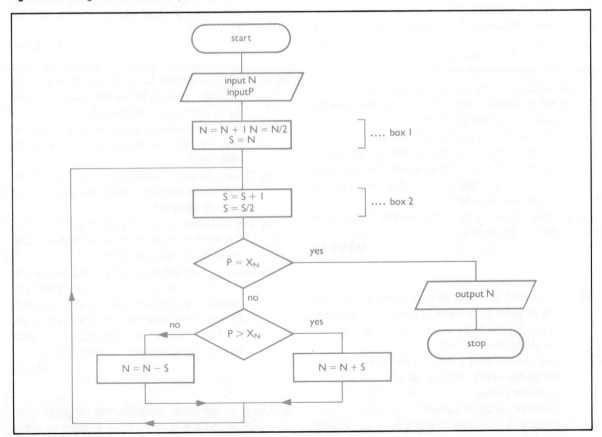

Figure 14.19   Diagram for exercise 14, question 34

34 The cells $X_1, X_2, X_3, \ldots, X_N$ contain a sorted list of numbers the smallest number being in X_1. The algorithm described in the flowchart in figure 14.19 finds which of these cells contains a particular number P. The algorithm uses integer division which means that whenever a division sum is carried out any remainder in the answer is ignored. For example when integer division is used

$$\frac{3}{2} = 1, \qquad \frac{4}{2} = 2, \qquad \frac{5}{2} = 2$$

Answer the following questions given that the cells contain the numbers shown in this list:

X_1	X_2	X_3	X_4	X_5	X_6	X_7	X_8
2	4	7	17	20	22	26	34

and the input data is 8, 7.
a) What will be the value of N immediately after the instructions in BOX 1 have been obeyed?
b) State the value of S immediately after the instructions in BOX 2 have been obeyed
   (i) for the first time
   (ii) for the second time
   (iii) for the third time.
c) State the value of N immediately before BOX 2 is entered
   (i) for the second time
   (ii) for the third time.
d) What will be the output from the algorithm?
e) What special name is given to the process described by this algorithm?
f) This particular algorithm will only work correctly if the smallest number in the list of sorted numbers is in X_1. How would the flowchart have to be changed if the numbers were sorted in the reverse order?
g) What would happen if the number P was not in the list of numbers?

WMEB 80

35 A firm which sells and services washing machines wants to know how much is spent by customers who pay for machines to be serviced but do not buy anything from the firm.
   The firm maintains a card file. For each customer, the file has a card which contains:
   customer's name,
   customer's account number,
   customer's sales account giving the total value of purchases,

customer's service account giving the total he has spent on servicing.
   The flowchart in figure 14.20 illustrates a program to print details from this file. Read the flowchart and then answer the following questions. Notice that the flowchart boxes have been numbered.
a) The page number is printed at the top of each page by the instruction in BOX 3.
b) Without changing BOX 2, how could you alter the flowchart so that the number 1 is printed at the top of the first page?
c) Excluding page number, how many lines are there in a full page of output?
d) When the last card has been processed, what does the value of CUSTOMER COUNT represent?
e) How would you alter the flowchart so that the total number of customers is printed out after the last card has been read?
f) How would you alter the flowchart so that the average amount spent by all customers on servicing is printed out after the last card has been read?

WMEB 81

36 a) Draw a flowchart to input two numbers into locations A and B, to find their sum and store it in S, and to output the result.
b) Why is it useful to use a loop when it is required that the sum of many numbers is to be calculated?
c) Draw a flowchart which uses a loop to find the sum of ten numbers, places the sum in S and outputs the result.
d) The flowchart used in (c) could not be used if the number of numbers is not known. State the method used in this case.
e) Draw a flowchart which uses a loop to find the sum of a set of numbers when the quantity of numbers is unknown and it is also necessary to determine how many numbers are in the set. Store the sum in S and output the result and also the quantity of numbers in the set.

YREB 78

37 Using a high-level programming language with which you are familiar, write sections of programs to perform the operations indicated below.

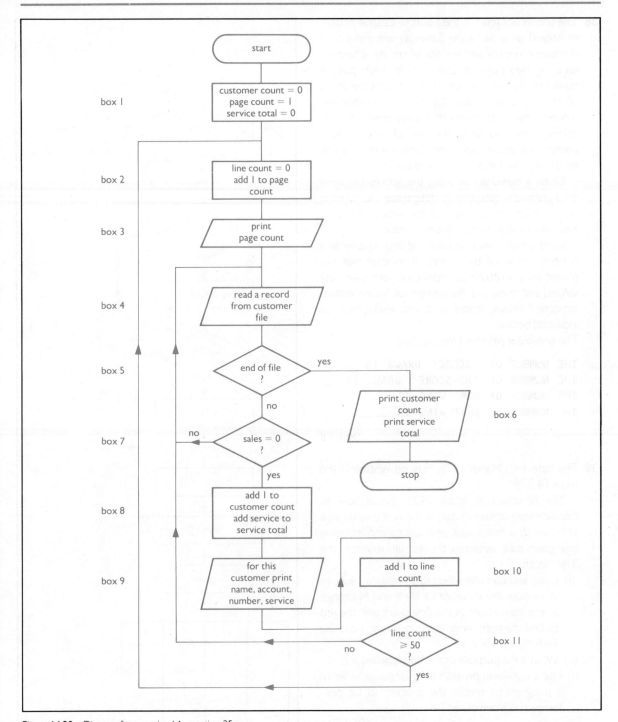

Figure 14.20 Diagram for exercise 14, question 35

a) Place the number 82.7 in location X.
b) Interchange the contents of locations P and Q.
c) If the contents of A are larger than 1000, jump to the end of the program.

d) When X lies between −5 and +5, output the message 'VALUE WITHIN RANGE'; otherwise jump to the end of the program.

YREB 78

38 The scores obtained in the Football League matches played on a particular Saturday are input to a computer in pairs and the list of results is terminated by two negative numbers. In each pair of numbers the first number given indicates the score of the home team and the second number the score of their opponents (the away team). If both teams score the same number of goals, this is known as a 'score' draw, and if there is no score at all, this is known as a 'no-score' draw.

Draw a flowchart to input the scores obtained on a particular Saturday to determine the number of 'score' draws, 'no-score' draws, home wins and away wins and to output this information.

Using a high-level programming language, write a program to input the scores of football matches played on a particular Saturday (use your own data values) and to output the number of 'score' draws, 'no-score' draws, home wins and away wins, as indicated below.

The computer print-out should state:

```
THE NUMBER OF 'SCORE' DRAWS IS _____
THE NUMBER OF 'NO-SCORE' DRAWS IS ___
THE NUMBER OF HOME WINS IS _____
THE NUMBER OF AWAY WINS IS _____
```

YREB 78

39 The date 14th March 1978, may be written in the form 14.3.78.

The flowchart in figure 14.21 shows how to calculate the number of days in the first quarter of a year, which is not a leap year, up to and including any given date between the 1st January and the 31st March.

(i) Copy and complete the table in figure 14.21 to show how the values of D, M, Y and N change as the instructions in the flowchart are obeyed to find the number of days up to and including 14th March, 1978.

(ii) What is the purpose of the box labelled ★ ?

b) Use a high-level programming language to write a program to enable the process to be performed on a computer.

YREB 78 II

40 a) Two unequal numbers are stored in locations A and B.

The flowchart boxes in figure 14.22 can be linked to show the method used to arrange that

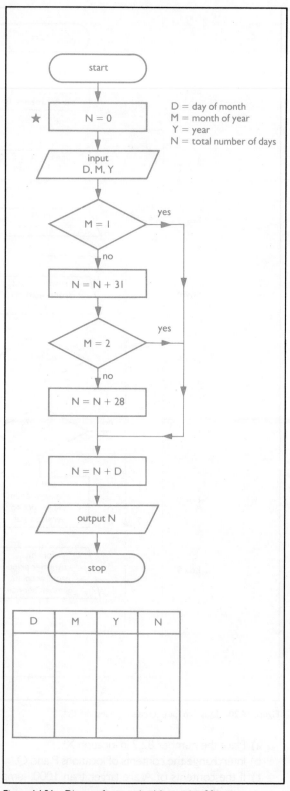

D = day of month
M = month of year
Y = year
N = total number of days

D	M	Y	N

Figure 14.21 Diagram for exercise 14, question 39

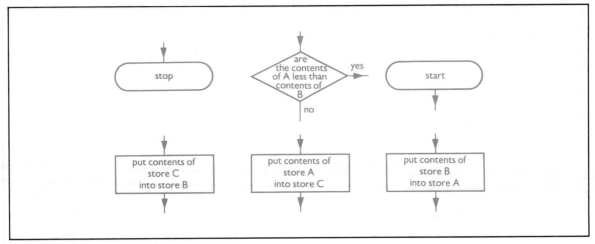

Figure 14.22 Diagram for exercise 14, question 40

the larger of the two numbers will be stored in location A and the smaller in B. Draw a flowchart which uses each of these boxes once only to provide a solution to the problem.

b) Write a program to input 5 pairs of unequal numbers and to output the larger of each pair followed by the smaller of each pair. If one pair of numbers input were 9 and 20, your output might be as follows:

`THE LARGER NUMBER IS 20 THE SMALLER NUMBER IS 9`

YREB 79

41 The flowchart in figure 14.23 is designed to be used with any numbers as input values. Look at the flowchart carefully, then answer the following questions.

  (i) Use the list of data values below to follow through the flowchart from START to STOP. Dry run the flowchart by copying and completing the table in figure 14.23.
  Data values
  5 −3 −18 0 80 −11 12 16 −1

  (ii) How many data values did you need to input?

  (iii) What were those values?

  (iv) What is the problem this flowchart is designed to solve?

  (v) What is the purpose of location P?

  (vi) What is the purpose of location M?

  (vii) Why is the instruction in box 2 used?

  (viii) If box 10 were removed, what effect would it have on the solution of the problem?

  (ix) Use a high-level language to write a program to enable the process shown in the flowchart to be performed on a computer.

YREB 79

42 At Highgrade Comprehensive School it is possible to take Computer Studies as an optional subject. When options were chosen too many pupils in the fourth year wanted to take the subject. It has been decided that two groups of pupils will be allowed to take Computer Studies. Fourth form pupils will be given an aptitude test to decide whether they will be allowed to do the subject, and, if so, in which group they will be placed.

Pupils who obtain marks below 30% in the aptitude test will not be allowed to take Computer Studies.

Pupils who obtain 60% or more will be placed in Group A and the remaining pupils in Group B.

A typical set of data is given below. The mark for each pupil is given as a percentage with the marks in pupil number order, i.e. pupil number 1 obtained 68%, pupil number 2 obtained 53%, pupil number 3 obtained 27% and so on.

68 53 27 63 20 61 29 21 14 59 95 89
32 54 68...87 47 25 31 3 101.

  (i) Why does the list finish with the number 101?

  (ii) Draw a flowchart to help in the writing of a program to print a list of pupils (using pupil numbers) and to indicate the group to which a

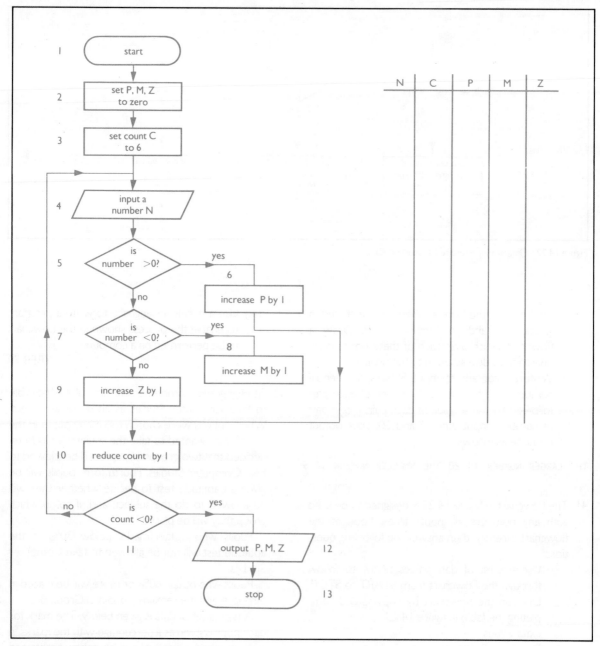

Figure 14.23   Diagram for exercise 14, question 41

pupil has been allocated if he or she has obtained 30% or more. Your output should be in the form below.

PUPIL NUMBER	MARK	GROUP
1	68	A
2	53	B
4	63	A

(iii) Use a high-level language to write this program.

YREB 79

43 A school has a class of 30 pupils. Each pupil takes six examinations and it has been decided that a computer will be used to read the six examination marks for each pupil and calculate that pupil's average mark.

The output will be in the following form:

EXAMINATION RESULTS FOR 30 PUPILS

PUPIL NUMBER	AVERAGE MARK
1	55.0
2	57.3

Using the flowchart in figure 14.24 write a computer program in a suitable high-level language, e.g. BASIC, to carry out the desired task.

Your program should include a DATA line for one pupil only.

YREB 80

44 Draw a flowchart and write a program in a suitable high-level language. e.g. BASIC, to read in a set of numbers greater than 0, terminated by a suitable rogue value, and print out with suitable text
a) the largest number,
b) the smallest number,
c) the number of numbers read in.
Include a suitable DATA line in your program.
Note that your program should work with any number of numbers read in.

YREB 80

45 On a certain bus route, tickets cost 5p, 10p, 15p, 20p, 25p, 30p, 35p, 40p, 45p and 50p. At the end of the day the serial number of the first 5p ticket sold that morning followed by the serial number of the first 5p ticket to be sold on the following day are used as data for a computer program. These numbers are followed by a similar pair of serial numbers for each of the other prices.

Draw a flowchart and write a program in a suitable high-level language, e.g. BASIC, which will accept the above data as input and which will output with suitable text
a) the number of tickets sold at each price,
b) the total amount of money collected during the day,
c) the total number of tickets sold.
Note that credit will be given to candidates who include a loop as part of their solutions.
In your program include specimen DATA for the 5p and 10p tickets only.

YREB 80

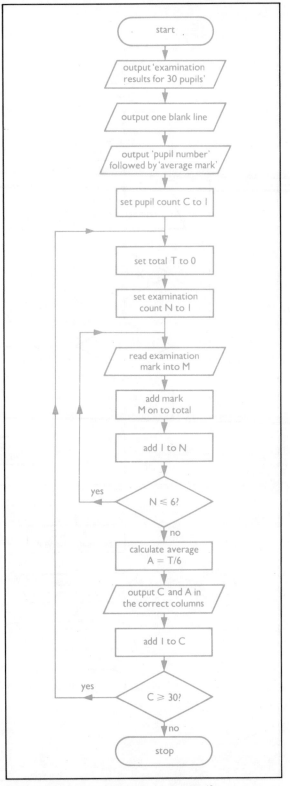

Figure 14.24 Diagram for exercise 14, question 43

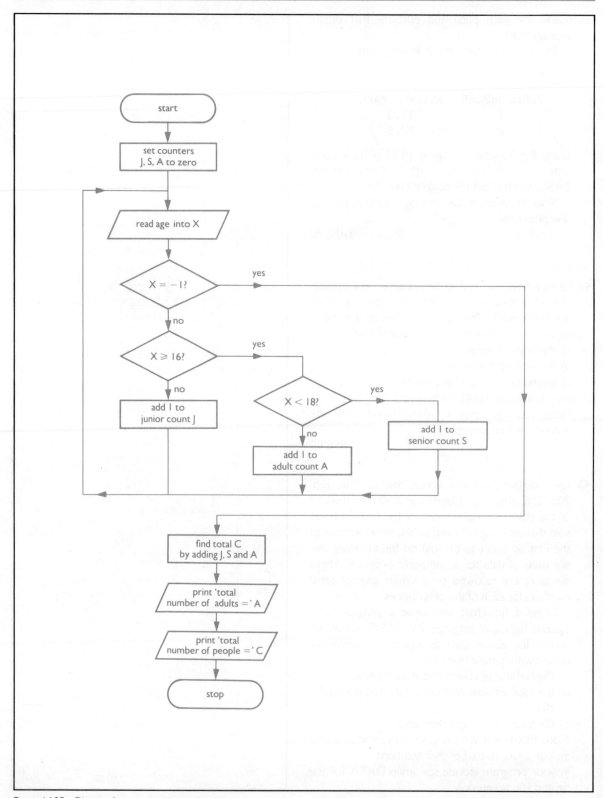

Figure 14.25 Diagram for exercise 14, question 46

46 The flowchart in figure 14.25 can be used to classify people into three age groups: juniors under 16 years old; seniors aged 16 or 17; adults aged 18 or over. The output is printed in the form

```
TOTAL NUMBER OF ADULTS =
TOTAL NUMBER OF PEOPLE =
```

Using the flowchart in figure 14.25, write a computer program in a suitable high-level language, e.g. BASIC, to carry out the desired task. Include a DATA line which will test each branch of the program.

YREB 81

47 An employer uses a computer to help him select and count suitable applicants for a post which he has advertised. He decides that the successful applicant will have an average of Grade 4 or better in five subjects taken at CSE level. There are 50 applicants for the post and if the sum of the applicant's grades is 20 or less, the name will be printed followed by an appropriate message, e.g.

JOHN SMITH IS SUITABLE

Draw a flowchart and use it to write a program in a suitable high-level language, e.g. BASIC, which will
  (i) read in the applicant's name followed by the five grades for that applicant,
 (ii) add the grades for that applicant,
(iii) if the sum of the grades is 20 or less, print the applicant's name and a suitable message, at the same time adding one to the total number of suitable applicants,
(iv) finally, print the number of suitable applicants with an appropriate message.

Include a suitable DATA line for one applicant in your program.

 NOTE that your program should include a loop allowing the data for 50 applicants to be processed.

YREB 81

48 A petrol station sells three grades of petrol as follows:
2 star at £1.25 per gallon,
3 star at £1.30 per gallon,
4 star at £1.35 per gallon.
After each sale of petrol the attendant types in the grade, followed by the number of gallons which he had just sold, e.g. a sale of 7 gallons of 2 star petrol would be entered as 2,7.

At the end of the day the computer should print out the total number of gallons sold and the total amount of money taken, with suitable messages.

 Draw a flowchart and from it write a program in a suitable high-level language, e.g. BASIC, which will accept as input a number of sales as described above, terminated by a suitable rogue value.

 Your program should
  (i) calculate the cost of each sale, adding it to the total amount,
 (ii) add the number of gallons sold at each sale to the total quantity sold,
(iii) upon receipt of the rogue value, print out the total number of gallons sold and the total amount of money taken together with suitable messages.

YREB 81

49 The discount prices of baked beans are worked out for a supermarket using the method shown in the flowchart in figure 14.26.

 Write a program in a high-level language to calculate the discount price and to output a table as shown below:

Baked Beans — cost per case	
Discount %	Cost £

WJEC 78 (CSE)

50 Three numbers are to be input as data to a program which is to be developed in stages as follows:

Stage 1 Check to see if the three numbers could be the lengths of the three sides of a triangle, that is, the sum of any two sides must be greater than the third side.

Stage 2 Calculate the length of the perimeter of the triangle and print out the answer in a suitable message.

Stage 3 Calculate the area of the triangle using the formula

$$\text{Area} = \sqrt{s(s-a)(s-b)(s-c)},$$

where a, b and c are the lengths of the three sides of the triangle and s is half the perimeter.

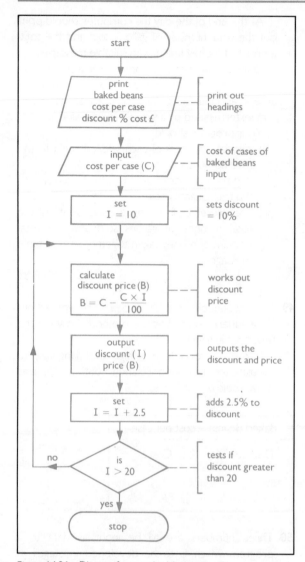

Figure 14.26 Diagram for exercise 14, question 49

Stage 4   Allow for the input of many sets of three numbers, this data to be terminated in a suitable manner.

By following through each stage, build up in stages a flowchart for the total program. Indicate clearly the development of the flowchart necessary at each stage.

AEB 78

51 A program has been written for an application in some subject at school. (You may choose the subject.) Outline the application you have chosen and then describe, in detail, the documentation which must accompany this program to make it usable by anybody with minimal computing knowledge.

AEB 78 1

52 Write a program in any high-level language for a Geography test as follows: the program, which must be interactive, is to ask for the capital city of the following countries, one at a time: France, Wales, Spain, Australia and Japan (capitals are Paris, Cardiff, Madrid, Canberra and Tokyo, respectively).

Two points are to be awarded for a correct answer and the program must state this. An incorrect answer must be stated as incorrect. After the last answer, the program must print out the score as a percentage.

AEB 78

53 The flowchart in figure 14.27 shows the necessary steps to solve a particular problem. Construct a 5-column table with each of the variables K, P, Q, R and S as a column heading.
a) Dry run the flowchart with $K = 12$, showing in your table the value of each variable at each step (working correct to 2 decimal places).
b) What is the name given to the type of process effected by the section of the flowchart labelled A—E?
c) What is the mathematical name given to the process as the value of P approaches that of R?
d) Give one advantage and one disadvantage of changing the check 'Is $S < 0.1$' to the check 'Is $S < 0.0001$'.
e) What would be the effect of changing the check to 'Is $S < 0.0001$' if $K = 16$?
f) What arithmetic problem does the flowchart solve?

AEB 78

54 Draw a flowchart to simulate the deal of a pack of 52 playing cards equally to four persons. (The flowchart should be programming language independent.)

AEB 79

55 Draw a flowchart to illustrate the process to read any amount of dollars and convert it into sterling. The output must be in pounds and pence as integer values ($£1 = \$1.94$).

AEB 79

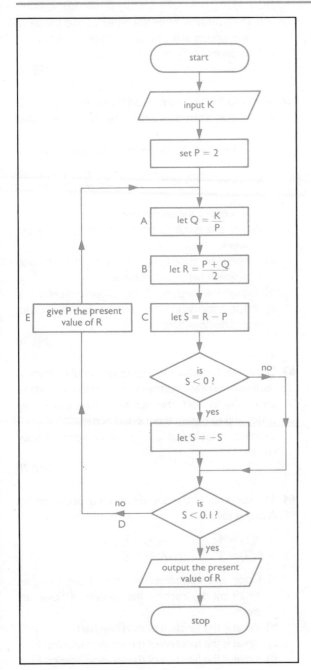

Figure 14.27   Diagram for exercise 14, question 53

56 It is required to calculate, and print out, the sum of the squares of all the odd numbers from P to Q inclusive (P < Q), where P and Q are both positive numbers.
a) Draw a programming language independent flowchart to solve the problem above.

b) Write a program in any high-level language to solve the problem.
c) Dry run your program using values of 3 and 9 for P and Q, respectively. Show the value of each variable used at each step of the program.
AEB 79

57 The following computer print-out, listing the numbers of the houses to which each paper is to be delivered, is designed to assist a newsagent in sorting his morning papers.

```
ROSE  GARDENS
FULCHESTER
MAIL 3,6,8,9
SUN 2,5,6,7,11
TELEGRAPH 1,4,9
GUARDIAN 3,8,12
EXPRESS 7,10
```

```
PRIMROSE  WALK
FULCHESTER
MAIL 2,3,5,6
SUN 4,7,9
TELEGRAPH 5,6,7
GUARDIAN 1,2,9,10
EXPRESS 1,8,9,12
```

a) Give two reasons why this information in this format is not very helpful to the paper boy.
b) Redraw the print-out in a format more useful to the paper boy explaining why you have used that format.
c) Using the data above describe an algorithm to convert the data into the new format suitable for the paper boy.
AEB 80

58 Your school introduces a new assessment scheme. For each subject studied the procedure is:
  (i) 3 assessments per term are given and a mark out of 10 awarded to each assessment,
  (ii) each term the 3 assessments are averaged,
  (iii) at the end of the year the best average over the three terms is printed on the pupil's report.
Consider a class of 20 pupils, studying several subjects. During one year each pupil will have 9 assessment marks for each subject. Draw that part of a flowchart (which must be language independent) that will read in the 9 marks for each pupil for one subject and will output

(i) the three termly averages for each pupil,

(ii) the best average for each pupil in this subject.

AEB 80

59 Read the following:

Situation On a long train journey to Marseilles, Michael Oldpound had become closely acquainted with a French girl, Susanne Brun, who lived in Marseilles. On his next visit to the city he decided to call on Susanne, but he had neither her address nor her telephone number.

Problem To contact Susanne Brun by telephone.

Analysis Michael remembered the following facts about Susanne;

(i) she lived by a lake,

(ii) she lived in a street named after a flower.

Michael also had the following aids available:

(i) a street map of Marseilles,

(ii) a telephone directory,

(iii) coins to make any number of calls.

a) Design an algorithm to help solve this problem, writing down the critical steps.

b) Draw the flowchart for your algorithm.

AEB 81 1

60 For a period of five days – Monday to Friday – a survey is made of every 100th passenger using a river ferry crossing. For each passenger the following data is collected and coded into a record on magnetic tape,

(i) whether male, female or child (of either sex),

(ii) whether using season, day return or other type of ticket,

(iii) whether on business, pleasure, shopping trip or other.

a) Draw a suitable data capture form for this survey.

b) Draw a flowchart for the analysis of the above data, i.e. to read, to calculate, to print out for a Wednesday:

(i) the total number of passengers travelling,

(ii) the number of children with season tickets,

(iii) the number of females going shopping on a day return.

AEB 81

61 Using any high-level language write a program,

(i) to read in a piece of prose,

(ii) to count how often the letter 'a', and the word 'the' occurs in the piece of prose,

(iii) to print out the respective totals.

AEB 81

62 The flowchart in figure 14.28 is designed to provide information from data which are input as indicated below.

G values which represent the sex: male (1) female (0)

S values represent marital status: married (1) single (0)

A values are the ages in years

W values are the number of working hours per week.

a) Suggest an appropriate entry for the decision box which has been left blank.

b) Explain the purpose of your suggested entry.

c) What information is provided by the output from this flowchart?

JMB 78

63 Draw the flowchart to represent an algorithm to read ten unsorted numbers into a one-dimensional array, A, to sort the numbers into descending order and to output them in this order.

Select suitable test data giving reasons for your choice.

JMB 78

64 The contents of the one-dimensional array (or list) A are as follows:

$$A(1) = 4 \qquad A(3) = 7$$
$$A(2) = 3 \qquad A(4) = 6$$

a) Copy and complete the trace table in figure 14.29 by dry running the section of flowchart given.

b) What is the function of this flowchart?

c) What is the function of the location labelled X?

d) What is the function of the location labelled F?

JMB 79

65 Draw a flowchart to represent an algorithm which does the following:

accepts numbers intended to be in the range 0–10 but terminated by a rogue value of 999;

checks each input number to see if it is in this range or is the rogue value; (numbers failing this check produce an error message 'INVALID DATA'

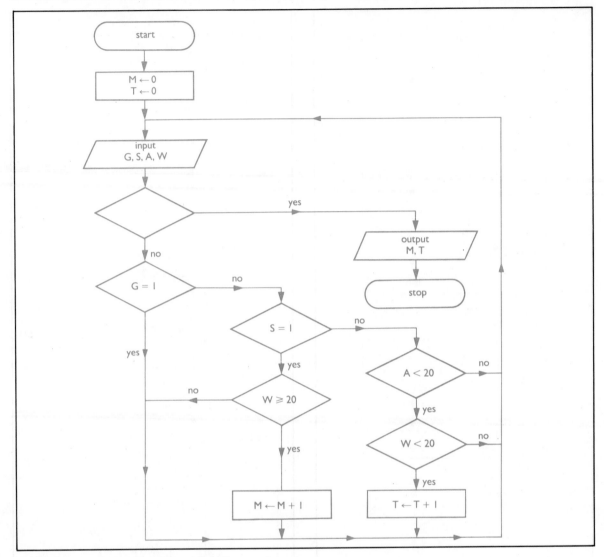

Figure 14.28 Diagram for exercise 14, question 62

and are not otherwise processed apart from in part 4 below);

  outputs the following:

1, the average of the valid numbers input,
2, the largest valid number input,
3, the smallest valid number input,
4, the number of invalid numbers detected in the input.

JMB 79

66 Copy and complete the trace table for the flowchart in figure 14.30.

JMB 80

67 The flowchart in figure 14.31 represents a subroutine.

  The values input to this are A1, A2 and L, where A1 is a string consisting of L characters and A2 is a string consisting of one character. The subroutine finds the value of a number R.

  SEG(A, J) is a function which returns the Jth character of the string A, e.g. given that A contains the characters XYZ and J has the value 2 then S ← SEG(A, J) stores the character Y in variable S.

  State the use of this subroutine, making clear what the value of R represents.

JMB 81

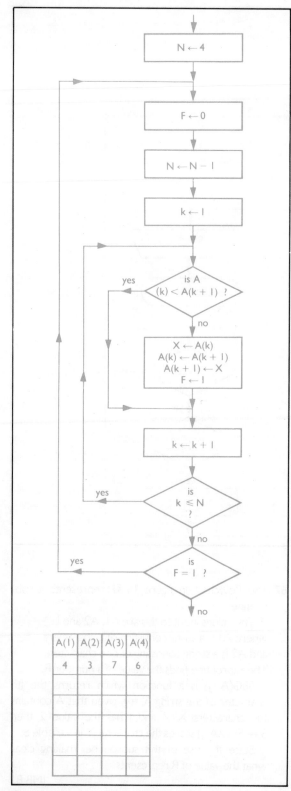

Figure 14.29 Diagram for exercise 14, question 64

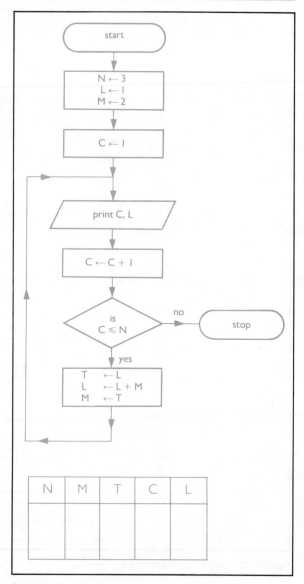

Figure 14.30 Diagram for exercise 14, question 66

68 Draw a flowchart to represent an algorithm to process a number of examination results as follows.

For each candidate the input consists of a candidate code (a 3-digit number) and a mark in the range 0–100.

For each candidate the required output is the candidate code followed by one of FAIL, PASS or CREDIT. The pass mark is 40 and the minimum mark for a credit is 65.

It is also required to output at the end of the results the percentage of candidates processed that are in each classification.

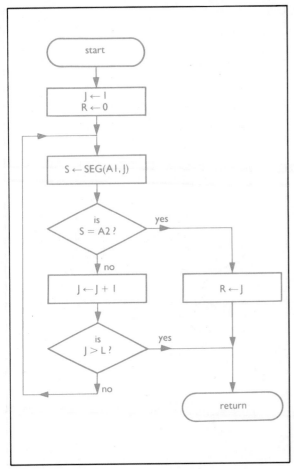

Figure 14.31   Diagram for exercise 14, question 67

All marks are recorded as whole numbers and a rogue value of −1 terminates the input.

Suggest suitable test data for your algorithm.

JMB 81

69 a) Explain why high-level languages are used for programming.

b) Name a high-level language, and use it to write a program, including explanatory remarks (comments), which reads a value for each of the variables a and b, and calculates and prints a headed table of the function

$$y = b\sqrt{\left(1 + \frac{x^2}{a^2}\right)}$$

for values of x from 0 to 10 in steps of 0.5.

OLE 79

70 A comparison is being made of the relative popularity of two television programmes. A number of viewers complete questionnaires in which they state whether they are male or female, and give marks, from 1 (meaning very bad) to 9 (meaning very good), for each of the two programmes. If a viewer misses a programme its mark is entered as 0.

Draw a flowchart to work out from these questionnaires:
  (i) the number of men and the number of women in the sample;
  (ii) the total number of viewers who watched the first programme, the total number who watched the second programme, and the number who watched neither;
  (iii) the average score for those men who watched each programme, and the corresponding average score for the women;
  (iv) which programme was preferred by the men, and which was preferred by the women.

OLE 79

71 Draw a flowchart and write a program to work out and print how much money a customer owes for a quarter's gas bill. The input to your program is the customer's code number and the number of units of gas used in the quarter. The output, which should be self-explanatory and printed at the top of a page, should include the customer's code number, the number of units used, and the cost. The cost is worked out as follows:
  there is a standing charge of £1.50,
  the first 52 units cost 19.3p each,
  the remaining units cost 15.3p each.

OLE 80

72 a) Explain what is meant in programming by a loop and a subroutine, showing clearly the differences between them, and explain why the use of loops and subroutines is advantageous.

b) What types of documentation should be provided for a program written by a candidate as project work for this examination?

OLE 80 ||

73 An electricity board requires a computer program to work out the bills for its clients. After inputting the previous meter reading and the present meter reading, the program must calculate the number of

units used, work out the cost in pounds and print this amount. If the client has used fewer than 1000 units the cost of each unit is 3p. If more than 1000 units have been used the cost is £30, plus 2p for every unit used in excess of 1000.
a) Draw a flowchart for this program.
b) Write a program corresponding to the flowchart.
c) How could you modify the program so that it will detect of the meter readings have been entered in the wrong order?

SUJB 80

74 Explain what the following program does, given that X$ and Y$ are the names of two children and A and B are their respective ages.

```
 10  INPUT X$, A, Y$, B
 20  IF X$ < Y$ THEN 90
 30  LET Z$ = X$
 40  LET X$ = Y$
 50  LET Y$ = Z$
 60  LET C = A
 70  LET A = B
 80  LET B = C
 90  PRINT X$, A
100  PRINT Y$, B
110  END
```

Explain how you would modify the program so that the first name printed is that of the younger child.

SUJB 81

75 The flowchart in figure 14.32 can be used to work out the cost of theatre tickets for a group of adults and children.
a) Find the total cost printed for 3 adults and 2 children.
b) Find the total cost printed for 4 adults and 8 children.
c) Write a program corresponding to this flowchart.
d) Modify your program to allow a 20% discount if the total number of people is more than 100 whilst still offering the 10% discount if the total exceeds 10.

SUJB 81

76
```
10  LET X = 0
20  PRINT X, SQR(X)
30  IF X = 10 THEN 60
```

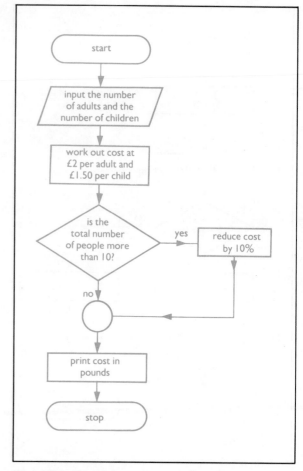

Figure 14.32   Diagram for exercise 14, question 75

```
40  LET X = X + 0.2
50  GO TO 20
60  END
```

The above program outputs a table of numbers and their square roots. Explain why the program might never terminate.

UCLES 78

77 The flowchart in figure 14.33 indicates a procedure for storing a set of positive numbers (which are followed by a rogue value −1) in an array and for finding and outputting the average (mean) of the set of positive numbers.
(i) Write a BASIC program corresponding to the flowchart, incorporating suitable data in a **DATA** statement. (You may assume that there are less than twenty but at least two values in the set.)

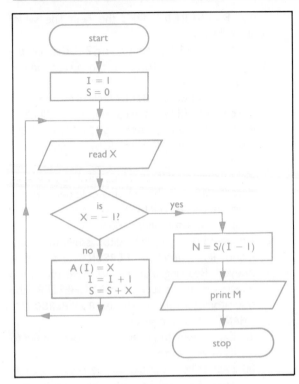

Figure 14.33   Diagram for exercise 14, question 77

(ii) Write out suitably line-numbered statements, for insertion into your BASIC program, which would cause the output of those numbers in the set which are greater than the average.

UCLES 78

78 a) Using a simple diagram, show how subscripts are associated with the elements of a two-dimensional array which has three rows and four columns.

b) The following program is designed to read a two-dimensional array and to evaluate and output the ratio:

$$\frac{\text{number of array elements which are zero}}{\text{total number of array elements}}$$

```
100  DIM A (20,20)
110  READ M, N
120  FOR I = 1 TO M
130  FOR J = 1 TO N
140  READ A(I,J)
150  NEXT J
160  NEXT I
170  LET T = M*N
```

```
180  LET K = 0
190  FOR I = 1 TO M
200  FOR J = 1 TO N
210  IF A(I,J) <> 0 THEN 230
220  LET K = K + 1
230  NEXT J
240  NEXT I
250  LET R = K/T
260  PRINT R
270  DATA 8,7
280  DATA 0,0,0,0,0,5,10,0,0,0,0,5,
     12,6,0,0,0,5,14,6,0,0,0,5,16,6,0,0
290  DATA 0,5,14,6,0,0,0,5,12,6,0,0,
     0,0,10,6,0,0,0,0,0,6,0,0,0,0,0,0
300  END
```

What is the significance of the following parts of the program
  (i) line 100,
  (ii) line 110,
  (iii) lines 120 to 160 inclusive,
  (iv) lines 190 to 240 inclusive.
c) Suggest suitably numbered statements to
    (i) check that the values of M and N are within the required limits,
    (ii) print the elements of the array so that they may be checked,
    (iii) insert a suitable comment before the value of R is printed.

UCLES 79

79 The following program is designed to find sets of positive whole numbers a, b, c such that $a^2 + b^2 = c^2$ with a and b both less than 100.

```
100  DIM S (100)
110  FOR A = 1 TO 100
120  LET S(A) = A*A
130  NEXT A
140  FOR A = 1 TO 100
150  FOR B = A TO 100
160  LET T = S(A) + S(B)
170  LET C = SQR(T)
180  LET C = INT (C + 0.001)
190  IF ABS (T-C*C) > 0.001 THEN 210
200  PRINT A; B; C
210  NEXT B
220  NEXT A
230  END
```

(i) State the purpose of line 100.

(ii) Describe the contents of the array S after the complete execution of lines 110 to 130.

(iii) State the purpose of the two lines 160 and 170.

(iv) Suppose that, immediately prior to the execution of line 180, C contains 47.6254. State the value of C immediately after the execution of this line.

(v) State, in general terms, the purpose of the set of instructions 180, 190 and 200.

UCLES 80

80 a) Draw a flowchart for an algorithm to read in a sequence of characters, character by character, ending with an asterisk (✱), and then to print out
   (i) the number of vowels (A, E, I, O, U),
   (ii) the number of consonants,
   (iii) the number of characters which are not letters,
   (iv) the number of occurrences of the letter P.

b) When a program is written for this algorithm a number of variables will be used. List the variables you would use, stating the purpose of each.

c) Dry run your flowchart for the following data:
PETER PAN✱

UCLES 81

81 A particular text editor operates on a file of text which is stored as lines of eighty characters. If a line of text is shorter than eighty characters then the system makes it up to eighty characters by adding spaces to the end of the line: edits which increase the text on a line will absorb as many of these spaces as are required. The text is stored on disk and blocks of text are copied into the main store when needed.

Three of the functions offered by the system are given below.

F, 'string' finds the next line which contains 'string'.

e.g. **F, 'FRED'** finds the next line which contains 'FRED'.

C, 'string1', 'string2' changes the next occurrence of 'string1' in the current line to 'string2'.

e.g. **C, 'FRED', 'BILLY'** changes the next occurrence of 'FRED' in the current line to 'BILLY'.

R, 'string1', 'string2' replaces all the occurrences of 'string1' in the file by 'string2'.

a) If no line can be edited to become longer than eighty characters and words must not be split, describe an algorithm which would perform the functions carried out by R.
   State any assumptions you make.

b) An operator using the editor issues the command **R, 'MAN', 'PERSON'** and this is obeyed. Realising that this will have unwanted effects on strings such as 'MANCHESTER', the operator issues the instruction **R, 'PERSON', 'MAN'** and this is obeyed.
   (i) Explain why this might not restore the file to its original form.
   (ii) Explain how the file can be restored to its original form if the updating was performed by
      (1) using the grandfather-father-son system,
      (2) overwriting the disk file.

UL 81

82 When supermarkets buy tinned food they are often given a discount on the purchase price depending on the number of cases bought. The list in table 82.1 is an example.

Draw a flowchart and write a program in a high-level language to
a) input a purchase price per case,
b) output a table giving the prices (with the above discounts allowed) in the form shown in table 82.2

WJEC 78 O-Level

Table 82.1

Number of cases of baked beans 8 oz tins (48/case)	1	2–4	5–9	10–14	15–19	20+
Discount %	0	10	12½	15	17½	20

Table 82.2

Number of cases	1	2–4	5–9	10–14	15–19	20+
Cost per case baked beans 8 ozs £						

15

Basic summary

This chapter presents a brief summary of the essential features of the version of Basic used in this book.

Program structure

A program is a set of instructions to a computer. In Basic, each instruction forms a statement. A Basic language program may contain one or more subprograms.

Line numbers

One line of a Basic program generally contains one statement. The line starts with a line number. Program lines are executed in order of line number.

Variables

A variable represents a number or literal data item. A numeric variable is a single letter or letter followed by a single digit, e.g. **X**, **A3**, **P0**. A literal variable is a single letter, followed by a $ sign, or a letter, or digit and a $ sign, e.g. **X$**, **A3$**, **P0$**.

Numbers

Numbers may be positive or negative (no sign means positive), with or without a decimal point. The **E** notation is used for powers of ten. Examples of valid numbers are **5**, **6.7**, **−369.25**, **1.3E5** ($= 1.3 \times 10^5$), **3.21 E−6** ($= 3.21 \times 10^{-6}$).

Statements

Statements are identified by an instruction word. The instruction words introduced in this book are as follows:

DATA

Supplies variable values for a **READ** statement. For example:

```
235  DATA 6, -6.2, 9.5E7, "ABERDEEN"
```

DEF

Defines a function for use later in the program. The function is given a name, starting with the letters FN, and a formula is provided to evaluate the function. For example:

```
170  DEF FNS(X) = X*X
205  DEF FNJ$(X$) = MID$(X$, 1,1)
```

DIM

Declares the size of one or more arrays. For example:

```
310  DIM X(3), Y(25), Z$(6), A(4,6)
```

END

Marks the end of a program.

FOR...TO

Marks the start of a program loop to be repeated a specified number of times, using a counter. The word **STEP** may be used to specify the amount of increase of the counter. For example:

```
150  FOR N = 1 TO 10
180  FOR J = 2 TO 30 STEP 2
290  FOR K = 6 TO 1 STEP −1
```

GO TO

Transfers control to the line number quoted. For example:

```
200  GO TO 100
```

GOSUB

Transfers control to the subprogram quoted. For example:

```
155  GOSUB 850
```

IF...THEN

Conditional transfer of control. If the condition is true, then control is transferred to the line number following the word **THEN**. If the condition is not true, then control is transferred to the statement after the **IF...THEN** statement. The condition must contain one of the following relations:

equals	=
greater than	>
greater than or equal to	>=
less than	<
less than or equal to	<=
not equal to	<>

Conditions may be joined by the words **AND** or **OR** and negated by the word **NOT**. For example:

```
150  IF A=2 THEN 200
185  IF X <> −1 THEN 300
200  IF B=0 AND A=1 THEN 250
235  IF A$=" ENDFILE" OR S$="OFF" THEN 100
240  IF C$ = " START" THEN GOSUB 600
```

Note that the last example is used to transfer control to a subprogram.

INPUT

Inputs values of variables quoted from the keyboard. For example:

```
105  INPUT N$
115  INPUT P, Q, R, S$
```

LET

Used to assign a value to a variable, or carry out a calculation. The statement contains an equals sign, with a variable to the left of it, and a constant, variable or expression to the right of it. Symbols in expressions are, in order of precedence:

( )	brackets
↑	powers and roots
* /	multiplication and division
+ −	addition and subtraction

For example:

```
115  LET X = 0
160  LET Y = 3*(X↑4 − 9)/2
175  LET M$ = " XXX "
180  LET J$ = " * " + K$ + " * "
195  LET X = X + 1
```

Note that the **+** operator is also used to join character strings or literal variables.

NEXT

Marks the end of a loop controlled by a **FOR...TO** statement. The loop counter is included. For example:

```
135  NEXT J
```

ON...GO TO

Controls a multi-way branch. If the expression or control variable has the value n, then control is transferred to the nth statement number quoted. For example:

```
200  ON X GO TO 300, 400, 500
325  ON A − B + 1 GO TO 350, 360, 370
```

ON...GOSUB

Controls a multi-way branch to one of a number of subprograms. If the expression or control variable has the value n, then control is transferred to the subprogram at the nth statement number quoted. For example:

```
650  ON P GOSUB 200, 250, 300
```

PRINT

Prints or displays values of variables or constants listed. Commas between variables cause output to be set out in columns; semicolons cause close spacing of output. For example:

```
125  PRINT " NOW IS THE TIME "
140  PRINT 1, X1, X2
145  PRINT A$; B$; " --- "; C$
```

```
150  PRINT                    (prints a blank line)
165  PRINT X$;
```

Note that in the last example printing resumes on the same line when the next **PRINT** statement is encountered.

READ

Reads values of variables listed from a **DATA** statement. For example:

```
120  READ X, Y$
```

REM

Remark statement. It supplies information for the use of the programmer. It is strongly advised that all subprograms start with a **REM** statement. For example:

```
200  REM INPUT VALIDATION SUBPROGRAM
```

RETURN

Returns control from a subprogram to the statement following the **GOSUB** statement from which the subprogram was called. For example:

```
285  RETURN
```

STOP

Halts the execution of a program. For example:

```
350  STOP
```

Functions

ABS(X)

Returns the absolute value of its argument. For example:

```
ABS(6) = 6
ABS(-5) = 5
```

ASC(X$)

Returns the ASCII code of the first character of its argument. For example:

```
ASC( "A") = 65
```

ATN(X)

Returns the angle (in radians) having the tangent of its argument. For example:

```
ATN(1) = 0.7855
```

CHR$(X)

Returns the character having the ASCII code of its argument. For example:

```
CHR$(65) = "A"
```

COS(X)

Returns the cosine of its argument, which is in radians. For example:

```
COS (1.571) = 0.000
```

EXP(X)

Returns the value of e raised to the power of its argument. For example:

```
EXP(1) = 2.71828
```

INT(X)

The integer function, returns the whole number part of its argument. For example:

```
INT (10.5) = 10
INT (-6.2) = -7
INT (3.998) = 3
```

LEN(X$)

Returns the number of characters in its argument. For example:

```
LEN( "CAT") = 3
LEN ("TO BE OR NOT TO BE") = 18
```

LOG(X)

Returns the natural logarithm of its argument. For example:

```
LOG (2.71828) = 1
```

MID$(X$, A,B)

Returns a substring of **X$**, length **B** characters, starting at the **A**th character. For example:

```
MID$ ("22/08/49", 4, 2) = "08"
```

RND(X)

Returns a random number in the range 0 to 1. A negative value of **X** is used to 'seed' the random number generator. A positive value of **X** produces the next random number in the sequence. A zero value of **X** repeats the previous random number.

SGN(X)

Returns +1 if **X** is positive
       0 if **X** is zero
     -1 is **X** is negative

SIN(X)

Returns the sine of its argument, which is in radians. For example:

SIN(1.571) = 1.000

SQR(X)

Returns the square root of its argument, which must be positive. For example:

SQR (25) = 5
SQR (1.44) = 1.2

STR$(X)

Returns the string equivalent of the number which is its argument. For example:

STR$ (1066) = "1066"

TAB(X)

Tabulates printed or displayed output to commence **X** character positions from the start of the line. For example:

```
100 PRINT TAB(5); " NAME " ;TAB(20); " ADDRESS "
105 PRINT TAB(5);N$;TAB(20);A$
```

TAN(X)

Returns the tangent of its argument, which is in radians. For example:

TAN (0.7855) = 1.000

VAL(X$)

Returns the numerical value of the character string which is its argument. For example:

VAL (" 1066 ") = 1066